THE MAKING OF EU FOREIGN POLICY

The Making of EU Foreign Policy

The Case of Eastern Europe

Karen E. Smith
Lecturer
Department of International Relations
London School of Economics and Political Science

Published by PALGRAVE
Houndmills, Basingstoke, Hampshire RG21 6XS and
175 Fifth Avenue, New York, N. Y. 10010
Companies and representatives throughout the world

PALGRAVE is the new global academic imprint of
St. Martin's Press LLC Scholarly and Reference Division and
Palgrave Publishers Ltd (formerly Macmillan Press Ltd).

Outside North America
ISBN 0–333–72605–7

In North America
ISBN 0–312–21582–7

This book is printed on paper suitable for recycling and
made from fully managed and sustained forest sources.

A catalogue record for this book is available from the British Library.

Library of Congress Cataloging-in-Publication Data
Smith, Karen Elizabeth.
The making of EU foreign policy : the case of Eastern Europe /
Karen E. Smith.
   p.   cm.
Includes bibliographical references and index.
ISBN 0–312–21582–7 (cloth)
1. European Union countries—Foreign relations—Europe, Eastern.
2. Europe, Eastern—Foreign relations—European Union countries.
I. Title.
D1065.E852S63   1998
327.4047—dc21   98–23464
                                                          CIP

9   8   7   6   5   4   3   2
08   07   06   05   04   03   02   01

Printed and bound in Great Britain by
Antony Rowe Ltd, Chippenham, Wiltshire

Contents

List of Tables

Preface

This is a book about European Union (EU) foreign policymaking. It is not a complete history of the relationship between the EU and Eastern Europe; the emphasis is squarely on the EU side, and on the process of foreign policymaking within the EU.

The book argues that there has been a common EU foreign policy towards six countries of Eastern Europe (Bulgaria, Czech Republic, Hungary, Poland, Romania, Slovakia), and analyzes why the EU member states have agreed to the policy. The objective of the EU's policy is to support the economic and political transformation in Eastern Europe and thus ensure security and stability. The policy instruments that it has used include trade agreements, financial assistance, loans, association agreements, political dialogue and, most importantly, the prospect of enlargement.

Enlargement (along with the creation of Economic and Monetary Union) has become the biggest challenge facing the EU, yet there are few books (but many articles) on the EU's relations with Eastern Europe. This book analyzes why the EU is now at the point at which it is poised to enlarge to several new members from Eastern Europe.

The empirical work is based largely on official primary sources and news reports, and two dozen interviews conducted with officials in Brussels, London, Florence and Rome. I would like to thank all those whom I interviewed for taking the time to talk with me about the policymaking process. Several officials did not wish to be identified, so the identity of all of those interviewed has not been revealed. I also thank Emir Lawless of the European University Institute library, who helped track down important documents.

This book began life as a PhD thesis, which I wrote at the London School of Economics under the supervision of Professors Christopher Hill and Paul Taylor. Both supervisors inspired and encouraged me, and offered invaluable, constructive comments on my work. The book was later revised during a fellowship year at the European University Institute in Florence, Italy. I am very grateful to have had the opportunity to study at both institutions, as they are dynamic and intellectually stimulating places for learning.

Several people offered extremely useful comments on drafts of part or all of this book and I cannot thank them enough: Christopher Hill (in particular), Jan Zielonka, William Wallace, Rodolfo Ragionieri and Federica Bicchi.

List of Abbreviations

ACP	African, Caribbean, and Pacific countries
ASEAN	Association of South-East Asian Nations
CAP	Common Agricultural Policy
CBSS	Council of Baltic Sea States
CCP	Common Commercial Policy
CEECs	Central and East European Countries
CEFTA	Central European Free Trade Agreement
CFSP	Common Foreign and Security Policy
CIS	Commonwealth of Independent States
CMEA	Council for Mutual Economic Assistance (also known as Comecon)
COCOM	Coordinating Committee for Multilateral Export Controls
COGECA	General Committee for Agricultural Cooperation in the EC
COPA	Committee of Professional Agricultural Organisations
Coreper	Committee of Permanent Representatives
CSCE	Conference on Security and Cooperation in Europe (later became the OSCE)
CSFR	Czech and Slovak Federal Republic
DG	Directorate-General
EBRD	European Bank for Reconstruction and Development
EC	European Community
ECJ	European Court of Justice
Ecofin	Economic and Finance Ministers Council
ECSC	European Coal and Steel Community
ECU	European Currency Unit
EEA	European Economic Area
EEC	European Economic Community
EFTA	European Free Trade Association
EIB	European Investment Bank
EMS	European Monetary System
EMU	Economic and Monetary Union
EP	European Parliament
EPC	European Political Cooperation
EU	European Union

Euratom	European Atomic Energy Community
fn	footnote
FRG	Federal Republic of Germany
FYROM	Former Yugoslav Republic of Macedonia
G7	Group of 7 most advanced industrialized countries
G-24	Group of 24
GATT	General Agreement on Tariffs and Trade
GDR	German Democratic Republic
GSP	Generalized System of Preferences
ICJ	International Court of Justice
IGC	Intergovernmental Conference
IMF	International Monetary Fund
JOPP	Joint Venture PHARE Programme
MEP	Member of the European Parliament
MFN	Most Favoured Nation
NACC	North Atlantic Cooperation Council
NATO	North Atlantic Treaty Organization
NGO	Non-Governmental Organization
OECD	Organization for Economic Cooperation and Development
OJ	Official Journal of the European Union (previously European Communities)
OOPEC	Office for Official Publications of the European Communities
OSCE	Organization for Security and Cooperation in Europe
PHARE	Poland/Hungary: Assistance for Restructuring Economies
pt	point
QMV	Qualified Majority Voting
QRs	Quantitative restrictions
SEA	Single European Act
TACIS	Technical Assistance for the Commonwealth of Independent States
Tempus	Trans-European Mobility Scheme for University Studies
USSR	Union of Soviet Socialist Republics
WEU	Western European Union

1 Conceptualizing EU Foreign Policymaking

During the first decade of the 21st century, the EU is set to enlarge to up to ten East European countries: Bulgaria, the Czech Republic, Estonia, Hungary, Latvia, Lithuania, Poland, Romania, Slovakia and Slovenia. EU enlargement has been agreed because it is believed that this will ensure security and stability in Eastern Europe. Yet enlargement will fundamentally alter the Union itself: along with the creation of an Economic and Monetary Union, it is the biggest challenge facing the Union.

The prospect of enlargement is an integral part of the EU's policy towards Eastern Europe. This book will trace the evolution of that policy and analyze why the EU member states agreed to it. In spite of the grandiose declaration in the 1993 Maastricht Treaty[1] that a 'common foreign and security policy is hereby established', the member states clearly do not often act together (much less, effectively) on international issues. Since the late 1980s, however, the European Community/Union has conducted a common, consistent foreign policy towards Eastern Europe. The policy's principal aims have been to support the economic and political transformation in Eastern Europe and thus ensure security and stability in Europe; as circumstances have changed, the Community/Union has used different policy instruments to fulfill those aims, from trade agreements to the offer of EU membership. The policymaking process has, at times, been marked by considerable differences among the member states, and the East European countries have frequently expressed their dismay with the outcome. But the member states have nonetheless overcome their differences to reach agreement on a series of crucial decisions, most importantly that on enlargement.

The policy towards Eastern Europe is a very unique one. The end result will be the incorporation of the former 'objects' of foreign policy into the EU as member states. The EU cannot enlarge forever: the offer of membership is a foreign policy tool nearing its sell-by date. The prospect of enlargement to Eastern Europe has been a very powerful instrument: because membership is to be offered only if certain conditions are met, the EU has been able to influence East

1

European countries' internal and external policies. But since membership may not be on offer to many more countries, the EU could be less able to influence developments elsewhere. Implementation of the enlargement decision also entails fundamental reform of the Union itself: 'widening' and 'deepening' must occur at the same time. Because of this, foreign policy towards Eastern Europe is closely intertwined with internal debates on institutional reform.

In spite of this uniqueness, analysis of the making of a policy towards Eastern Europe offers insights about EU foreign policymaking of use in other cases; many precedents have been set in the process – from strengthening the Commission's role in policymaking, to applying conditionality in the EU's relations with other countries. It also provides an opportunity to evaluate the usefulness of different explanations of EU foreign policymaking for explaining this particular case.

1.1   SOME DEFINITIONS

'Eastern Europe' refers here primarily to the following six countries: Bulgaria, the Czech Republic, Hungary, Poland, Romania and Slovakia.[2] All of these countries were former members of the Council for Mutual Economic Assistance, or CMEA (Czechoslovakia was one country then) and were the first East European countries to sign association agreements with the Community. They were also the first to be considered for eventual EU membership. Focussing on these six countries allows us to trace the continuous development of the Community/Union's relations with them from the Cold War to the present. The Baltic republics (Estonia, Latvia, and Lithuania) and Slovenia have also negotiated association agreements with the EU, and Estonia and Slovenia are now at the front of the accession queue. But the EU's relations with these four countries have developed only since all four became independent states, and along the lines established in the policy towards the first six countries.

Several of these countries prefer to be considered 'Central European'; the Union does in fact refer to them as the 'Central and East European Countries' (CEECs). For the sake of brevity, and to try to reduce the use of acronyms (already alarmingly high in any discussion about the EU), the term 'Eastern Europe' will be used here.

'Foreign policy' is another term to be clarified. Simply put, it is 'that area of governmental activity which is concerned with relationships between the state and other actors, particularly other states, in the international system.'[3] These relationships are not limited to diplomacy and war (the stuff of what was once called 'high politics'). Foreign policy differs from foreign economic policy, in that the latter involves economic aims and means, although the objectives may ultimately be political or security-related.[4] Foreign policy can also entail the use of economic instruments, but its aims are explicitly political or security-related. The EU's policy towards Eastern Europe is foreign policy, not foreign economic policy. The fungibility of military force is declining in an interdependent world (although peacekeeping forces have been more in demand), and foreign policy can certainly be conducted without using military instruments (indeed, the recourse to military instruments can indicate a failure of foreign policy).[5] That the EU lacks its own military instruments thus does not mean that it cannot conduct foreign policy.

Can only governments conduct foreign policy? As Michael Smith has noted, foreign policy has generally been seen as 'the embodiment of national aims and interests, pursued through the mobilization and application of national resources.'[6] David Allen has argued that it is difficult 'to separate the notion of a foreign policy from the idea of a state with a set of interests identified by a government.'[7] But this notion is stretched by the ways statehood has been changing and the involvement of non-state bodies in performing governance roles. A broader view would consider that 'actions with meaning and effect can be produced by a range of actors and from a variety of sources'.[8]

By this view, the European Union (a non-state actor) could formulate and implement foreign policy, even though foreign policy is an area traditionally considered to be at the 'heart' of state sovereignty and thus off-limits to international cooperation. Clearly, however, there is no *single* 'European foreign policy': no single European foreign ministry, no single set of armed services under centralized control, and so on.[9] And the member states still conduct their own foreign policies. Many crucial resources and powers remain under national competence. The EU is not yet a fully-fledged international actor, able to function actively and deliberately in relation to other actors in the international system.[10] Yet on some occasions and on some issues, the member states do agree on common foreign policies: they agree on common interests and objectives, and mobilize national and collective resources to fulfill them. The policy towards Eastern Europe is one such case.[11]

Breaking the two terms down ('foreign' and 'policy') raises further questions. As Brian White has noted, 'policy' has two very different connotations. It can mean an explicit plan of action, a strategy designed to serve specific objectives (an activist conception), or it can mean a series of habitual responses to events in the international realm.[12] The Union has frequently been criticized as capable only of reacting to outside events, rather than initiating active policies, in the sense of long-term strategies to pursue its interests.[13] Its reactions could, though, still be considered policy.

The meaning of 'foreign', on the other hand, is fairly clear-cut: the East European countries are 'third countries' (in EU jargon), or non-members and thus the object of policy. Although the East European countries will eventually join the EU, they are still now third countries.

Analyzing foreign policymaking in the Union is complicated by an institutional division between frameworks for making economic policy and for coordinating foreign policy. Responsibility for 'external economic relations' has largely been entrusted to European Community bodies, while the member states have formulated some common positions on some foreign policy issues in an intergovernmental framework (initially European Political Cooperation, or EPC; since the 1993 Maastricht Treaty, Common Foreign and Security Policy, or CFSP).[14]

Decisions taken in both frameworks are to be 'consistent',[15] although this term has not been officially defined. Simply speaking, consistency means that the policies decided in both frameworks should not cancel each other out, or pursue incompatible objectives. Consistency can also be seen as a two-step process: first a foreign policy is set out in the CFSP framework; then the Community's economic instruments are used to implement it. But the process may be less clear cut, and policymaking can cut across formal institutional divisions. 'Consistency' as used here implies a growing together of the two frameworks.[16] This mirrors the growing together of political/security and economic issues in a world characterized by interdependence.

Pulling together these various elements, a common, consistent foreign policy thus means that the member states and EC institutions have expressed a unified position in response to external events and/or formulated a plan of action directed towards the fulfillment of specified political/security objectives, and have agreed to use Community/CFSP instruments and/or instruments under national competence in a coordinated way to implement it.[17] A common foreign policy does not supersede completely national relationships, but the collective relationship is the most important.

Although there have been few EU common foreign policies, the member states have created institutions whose ultimate aim is that of making common foreign policies, in this ideal sense. The institutions have in turn influenced national policymaking, as discussed in the next two sections.

The division between the frameworks (pillars, in Maastricht Treaty parlance) creates further problems with terminology, which are compounded by the extent to which the division blurred in the case of the policy towards Eastern Europe. During the period under consideration here, the Maastricht Treaty was negotiated and entered into force (on 1 November 1993). It set up a European Union consisting of three pillars. In pillar one are revisions to the 1950s treaties establishing the three Communities; the EEC is renamed as the European Community (EC), reflecting an already widespread usage, which will be followed here.[18] In pillars two and three are the separate intergovernmental frameworks, the CFSP and justice and home affairs cooperation.

Pre-Maastricht, the European Community and EPC will be indicated separately here, although this means that referring to the 'collectivity' is awkward (Community/EPC).[19] European Union can thankfully be used more generically for events since November 1993, although attention must still be paid to the differences between the pillars. The foreign ministers acting in EPC/CFSP are also often referred to as the 'Twelve' or 'Fifteen', according to the current number of member states. A further problem arises in referring to the collectivity across time, before and after the Maastricht Treaty: for this, the awkward term 'Community/Union' will be used when necessary.

1.2   THE COMMUNITY AND EPC/CFSP

So how is foreign policy made in the EU? A brief digression on the respective powers and decisionmaking procedures of the separate pillars will help clarify the nature of the Union as an international actor, and the resources that could be mobilized should the member states agree to pursue a common foreign policy. What is striking is that in the making of a policy towards Eastern Europe, the formal rules were neither a constraint (an excuse for inaction or ineffectiveness) nor a spur (in and of themselves) for policymaking.

On the Community side, the main decisionmaking bodies are the Commission, the Council and the European Parliament (EP). The Commission initiates proposals and defends the 'Community interest'.[20] The EP (now with 626 directly-elected members from across the EU) has some power to block or, since Maastricht, reject proposed legislation but not to initiate it.

Decisions on Commission proposals are taken by the Council of Ministers from the member states, whose membership varies according to the subject at hand: the General Affairs Council comprises the foreign affairs ministers, and is the 'senior' Council. Trade issues are usually handled by the General Affairs Council.[21] Every six months, a different member state assumes the Council presidency. The presidency organizes and manages the Council's business, and is a position from which member states can push specific priorities. A Committee of Permanent Representatives (Coreper) prepares the Council's discussions, with input from Council working groups. In 1974, the European Council of heads of state and government was established, and has met at least once per presidency. It has increasingly become the main arena in which decisions are ultimately endorsed or even settled.

The Treaty of Rome (establishing the EEC) set out several provisions under which the Community can conduct relations with non-member countries.[22] These were modified only slightly by the 1987 Single European Act (SEA) and the Maastricht Treaty. Articles 110–16 provide for a Common Commercial Policy (CCP) based on a common external tariff. Article 113 states that the CCP is to be based on uniform principles, regarding changes in tariff rates, the conclusion of tariff and trade agreements, liberalization measures, export policy, and anti-dumping and anti-subsidies measures. Exclusive competence for negotiating and concluding agreements in these areas lies with the Community. Such agreements are negotiated by the Commission, according to Council directives.[23] They are concluded by the Council by a qualified majority vote.

Under article 238, the Community can conclude association agreements with third countries. Association agreements are negotiated by the Commission and concluded unanimously by the Council.

The Community's competence to conclude international agreements does not cover areas outside its field of internal action. But under article 235, agreements can be reached in such areas if they are necessary to attain a Community objective.[24] Agreements that provide for economic cooperation with third parties (such as the trade and cooperation agreements with the East European countries) are based on this article. Article 235 was also used to conclude agreements on development cooperation and set up aid programmes (including the PHARE programme for Eastern Europe); this was replaced by the Maastricht Treaty provisions on development cooperation policy.[25]

'Mixed' agreements include areas within the Community's competence and within the competence of the member states (such as political dialogue). These must be ratified by the Community and the member states. The association agreements with the East European countries are mixed agreements.

The prospect of membership for European third countries has become a powerful policy instrument. Article 237 of the Rome Treaty provided for enlargement of the Community to other European states; this has since been replaced by article O (an EU-wide provision) of the Maastricht Treaty. Accession treaties must be ratified by all the member states and the acceding country.

Several areas of external economic relations are not controlled exclusively by the Community. The member states can grant export credits, promote investment and conclude economic cooperation agreements with third countries, as long as the provisions of their agreements do not violate the CCP. They can tax, and freeze, foreign assets. Member states can provide debt relief, which has been, for example, a major part of the West's efforts to assist Eastern Europe.

Under the Rome Treaty, the EP had few formal powers with respect to external relations. With the Single European Act, it acquired the right to approve association and membership agreements. This was extended under the Maastricht Treaty to all but very simple trade agreements (of which the EC concludes very few, nowadays); but even before Maastricht, the EP had been asked to approve the trade and cooperation agreements with the East European states.

The Community is the world's largest trading entity. Naturally, then, third countries want access to its market. The Community has concluded trade, trade and cooperation, or association agreements with most states in the world; these agreements often have considerable political implications.[26] Its attraction has grown particularly since the SEA, which set a deadline (31 December 1992) for the completion of the single European market, and provided for qualified majority voting for most measures relating to the single market. The late 1980s, during which the process of completing the single European market was launched, was an extremely dynamic period in the Community's history, and this strongly influenced its foreign relations (see Chapter 3).

On the foreign policy side, European Political Cooperation was established in 1970, well after the founding of the Community.[27] Its goals were modest: by consulting regularly, the member states would develop a mutual understanding of international problems; national views would be harmonized and positions coordinated; and, where possible and desirable, common actions could be taken.[28] EPC was formed for a number of reasons: to balance the EC's economic weight, to allow member states to speak with one voice in world affairs, and as a step towards political union. EPC was replaced by the CFSP for strikingly similar reasons: the CFSP was hammered out during the 1991 intergovernmental conference (IGC) on political union, which was to balance an IGC on economic union, strengthen the institutional framework binding a newly united Germany (see Chapter 5), and better equip the new Union to lead in the post-Cold War era. Dissatisfaction with the Union's ability to act in international affairs led to further revisions of the CFSP during the 1996–7 IGC, contained in the 1997 Amsterdam Treaty.

EPC was deliberately kept separate from the Community: of the EC's institutions, only the Commission played any role at all in the process. This suited 'supranationalists', concerned that EPC's inter-governmental procedures might contaminate the EC's supranational processes, and 'intergovernmentalists', concerned that the Community might encroach on national control of the foreign policymaking process. These concerns continue to influence the CFSP's development: under both the Maastricht and Amsterdam Treaties it remains a separate 'pillar'. Yet, right from the start of EPC, there has been a blurring of the line between them (see Section 2.2).

Until the 1987 SEA, EPC was based on three reports, which set out its principles and procedures: the 1970 Luxembourg Report, the 1973 Copenhagen Report, and the 1981 London Report. Although these were not legally binding, they can be seen as 'soft law', as EPC still exerted a constraining influence on the member states.[29] The SEA consolidated many of the practices and customs which had developed over the years (the '*acquis politique*'), but did so under a separate title (Title III) from that of the revisions to the European Communities treaties. The Maastricht Treaty further codified practice, such that 'the CFSP process is far more legalized, formal and bureaucratized than EPC ever was.'[30] The Amsterdam Treaty made further refinements, but disappointed those who hoped for more radical reforms, such as majority voting.

The European Council was the only framework in which both EC and EPC matters could formally be handled, though it rarely played a role in EPC. In the 1990s, it has become increasingly important. The Maastricht Treaty states that the European Council will define the CFSP's principles and guidelines; under the Amsterdam Treaty, it is to decide on 'common strategies'.

Decisions are taken in meetings of the foreign ministers, officially by unanimity. Under EPC, the foreign ministers met often (four times a year or more), and 'at the margins' of the monthly General Affairs Council meetings. EPC foreign minister meetings were not called Council meetings (thus emphasizing that the frameworks were separate), although both involved the foreign ministers. Since 1974, 'Gymnich-type'[31] meetings have been held, now once a presidency: they are informal meetings of the foreign ministers at which both EC and EPC/CFSP business is discussed, but no decisions are formally taken or official record made. The agendas of EPC foreign minister and EC Council meetings were separate until 1990, when the Irish and Italian presidencies merged them.[32] Since the Maastricht Treaty, this key body has been called the Council, thus confirming practice and ending some linguistic confusion.

EPC discussions were prepared by the Political Committee (the political directors of the foreign ministries).[33] Since Maastricht, the Political Committee and Coreper have been responsible for different items on the Council's agenda, although cooperation between them has increased.[34] EPC working groups have been merged with the Council working groups on the same geographical area (the East European working groups worked closely even pre-Maastricht).

From 1981, the Commission was officially associated with EPC and participated in meetings at all levels. Under the Maastricht Treaty, the Commission can submit CFSP proposals, a privilege hitherto granted only to the member states (though the Commission had made proposals regarding political relations with Eastern Europe before Maastricht). To reflect its new role, the Commission in early 1993 divided Directorate-General (DG) I, responsible for External Relations, into DG I, for External Economic Relations, and DG IA, for External Political Relations. This perpetuated the division between economic and foreign policy. The Commission president from January

1995, Jacques Santer, moved away from that division to one based on geography: responsibility for both political and economic relations with Eastern Europe was given to one Commissioner (Hans van den Broek) and to a new DG IA.

The Council presidency is responsible for setting agendas, circulating position papers and presenting the common view to the outside world. To lessen the load, particularly in contacts with third countries, the presidency has been accompanied by representatives of the previous presidency and the next, and the Commission: the troika. The Amsterdam Treaty states that the presidency will also be assisted in this task by the Council's Secretary-General, which could provide the Union with more continuity in its international representation.[35]

The SEA established a small, minimal secretariat, housed in the EC Council's headquarters in Brussels.[36] Since the Maastricht Treaty, an enlarged EPC Secretariat has been merged into the Council Secretariat as the CFSP unit. A confidential telex network known as Coreu connects the foreign ministries, the CFSP unit, and the Commission. Responding to concerns that the EU is too reactive in the face of international crises, the Amsterdam Treaty provides for a policy planning and early warning unit to be established in the Council Secretariat.

The SEA declared that the member states will 'endeavour jointly to formulate and implement a European foreign policy' (article 30.1). But since decisions were taken by consensus, often the member states could not reach agreement on international issues or could agree to only modest proposals. However, Simon Nuttall maintains that where EPC could set its own agenda, decisions did not represent the lowest common denominator, but a median of the range of national views.[37]

Under the CFSP, the member states are to ensure that 'their combined influence is exerted as effectively as possible by means of concerted and convergent action' (article J.2). For this purpose, two new procedures were laid out. The Council can agree on a 'common position', which is more formal than EPC/CFSP statements and tends to specify the EU's aims. Member states must ensure their national positions conform to CFSP common positions. The Council can also adopt 'joint action', essentially a decision to take action (and thus spend money), such as sending election observers or peace envoys.[38] Member states are bound to follow the position agreed in the joint action, although there are provisions for opting out of it. This is the first time such an obligation has been agreed. With respect to Eastern

Europe, no common positions and only one joint action have been agreed: the CFSP procedures have proved to be too limited. The Maastricht Treaty altered slightly the need for consensus on foreign policy. The Council could decide unanimously that further decisions on a joint action be taken by qualified majority voting (QMV), though this has yet to occur. Under the Amsterdam Treaty, QMV can be used to adopt joint actions and common positions that are part of a 'common strategy' (yet another new concept), or to implement joint actions or common positions. But a member state can oppose the use of QMV, and thus block decisions.

The policy instruments that the member states have agreed to use in EPC/CFSP are primarily diplomatic ones, including: declarations, confidential démarches to foreign governments, high-level visits, diplomatic sanctions, political dialogue with third countries and other regional groupings, making peace proposals and sending special envoys. In the 1980s, the EC's economic instruments were increasingly used to 'reinforce' EPC decisions. The Community/EPC first imposed trade sanctions with respect to the 1981 Polish crisis (see Chapter 2). It then became practice for a political orientation regarding sanctions to be defined in EPC and implemented by the EC.[39] Likewise, EC aid was extended or increased following EPC discussions to that effect.[40] There has been a growing tendency to formulate 'global approaches' that use instruments from both policymaking frameworks.[41]

As for military instruments, security was a touchy subject in EPC, because several member states did not want to challenge the primacy of NATO (and the US) in defence matters. In addition, Denmark, Greece and neutral Ireland opposed discussing defence issues in EPC. The SEA, though, included the political and economic aspects of security as areas that could be discussed within EPC (article 30.6). Most member states (not Denmark, Greece or Ireland) discussed defence issues in the Western European Union (WEU), a nominal defence grouping overshadowed by the US-led NATO. The Community/EPC was a 'civilian power', because it relied on economic and diplomatic policy instruments to influence other international actors.

The withdrawal of many US forces from Western Europe with the end of the Cold War, the Gulf War and the Yugoslav crisis seemed to indicate that the Community/EPC needed a military capability. The WEU was seen as a potential military arm, and under the Maastricht Treaty's CFSP provisions, the EU can request the WEU to elaborate and implement decisions and actions which have defence implications.[42] Although proposals for an EU-WEU merger were not accepted at the 1996–7 IGC, the Amsterdam Treaty states that the WEU could eventually be integrated into the EU if the European Council so decides. The EU could use the WEU to elaborate and implement decisions relating to humanitarian and rescue, peace-keeping, and crisis management tasks.

These developments seem to indicate that the EU is, however hesitantly, abandoning its civilian power image. A widespread assumption seems to be that the EU will be unable to act effectively in international affairs unless it can use military instruments.[43] Yet the policy towards Eastern Europe has been a civilian one, and it is in Eastern Europe that the EU arguably has the most influence. Civilian power still has its merits.

1.3   DIFFERENT THEORIES, DIFFERENT ANSWERS

No general theory has arisen to explain EU foreign policymaking, not surprisingly given the rather unique character of the enterprise. Martin Holland even warns that no single theory of EPC/CFSP should be promoted because '*different* conceptual approaches will be appropriate for *different* theoretical questions and illuminate a *different* set of empirical facts.'[44]

But which conceptual approaches should we turn to? Conventional foreign policy models, developed to explain *national* policymaking seem inadequate, because the key actors are still (however nominally) sovereign states, and are interacting within a *sui generis* organization.[45] EPC/CFSP is dominated by elites in national foreign ministries (and to a certain extent, the Commission), so that recent work on policy networks and policy communities within the Community does not really fit the phenomenon. In the area of external economic relations, interest groups are linked at the European level, but their influence seems to be exercised largely at the national level.[46]

Several different approaches have been used to explain EU cooperation or integration:[47] neorealism; neoliberal institutionalism and intergovernmentalism; two-level analysis; constructivism; and neo-functionalism.[48] These various approaches could also provide a useful starting-point for generating explanations of EU foreign policymaking. They direct attention to different answers to several key questions: who are the important decisionmaking actors (only the member states)?; how do they decide (by bargaining, on the basis of the 'lowest common denominator', by making compromises)?; and why do they act jointly (under external pressure, to pursue EU interests)?

The American debate on cooperation has been dominated by two systemic-level theories, neorealism and neoliberal institutionalism. Both theories posit that (rational, self-interested) states are the key actors in world politics.

Neorealists claim international anarchy constrains cooperation: states are thus concerned with whether or not other states (potential enemies) will gain more than they do in any cooperative venture, and international institutions cannot ease these concerns.[49] Neorealism emphasizes the limits to cooperation: it may thus help explain why the member states do not agree on certain foreign policy issues or why EPC/CFSP has not eroded national foreign policy competences.[50] But it appears of little use for explaining why and how the member states may conduct a common foreign policy. Neorealism stresses only two factors that may encourage cooperation: a common enemy and/or a hegemony, neither of which seem particularly relevant in post-Cold War Europe. While concerns about Russian intentions and US pressure for EU leadership are two possible spurs for a common foreign policy towards Eastern Europe, neorealism offers little to explain why and how the policy would be made.

In contrast, neoliberal institutionalists argue that cooperation among self-interested rational states with shared interests is possible.[51] Institutions, which states create to control increasing interdependence, facilitate cooperation by setting rules and providing enforcement and sanction mechanisms. They help overcome the obstacles posed by collective action.[52]

Intergovernmentalism follows in the tradition of neoliberal institutionalism. It has developed primarily to explain the 'defining moments' in European integration, notably the outcomes of the periodic IGCs that have revised the founding treaties. It posits that: states are the key actors; they pursue self-interested goals (which can be derived from within the state, rather than from the state's position in the international power structure, as neorealism would maintain); the Community is the forum in which they bargain to try to achieve those goals more effectively; and large states can block cooperation or prevent outcomes that are anything more than the lowest common denominator. Bargaining involves making side payments to small states and threatening sanctions to overcome resistance to an agreement.[53]

Applied to EU foreign policymaking, an intergovernmental approach would stress that a common foreign policy is possible if the member states have shared interests and consider collective action to be more effective and influential than separate national action (the 'politics of scale', in Roy Ginsberg's words).[54] When cooperation brings mutual benefits, member states will support a common foreign policy. They will bargain to ensure that their own interests are protected or advanced, and would be unwilling to make fundamental compromises. But if they do not share common interests, the member states may not agree to a common policy, even when collective action could bring mutual benefits. What Stanley Hoffmann termed a 'logic of diversity' could block cooperation: external developments and pressures would generate different responses because the member states have different histories, cultures and foreign policy traditions.[55]

Consociational theory – a theory of elites – has been used to analyze the Community and EPC. It is a modified form of intergovernmentalism. In a consociational system, consensus among a 'cartel of elites' is the guiding principle and decisions tend to represent the lowest common denominator. Paul Taylor argues that the Community does not challenge member state identity, but reinforces it; elites can manipulate the Community so as to consolidate their bases of authority.[56] EPC (and now CFSP) *has* been dominated by elites, and Joseph Weiler and Wolfgang Wessels use consociationalism to explain EPC's stability. They note that EPC reflected an elite consensus, and that change – particularly towards supranationalism – is unlikely.[57]

Intergovernmental approaches help demonstrate how cooperation can be fostered by institutions and why states abide by an institution's norms and rules. They also point to the limits that member states can put on cooperation. But they are insufficient explanations of cooperation within the EU, even in the area of foreign policy. Non-state actors, such as the Commission, and any external pressures on the member states to act jointly are given scant attention.

Intergovernmental approaches assume that states are self-interested actors. Yet Robert Keohane himself has relaxed this assumption, and put forward a concept of empathetic interdependence, or the interest of actors in the welfare of others for their own sake.[58] 'Governments that regard themselves as empathetically interdependent will be more inclined than egoists to reach for greater joint gains – solutions to international problems that lead to larger overall value – even at the expense of direct gains to themselves.'[59] As one observer noted, even in EPC 'bargaining appears to be the exception, not the rule ... EPC became directed more towards a "problem-solving", not bargaining, style of decisionmaking.'[60] A problem-solving style of decisionmaking relies on the appeal to common values and resort to exclusion as the ultimate sanction.[61]

The concept of empathetic interdependence appears quite helpful, but as Andrew Hurrell asks, 'Can one relax the basic assumption of rational egoism and accept the role of empathetic interdependence, without the overall force of the rationalist project being undermined?'[62] This point will be taken up below.

Several observers have argued that analysts must examine the domestic sources of national preferences and consider the limits that domestic constituencies can place on cooperation. The role of interest groups, bureaucracies, 'capital', should be taken into account.[63] Andrew Moravscik's 'liberal intergovernmentalism' combines a theory of domestic preference formation with an analysis of intergovernmental negotiation within the Community.[64] Robert Putnam has proposed that international negotiations be conceived of as a two-level game. At the international level, national governments seek to maximize their own ability to satisfy domestic pressures. International agreements must be ratified at the national level.[65] Transnational and supranational actors (such as the Commission) do not figure in these models. They also disregard the process by which the separate national positions are hammered into common policies and any international pressures on the EU to act as a unit despite domestic opposition.[66]

For the most part, domestic pressures did not intrude on EPC; EPC was controlled by government elites, who generally operated secretly.[67] But public awareness of the CFSP may be growing, sparked by the Yugoslav fiasco. And domestic-level interest groups can play an important role particularly in the making of EU trade policy – an important foreign policy instrument especially for a civilian actor. There is also bound to be some haggling between foreign and economic ministries (echoes of bureaucratic politics) before agreement on a common policy using economic instruments can be reached. Domestic-level pressures must thus be taken into account in explaining EU foreign policymaking.

Intergovernmental approaches have also been criticized because they treat state preferences exogenously. Alexander Wendt (citing Jeffrey Legro) describes them as the 'rationalist "two-step": first interests are formed outside the interaction context, and then the latter is treated as though it only affected behavior.'[68]

Academics are increasingly considering the ways in which membership in an international organization can change states' interests (what

Joseph Nye calls 'sociological liberalism').[69] This line of exploration seems particularly relevant in the EU context. As Wayne Sandholtz has argued, 'States define their interests in a different way as members of the EC than they would without it.'[70] Alexander Wendt maintains that investigating this requires a 'constructivist' approach, which considers identities and interests to be endogenous to interaction, rather than a rationalist approach which takes interests as given.[71]

Constructivists argue that through the process of cooperation (interaction), actors' interests and identities change. Actors acquire identities by participating in 'collective meanings'. Institutions (stable sets of identities and interests) are created through reciprocal interaction; institutionalization is then a process of internalizing new identities and interests.[72]

Collective identities and interests could even be formed in this process, thus redefining Mancur Olson's logic of collective action, which takes rational, self-interested actors as constant. Collective identity 'refers to positive identification with the welfare of another', a situation of empathetic interdependence: 'This is a basis for feelings of solidarity, community, and loyalty, and thus for collective definitions of interest.'[73] Collective identity does not supplant egoistic identity: there can be conflicts over 'multiple loyalties'. But *'to the extent that mechanisms are at work that promote collective identities, models that ignore them will understate the chances for international cooperation and misrepresent why it occurs.'*[74]

Wendt surmises that four decades of cooperation in Western Europe may have generated 'a collective "European identity" in terms of which states increasingly define their "self"-interests.'[75] Ole Wæver, backing this, maintains that the EU Council has become a 'Euro-organ', often acting according to EU interests.[76] A sense of a collective EU identity (on some occasions or some issues), overcoming the logic of diversity, would presumably facilitate (if not drive) the forging of common foreign policies.

Wendt maintains there are two ways in which empirical work could disprove the constructivist approach. If domestic factors are found to be more important determinants of states' interests, then a rationalist approach is appropriate because interests are in fact exogenous to interaction. If interests change only very slowly, then it may be appropriate to consider them as given.[77]

Wendt's approach is state-centric, focusing on the interaction of states. Yet transnational ties and interdependence (below the state level) may also influence identities and interests, as both Karl Deutsch and the functionalists argued.[78] A sense of community can arise from this sort of interaction. Given that EU foreign policymaking is fundamentally a process of interaction among a small group of national elites, it is difficult to translate this sense of community into explanations of it. But identity-shaping processes occurring below the level of the state could reinforce those occurring in interactions between states.

Wendt's approach also does not consider whether the specific organizational context in which states interact affects the development of a collective identity. Would states interacting in an organization like the EU be more likely to form a collective identity, than, say, 'the West' interacting in a multiplicity of frameworks?

Neofunctionalism, which developed in the context of European integration in the 1950s and 1960s, did consider that identities and interests could change in the process of interaction within the Community. Neofunctionalism has been criticized because it is not clear whether the processes that it highlights are supposed to lead to some form of super-state. But neofunctionalist insights could still be useful to explain why common policymaking can occur in specific cases. Although it has appeared to be of little use in explaining foreign policymaking, an area less institutionalized than the EC itself, one observer has argued that 'the case for the re-evaluation of neofunctionalism with respect to foreign policy is strong'.[79]

Neofunctionalism posits that integration proceeds gradually, via 'spillover'. Sector integration, as in that of the coal and steel sectors, will beget its own impetus toward an extension, or spillover, to the entire economy.[80] Two factors contribute to the process: the interdependence of the functional tasks, which can be mobilized by pressure groups, parties, or governmental agencies; and the 'creative talents' of political elites who seize opportunities to redefine and expand regional organization tasks.[81]

The fact that the Union still does not have the trappings of a traditional foreign policy (with a diplomatic service, intelligence service and military capability) has been seen as proof that there is a definite limit to spillover: economic integration will not lead to further integration in the area of foreign and security policy.[82] But this ignores the possibility that the Community's external relations could be highly political (indicating spillover between 'high' and 'low' politics), or that the EC and CFSP could collaborate (spillover leading to increased involvement of EC 'supranational' actors in CFSP, as the EC's instruments are used to back up CFSP decisions). Spillover can occur because separating out economic and political relations with outsiders is difficult in an inter-dependent world. Early neofunctionalist writings addressed the issue of changing interests and identities.[83] Ernst Haas defined political integration as a 'process whereby political actors in several distinct national settings are persuaded to shift their loyalties, expectations and political activities toward a new centre, whose institutions possess or demand jurisdiction over the pre-existing national states.'[84] He assumed that as integration proceeds, interests will be redefined in regional terms. Although the decision to establish or join an integrative institution is determined on the basis of national values, and those national values influence the officials in the new institution, there will also be a reverse process in which the new central decisionmakers will influence the national ones.[85]

Haas found in 1957 that a 'supranational' style of decisionmaking had begun to take shape in the ECSC. An 'atmosphere of cooperation' prevailed in the Council; governments preferred not to be the sole negative vote and were willing to negotiate until a consensus was obtained.[86] Leon Lindberg found that in the EEC Council, the member states made significant compromises to try to achieve a Community solution to joint problems. There was a clear awareness of running a common project.[87] Most decisions were not the lowest common denominator (determined by the most stubborn member state), but represented an 'upgrading of the common interest'. Crucial to the reaching of such decisions was the Commission, an institutionalized mediator with autonomous powers.[88]

The same socialization and identity-shaping processes could work even in EPC/CFSP, a less integrated framework than the Community. As Philippe de Schoutheete has noted, EPC brought a new 'European' dimension to the national foreign policy process. EPC multiplied the direct contacts between officials at different national levels. By constantly meeting and consulting with each other, officials acquired a 'réflexe européen', or coordination reflex. Whenever an international problem arose, officials would consider its 'collective dimension' and even adapt their initial position in accordance with those of the other member states. This facilitated the taking of common decisions.[89] 'Member states have got used to consulting each other on major international issues, to profiting from each other's advice and to paying due attention to each other's concerns.'[90]

Michael E. Smith considers the development of the coordination reflex as part of the 'Europeanization' of EPC. This is a process of institutionalization that results from three linked processes: 'the development of a decentralized but complex and resilient transgovernmental network; the codification of EPC habits as norms and rules; and the involvement in EPC of entrenched EC actors such as the Commission.'[91] EPC norms and rules had an increasingly binding influence on the member states, and 'state preferences were often formed endogenously, within the EPC system.'[92]

Endogenously-formed preferences could reflect a sense of a wider EU interest. Roy Ginsberg's 'self-styled logic' posits that the Union may formulate foreign policy that reflects its 'own foreign policy interests, and its own mission and initiative in the world independent of the phenomena that trigger other actions.'[93] This presupposes a collective identity: '[t]here is a symbiosis between the EC and member actors and institutions that produces joint actions that are uniquely European.'[94] A common policy that fit the self-styled logic would come closest to the traditional definition of national foreign policy (see Section 1.1), because it would embody collective interests and the sense of a collective identity.

While generally skeptical about the strength of a collective European identity, Christopher Hill and William Wallace warn that 'one should not dismiss the possibility that participation in EPC itself helps to foster a sense of shared identity.'[95] Constructivist and neo-functionalist insights help explain how identity can change in the process of interaction, and thus why the self-styled logic might fit with some cases of common foreign policies.

The stimulus for EU foreign policymaking in Ginsberg's self-styled logic arises from within the Union. The impact of the international system on EU foreign policymaking, however, has attracted less attention from theorists. International developments and crises do create strong pressures for common action. Panayiotis Ifestos, for example, finds that external demands are an important source of pressure for coordinated Community responses.[96] But international interdependence could also make it more difficult for the member states to act together, as they might prefer to work with other actors on certain issues.[97]

Neofunctionalists did not consider in much depth the impact of the outside world on the Community or the integration process. The externalization hypothesis, however, posited that EC policies, such as the Common Agricultural Policy, will adversely affect non-member states, which will demand relief from the Community (viewed thus as a single policymaking unit). The Community would then have to respond to the outsiders and in the process would be elaborating a common foreign policy.[98] Externalization serves as a catalyst for further integration in the Community sphere.[99]

Externalization could also be useful to explain EU foreign policy-making and integration in the foreign policy sphere: as EPC/CFSP's stature has grown, there have been increasing demands on it.[100] The Maastricht and Amsterdam Treaties were partially a response to this, though widely considered an inadequate one.

The approaches and theories that have been reviewed here thus offer different answers to our key questions and should help explain why the EC/EU formulated and implemented a common policy towards Eastern Europe. Which actors have played an important role in the making of a common foreign policy? Intergovernmentalist approaches consider the member states to be the only key actors in the foreign policymaking process; neofunctionalism points to the Commission's importance as a mediator. Spillover between economic and political issues in particular would make way for the Commission's involvement, with potentially positive implications for 'upgrading the common interest'.

How have the policy decisions been made? To what extent has the policy towards Eastern Europe been 'rational' and 'controlled'? For intergovernmentalists, bargaining is the predominant decision-making style, and decisions tend to be the lowest common denominator. Neofunctionalism and constructivism instead suggest that socialization processes lead to a different 'supranational' (or problem-solving) style of decisionmaking and that decisions represent a median of the various national preferences, or even an EU preference. Bargaining would tend to lead to a more incremental and less strategic foreign policy. A sense of EU interest, and the problem-solving style of decisionmaking, could result in a more strategic, long-term policy.

What have been the role of endogenous and exogenous factors? What role did third parties play in forcing the Community/Union to formulate a common policy? To what extent has the EU manifested a collective identity in its policy towards Eastern Europe? Domestic-level and two-level approaches emphasize the influence of domestic interest groups on policymaking. The externalization hypothesis and, to an extent, neorealism point to different external stimuli favouring the making of a common foreign policy. The self-styled logic empha-sizes that EU foreign policy could reflect EU interests and a sense of collective identity.

These questions and the answers proposed by the theoretical approaches outlined above will guide the analysis in this book. Some of these approaches will prove to more be helpful than others in explaining why the Community/Union has formulated and implemented a common foreign policy towards Eastern Europe.

1.4 OUTLINE OF THE BOOK

The next chapter will review the history of relations between the Community/EPC and Eastern Europe through 1988. Although those relations remained quite limited, a certain legacy of cooperation was established, which could be drawn on as the communist regimes collapsed.

The following five chapters will analyze the making of the policy since 1988, and are divided according to the different policy instruments that the Community/Union has wielded to support the East European reforms and ensure security in the region. Chapter 3 will cover the 1988–9 period, when the Community and EPC first worked out a common policy towards Eastern Europe and the Community negotiated trade and cooperation agreements with the fastest reforming states in the region. Chapter 4 will cover the measures the Community has taken to support financially the reforms in Eastern Europe. Association agreements, covered in Chapter 5, represented a further step in the strengthening of relations between the Community and the East European countries. The debate on integrating the associates into the Union and the steps taken on enlargement will be analyzed in Chapter 6. Measures taken to prevent conflicts in Eastern Europe – a particularly pressing problem as enlargement looms – are discussed in Chapter 7. The concluding chapter will consider which approaches and concepts prove most helpful in explaining the making of a common foreign policy towards Eastern Europe.

2. The Community's Relations with Eastern Europe through 1988

Until 1988, neither the Community nor EPC played a significant role in relations with Eastern Europe. Relations between Eastern and Western Europe were constrained by the Cold War, leaving little room anyway for the Community/EPC to act. But the member states also retained control over their bilateral relations with the East European states, thereby limiting any potential role for the Community/EPC. They did, however, cooperate on some aspects of relations with Eastern Europe: they forged a common position on the Community's relations with the CMEA, or Comecon and its members; they coordinated their positions on the Conference on Security and Cooperation in Europe (CSCE); and they agreed on a common response to the 1981 Polish crisis, in contrast to the US position. In so doing, the member states clarified their common interests and established precedents for cooperation.

Two broad themes stand out in this historical survey: the interrelation between economic and political issues, on the one hand, and between the external and internal factors pushing the member states to act jointly, on the other. Both themes are still very much in evidence in the making of a common policy towards Eastern Europe from 1988.

The distinction between 'external economic relations' and 'foreign policy' broke down frequently in practice. Trade with Eastern Europe was highly politicized and tensions arose over the degree to which the Community could handle economic relations with Eastern Europe, given the national economic and political interests involved. When the Community finally assumed control over trade with the East European countries, it became involved in making political decisions.

Internal and external pressures pushed the member states to cooperate. The Commission actively sought to extend its control over national trade policies. As this occurred, the East European states asked to negotiate trade access to the EC, which in turn forced the Community to formulate a collective response. Other external events – the CSCE negotiations and US pressures over sanctions during the Polish crisis – spurred the member states to act jointly. Member states themselves pushed for common positions, for a variety of domestic factors, including the desire to secure backing for their own national policies.

In the first part of this chapter, the formulation of the Community's position towards the CMEA and its East European member states will be examined. Attention will turn in Section 2.2 to the EPC/Community role in the CSCE process. The dispute with the US over the Polish crisis, in which the different US and West European approaches to trade with Eastern Europe were particularly clear, will be discussed in Section 2.3.

2.1 EC RELATIONS WITH THE CMEA AND ITS MEMBER STATES

When the ECSC Treaty was signed in 1951, at the start of the Cold War, relations between Eastern and Western Europe were frosty. The two sectors involved – coal and steel – did not directly affect the eastern economies, but the lifting of controls on West German industry had political implications. In the Soviet bloc, the Western moves were interpreted as the beginning of an American-German hegemony over the entire continent.[1] The EEC's establishment six years later provoked another hostile Soviet reaction. In 1957, the EEC was portrayed as the economic arm of NATO and an instrument serving the interests of the monopolist class. The contradictions inherent in capitalism would soon cause the EEC to disintegrate.

When the Community instead proceeded with integration and began to prosper, a 1962 article in *Pravda* acknowledged it as an economic and political reality that promoted investment, modernization, trade and wage increases. Yet until the 1980s, the Soviet Union and its allies refused to deal officially with the Community and tried to block its participation in international organizations.

From the Community side, the Cold War, and the US position on relations with the Soviet bloc (see Section 2.3), precluded close ties with Eastern Europe in the 1950s and early 1960s. East-West political dialogue was either absent or acerbic and East-West trade relatively insignificant. But after the Cuban missile crisis in 1962, East-West tensions relaxed somewhat, permitting freer exchanges between the two halves of Europe. CMEA members became increasingly aware that they lagged behind the West and needed to import Western technology. Trade between the Community and CMEA member states expanded (see Table 2.1).

Table 2.1   EC trade with Eastern Europe, 1958–87
(in ECU million)

Country	1958	1960	1965	1970	1975	1980	1985	1987
USSR								
Exports	386	604	563	1415	5064	7808	12 509	9189
Imports	477	706	1066	1554	4064	11 382	20 710	13 128
Balance	−91	−101	−503	−139	1000	−3573	−8201	−3940
GDR[1]								
Exports	57	95	177	219	494	865	947	1086
Imports	61	91	166	230	519	951	1832	1390
Balance	−4	3	11	−10	−25	−86	−884	−304
Poland								
Exports	197	209	315	604	2745	2892	2733	2332
Imports	229	278	438	689	1733	2805	3572	2907
Balance	−32	−69	−123	−85	1013	87	−839	−575
CSFR								
Exports	136	178	283	565	1068	1405	1966	2078
Imports	143	184	281	478	874	1544	2272	2055
Balance	−7	−6	2	87	194	−139	−306	23
Hungary								
Exports	72	134	195	416	980	1619	2486	2372
Imports	70	103	198	372	713	1430	2014	1996
Balance	2	32	−4	44	267	189	473	375
Romania								
Exports	56	105	256	500	1105	1772	1157	651
Imports	72	111	224	462	989	1826	2910	2429
Balance	−16	−7	31	38	116	−55	−1753	−1778
Bulgaria								
Exports	30	63	152	231	689	805	1639	1453
Imports	33	50	127	191	222	507	586	517
Balance	−2	13	25	40	466	299	1053	936

Source: Eurostat.
Note: [1]Excluding intra-German trade.

2.1.1   Towards a Common Commercial Policy

Trade with the CMEA countries burgeoned as the member states were supposed to allow the Community to assume jurisdiction over trade policy. But they were quite reluctant to cede their powers over trade with the communist bloc by 1 January 1970, as required by the Rome Treaty: they vied with each other to meet the demand from the east. Trade with the USSR and Eastern Europe was an integral part of both France's anti-bloc foreign policy and West Germany's *Ostpolitik*.[2] Member states (particularly France under President de Gaulle) jealously guarded national prerogatives. They also wanted to be able to protect their economies from potentially distorting trade with 'state-trading countries'.[3] External factors eventually helped push the member states to agree on a position on trade with the Soviet bloc. In particular, the prospect of a pan-European Security Conference convinced them of the need for a common approach to relations with Eastern Europe (see Section 2.2).[4]

During the 1960s, the Commission had found it difficult to gain control over the member states' conventional trade activities, such as import quotas and tariffs.[5] In December 1969 the Council finally agreed that member states could not unilaterally impose new quotas on a list of liberalized imports from state-trading countries; instead, the Community could take safeguard measures.[6]

Member states, however, still insisted on holding on to their right to negotiate trade treaties with state-trading countries. In December 1969 the Council authorized member states to continue negotiating bilateral agreements with the CMEA members until 31 December 1972, because the CMEA's policy of non-recognition precluded the CMEA states from negotiating with the Community (see Section 2.1.3).[7] The Community would negotiate trade agreements with the eastern bloc countries only as of 1 January 1973. In practice, this deadline was put off again, as most bilateral agreements expired at the end of 1974.[8] Finally, in May 1974 the Council reaffirmed that from then on, all trade negotiations with state-trading countries were to be conducted through the Community.[9]

The Commission then proposed two commercial policies to replace member states' agreements with the CMEA states. One, the so-called 'autonomous policy', would simply incorporate all of the different national restrictions on imports from the state-trading countries into an EC framework, in recognition of the difficulty of harmonizing the varying policies. The other would entail drafting an agreement between the EC and each CMEA member state that provided for trade liberalization, the reciprocal granting of most-favoured-nation (MFN) status, and supervision by a joint committee.[10]

In September 1974, the Council decided to deliver the sample agreement to the state-trading countries, to show that the Community was ready to negotiate new trade agreements with them. In November the Commission did so, offering to open negotiations.[11] No replies came back, consistent with their traditional hostility to the Community and with the CMEA's attempt to negotiate a bloc-to-bloc trade agreement with the EC (see Section 2.1.3). The Council then decided in April 1975 that the Community would proceed with the autonomous policy.[12] Member states' quotas on goods from state-trading countries were incorporated into an EC list; each year, the Council revised the list, usually liberalizing imports. The member states maintained more quantitative restrictions (QRs) on goods from CMEA countries than on those from other countries.[13] Community anti-dumping and anti-subsidy procedures could be – and often were – used in response to complaints that artificially low priced goods from state-trading countries were hurting EC producers.

Although the Commission had managed somewhat to 'communitarize' trade policy, the member states still used export credits and cooperation agreements to secure advantages for their businesses in Eastern Europe. West European governments promoted national exports to the CMEA countries with an assertive use of credit guarantees.[14] In 1962, the Council decided that member states were to consult each other when they intended to breach the Berne Union of Credit Insurers agreement, but the decision was frequently ignored.[15] The West European countries competed to extend favorable terms to the East European countries and the Soviet Union.

The Commission, supported by West Germany and the Netherlands, tried unsuccessfully to coordinate member states' credit policies. France, for example, maintained that export credits were an element of foreign policy, which remained the prerogative of the member states.[16] In 1975 the ECJ held that export credit policy fell under the Community's competence, but the OECD became the forum in which export credit guidelines were stipulated.[17]

As the Community assumed responsibility for trade negotiations with state-trading countries in 1973–4, the member states negotiated long-term economic cooperation agreements with communist countries. *Commercial* cooperation agreements, aimed at developing trade, fall under article 113; *economic* cooperation agreements do not (although this view is not accepted by the Commission in particular). Such agreements provided a framework for economic relations and, in particular, were to ensure that Western companies could operate in the CMEA country concerned.[18] By concluding them, the member states could still conduct national economic policy towards the CMEA countries.[19] In addition, West European businesses and the East European countries preferred the bilateral cooperation links.[20]

Most member states, however, could agree on the need for minimum Community coordination of such agreements and in July 1974, the Council set up a consultation procedure for cooperation agreements with state-trading countries.[21] The Commission would be able to ensure that their provisions did not violate the CCP. These procedures, however, frequently went unobserved.[22]

The absence of Community cooperation agreements with the East European countries contrasted with its ties in other regions: in the 1970s and early 1980s, it concluded cooperation agreements (based on article 235) with, among others, Canada, ASEAN, India, Brazil and the Andean Pact countries. The member states' reluctance to allow the Community to do the same with the East European countries partly reflects the degree to which they guarded their own national economic and political interests in the region and partly the effects of the Cold War and of Soviet dominance in Eastern Europe.

The Community thus suffered from a lack of positive instruments (credits, guarantees and so on) for conducting commercial relations with Eastern Europe.

So far, EC member states have (under Article 113) only transferred to the Community the authority to wield the stick, which also includes restrictive import policy measures. But – notwithstanding Article 113 – they have largely reserved the carrot for themselves as an instrument of their export policies.[23]

And the member states preferred to use 'carrots' to encourage liberalization in Eastern Europe (see Section 2.3).

But as the Community proceeded with integration, the East European states and CMEA approached the Community for trade negotiations. This in turn forced the EC to come up with a common response.

2.1.2   The Community's Relations with Individual CMEA States

As the Community developed its internal policies on agriculture, industry, and fisheries, beginning in the 1960s, non-member states often found that their trade with the Community was adversely affected. They frequently approached the Commission – the only body authorized to conduct trade negotiations – to seek concessions. This held true for the East Europeans as well, the official policy of not recognizing the EC aside. Their exports (agricultural goods, chemicals, machinery, iron and steel, and textiles) met with tariffs and restrictive quotas at EC borders, while Soviet exports of raw materials entered the Community duty free. Trade with the EC accounted for 25 per cent of the East Europeans' total foreign trade, so they had good reason to approach the Commission asking for concessions.[24] As the Hungarian Prime Minister noted in 1968:

> The Common Market is a fact and we, who are always realists have to acknowledge its existence.... If our trade relations required us to call on some of the Brussels offices of the Common Market, we would not consider this step a renunciation of our principles.[25]

The creation of the Common Agricultural Policy (CAP) in 1960 spurred several CMEA member states to break ranks with the official policy of hostility towards the EC. Between 1965 and 1982, Bulgaria, Czechoslovakia, Hungary, Poland and Romania concluded informal agreements on agricultural products with the EC.[26]

From the mid-1970s, the Community acted to protect EC textile suppliers from low-cost competitors. Voluntary export restraint agreements in the textiles sector were then signed with Romania in 1976, Hungary in 1978, Bulgaria and Poland in 1979 and Czechoslovakia in 1981.[27] Similarly, the increase in Community protection of the steel industry in 1977–8 prompted East European states to negotiate access for their steel products with the Commission. Czechoslovakia, Hungary, Poland and Romania all reached informal voluntary restraint agreements with the Commission in 1978–9.[28]

The Community's growing management of sectoral trade problems thus

> helped move the socialist states away from a policy of non-recognition of the EEC's competence in trade matters and towards direct engagement in political bargaining with the Commission on crucial issues of East-West trade, on an informal basis.[29]

Further integration in the Community even induced the Soviet Union to approach the Commission. In 1976, the member states agreed to transfer jurisdiction over a common fishing zone to the Community. The Soviet Union, with a large economic interest in the fishing zone, sought an agreement on access to it (as did Poland and the GDR). Yet it still refused to recognize the Community and by September 1977, negotiations were suspended.[30]

In contrast, the Community 'rewarded' Romania's independent foreign policy. In 1972, Romania asked to begin negotiations on a trade agreement with the EC.[31] In 1974, Romania requested and obtained special treatment under the EC's Generalized System of Preferences (GSP).[32] Two agreements were concluded in 1980: the first created a joint committee on trade matters and the second provided for some liberalization of import quotas on industrial goods.[33] Romania agreed that it would expand and diversify its imports from the EC at a rate not smaller than that of its imports from other GATT countries. Attempting to keep up the facade of non-recognition, Romania intended the trade agreement to be regarded officially as another sectoral agreement, which is why the joint committee was established by a separate agreement.[34]

In the 1970s, the Community also moved to strengthen its relations with Yugoslavia, which was only associated with the CMEA.[35] By reaching agreements with Romania and Yugoslavia, the Community sent the very political message that it would extend benefits to countries that had fewer qualms about dealing with it.

By the early 1980s, then, the Community was playing a greater role in trade relations with Eastern Europe. But these relations were fairly low-key, and the member states still controlled most economic instruments. The Community's role was also constrained by Cold War realities and, in particular, difficult relations with the CMEA.

2.1.3 EEC-CMEA Relations

From 1973 through to 1981, the possibility of the Community and the CMEA concluding some sort of agreement was discussed. Although talks between the two sides were held, they came to nothing as the respective positions could not be reconciled. Only after Gorbachev launched a more open Soviet foreign policy could an agreement be realized. The standoff meant in practice that the member states had greater freedom to pursue their own policies in Eastern Europe.

In the early 1970s, the Soviet Union began to promote the CMEA as an equal negotiating partner of the Community. The Soviet Union sought to strengthen the organization. During this period, EPC and the Community played an active role at the CSCE negotiations (see Section 2.2), so there was a 'demonstration effect'. In addition, the Soviet Union was anxious to keep the economic relations between the East European states and the West under control. Mindful of the 1968 intervention in Czechoslovakia, it also hoped that economic integration in Eastern Europe would stimulate growth and help maintain stability.[36]

In 1972 Soviet leader Leonid Brezhnev declared that relations with the Community would depend on the EC recognizing realities in the socialist part of Europe, which signalled a softening in hostility towards the Community.[37] The CMEA then contacted the Community in 1973. In August CMEA Secretary Nicolai Faddeyev approached the Council president (the Danish foreign minister) to propose talks between the two organizations.[38] The Soviets sought an overarching agreement between the EC and the CMEA which would strengthen institutional – and therefore Soviet – control over the foreign trade policies of the CMEA member states. The East Europeans, for their part, hoped only for an agreement on general principles; they wanted to continue negotiating sectoral agreements with the EC and cooperation agreements with the EC member states.[39]

In both the EPC and EC frameworks, the issue of an agreement with the CMEA was considered. The EPC Political Committee examined the relationship between the Community and the CMEA, in the course of coordinating the EPC position in the CSCE. The 1972 EPC document pointed to the CMEA's lack of powers in areas where the EC did have control.[40]

The Commission's view on negotiations with the CMEA, elaborated in September 1974, was that the CMEA could not be considered a parallel organization since it did not possess supranational powers over the external commercial and trade policies of its member states.[41] Relations with the CMEA could only complement separate relations with its members; the two organizations should discuss issues such as environmental problems.

In September 1974, the Council thus responded to the CMEA that the Community (and specifically the Commission) – not the member states – was responsible for trade policy.[42] In addition, the Community would only negotiate with the CMEA member states individually. In November 1974, the Commission tried to establish trade links with the separate CMEA member states, but was rebuffed (see Section 2.1.1). The Community's stance was maintained in all dealings with the CMEA, right up to the CMEA's demise.

Relations with each CMEA member state would allow the Community to take into account that state's specific characteristics ('specificity'). An EP report pointed to another reason for dealing with the CMEA states individually:

> while one superpower, the United States, does not belong to the European Community, the Soviet Union, the other superpower, is the leading member of the CMEA.... [F]or this reason alone the European Community must make a clear distinction between trade, economic, cultural and other relations with the Eastern European CMEA countries on the one hand and with the Soviet Union on the other.[43]

The CMEA's lack of supranationality was not the primary reason why the Community refused to negotiate an agreement with it; the EC has concluded agreements with other blocs, such as ASEAN and the Andean Pact, which are not as integrated as the Community. More importantly, the Community sought to weaken the Soviet Union's domination of Eastern Europe. By minimizing the CMEA's potential role in trade negotiations, the Community might prevent the Soviet Union from limiting the autonomy of the East European countries.[44] The Community wanted to ensure that the East European states conducted their external economic relations freely, even though the CMEA's unanimity rule would have made it difficult for the Soviet Union to restrict the foreign trade practices of the other members.[45]

In addition, over and above the EC's politically motivated reticence to negotiate a trade agreement with the CMEA, John Pinder has pointed to another obstacle to an EC-CMEA agreement: neither the Soviet Union nor the Community had much economic interest in trade negotiations.[46] The EC was running surpluses in its trade with the CMEA (see Table 2.1) and, given the nature of state-trading economies, could not be assured that trade concessions would be fully reciprocated. Soviet exports to the EC (mostly raw materials) were not subject to tariffs or quotas. Only the East European countries, with the exception of East Germany, encountered protectionism in exporting to the EC and needed to negotiate concessions.

Not surprisingly then, EC-CMEA talks during the 1970s did not proceed smoothly. Faddeyev contacted Commission President Ortoli (in accordance with the Council's demands) in September 1974. Preparatory talks were then held in February 1975 between Commission and CMEA representatives, but they only resulted in an EC invitation to further talks in Brussels.[47]

In February 1976, shortly after the CSCE Helsinki summit conference, the CMEA wrote to the EC Council president to propose EC-CMEA negotiations on trade issues. The agreement would lay down principles governing trade between CMEA countries and the Community, and a joint committee would oversee the implementation of these principles, thus giving the CMEA powers over the trade policies of its members.[48]

In November the Community replied, reiterating that the EC sought trade agreements with the individual CMEA states and an agreement on areas outside trade policy with the CMEA itself.[49] Negotiations between the EC and the CMEA were then held from 1978 to 1980, without success, reflecting the incompatibility of their respective positions. In 1981, the negotiations petered out.[50] The tense international political atmosphere of the early 1980s then precluded the resumption of talks.

A change in the CMEA's stance began to occur in 1983–4. Hungary and Czechoslovakia started talks with the Commission in 1983 about expanding their sectoral trade arrangements (see Chapter 3). Then the June 1984 CMEA summit meeting affirmed that the CMEA members were ready to conclude an appropriate agreement with the Community, to promote trade and economic relations between the members of both organizations. An October 1984 message to the EC repeated the CMEA's readiness to resume negotiations.[51]

When Italian Prime Minister Bettino Craxi, then Council president, visited Moscow in May 1985, it became clear that hostility to the Community was in sharp decline and that the CMEA's position was edging closer to the EC's. On that occasion, the new Soviet leader, Mikhail Gorbachev, declared that it was time 'to organise mutually advantageous relations between (the CMEA and the EEC) in economic matters. To the extent that EEC countries act as a "political entity" we are ready to seek a common language with it, too, over international problems.'[52]

In June 1985, the CMEA Secretary Vyacheslav Sychov wrote to Commission President Delors proposing to establish official relations between the two organizations. The European Council, meeting in

Milan the same month, agreed that the Commission should explore the proposal. The Commission replied to the CMEA that it was willing to resume dialogue, but that the normalization[53] of relations between the two organizations should occur alongside normalization of relations between the Community and the CMEA member states. It asked for further details.[54] In September, Sychov sent a draft EEC-CMEA declaration: in it, the two organizations would establish official relations and state that the form of those relations would be decided in subsequent meetings. The CMEA had thus abandoned its attempt to conclude a trade agreement with the Community. However, relations were to be established between the two organizations – creating a 'favourable climate' – before they were developed with the CMEA states.[55]

The reasons for the CMEA's change of attitude stem primarily from Gorbachev's ascendence to the top of the Soviet leadership and his more open and flexible foreign policy, although the change pre-dates his election as Secretary-General of the Soviet Union's Communist Party in March 1985. The Soviet Union's economic interest in developing relations with the Community now outweighed its previous reluctance to deal with it at all. The economic situation in Eastern Europe was declining rapidly; several countries, most notably Poland, were heavily in debt to the West and oil prices had fallen, worsening the Soviet Union's trade balance. The transatlantic tensions over the gas pipeline in the early 1980s (see Section 2.3) helped ease Soviet hostility towards the Community.[56] Concern over access to the single European market spurred CMEA member states to make compromises. They probably also took into account the Community's increased economic weight after the 1986 accession of Spain and Portugal.

The Community's position on resuming negotiations was to pursue its usual parallel approach: the Community would seek to develop normal relations with the separate CMEA countries at the same time as it developed relations with the CMEA itself. In January and February 1986, External Relations Commissioner Willy De Clercq wrote to the CMEA Secretary and to the East European members of the CMEA, setting out this position. In their replies, the East European states and the CMEA accepted it; Sychov indicated that each CMEA member would decide whether to reach an agreement with the Community. By mid-1986, talks on separate agreements were beginning with Bulgaria, Czechoslovakia, Hungary, Poland and Romania, so the Community felt it could proceed with discussions with the CMEA. East Germany and the Soviet Union made normal-ization of relations conditional upon the adoption of a joint EEC-CMEA declaration.[57]

Talks on the CMEA's proposal began in September 1986 and con-tinued through 1988. The principal contention arose over the Community's insistence on including a territorial clause regarding the application of the Rome Treaty to West Berlin, to which the CMEA objected.[58] The EC, however, refused to budge from its position; West Berlin had to be acknowledged as being part of the Community.

Only in May 1988 was the question settled in the EC's favour. West Germany, which held the Council presidency during the first half of 1988, pushed hard for a solution so that the declaration could be signed by the end of its presidency. Martin Bangemann, the West German Minister for Economic Affairs, met with Gorbachev and Soviet Prime Minister Nikolai Ryzkhov in mid-May and apparently hammered out a new formulation of the Berlin clause.[59] The 'Hungarian formula' (so named because it was used in the 1978 EEC-Hungary textiles agreement) would be adopted: without explicitly mentioning West Berlin, the declaration states that it applies in all areas where the EEC Treaty is valid. Later it was agreed that the CMEA would add a statement stressing that the declaration did not affect the four-power supervision of Berlin by France, the Soviet Union, the US and the UK.[60]

The Joint EEC-CMEA Declaration was initialed on 9 June in Moscow and signed on 25 June in Luxembourg, after Council and EP approval. In it the EEC and the CMEA establish official relations and undertake to cooperate 'in areas which fall within their respective spheres of competence and where there is a common interest.' No institutions are provided for and even the cooperation element is vague, the parties agreeing that they 'will, if necessary, examine the possibility of determining new areas, forms and methods of cooperation.'[61]

The limited substance of the declaration is a result of the Community's attitude towards relations with the CMEA. 'The EC accepted the Joint Declaration with the CMEA as the entrance ticket to bilateral agreements with individual countries, not as a framework agreement that fixed an agenda for further bilateral cooperation.'[62] The CMEA had been forced to reverse its original position and accept the Community's demands, recognizing 'the Community's identity both in terms of its territory and of its competences.'[63] The Community could thus be quite satisfied, although its tenacity really paid off only with the extraordinary changes in Eastern Europe.

Within a few months of the signing of the Joint Declaration, almost all of the East European states established diplomatic relations with the Communities.[64] Trade and cooperation agreements (discussed in Chapter 3) were then concluded with the CMEA member states.

2.2 EPC, THE EC AND THE CSCE

In the 1950s and 1960s, the Soviet Union periodically floated proposals for a pan-European conference on security and economic cooperation. The West rejected them as attempts to legitimize the unsatisfactory status quo in Europe and reinforce Soviet domination over Eastern Europe. But with detente in the late 1960s, NATO agreed to the proposal provided that talks on force reductions in Europe started at the same time.[65] Along with 33 European states, the US and Canada also took part.

The CSCE provided an ideal opportunity to inaugurate the new EPC machinery. At the first EPC meeting of the foreign ministers in November 1970, it was agreed to handle the CSCE in that framework. Cooperation would allow EPC to evolve a separate European policy, so important to France. West Germany strongly favoured coordination in the CSCE forum, as a way of garnering support for *Ostpolitik*.[66] The looming transfer of national powers over trade policies towards Eastern Europe to the Community (from May 1974) was an added incentive to cooperate: by coordinating their positions on political relations with the eastern bloc, the member states could ensure they set the political guidelines by which the CCP would operate.[67]

The US, preoccupied with the Vietnam War and sceptical about the benefits of conference diplomacy, demonstrated a striking lack of interest in the CSCE and was willing to let EPC take the lead. An atmosphere of detente also 'created more room for manoeuvre for the non-military powers and blocs.'[68] The 'civilian' character of the CSCE appealed to a 'civilian' EPC: military issues did not figure prominently in the early negotiations, while NATO coordinated the Western position on confidence building measures.[69]

A common EPC approach was considered necessary to oppose more effectively Soviet attempts to control the CSCE's agenda and purpose. The USSR sought a treaty-based pan-European security system which would legitimate the division of Europe and Germany.[70] Accordingly, the CSCE would declare the immutability of frontiers and noninterference in internal affairs. The member states sought to block such an outcome: the immutability principle could be used to freeze the status quo in Europe and as grounds for the Soviets to oppose further West European integration. Western countries wanted to stress human rights and contacts, in keeping with the general approach to foster detente and interdependence between Eastern and Western Europe. They also resisted the Soviet proposal to institute a permanent machinery for the CSCE, which might reinforce the status quo.

Coordination of the member states' positions began soon after the November 1970 foreign ministers' meeting, to prepare for the 1972–3 preparatory talks. The EPC Political Committee set up two committees in the spring of 1971: the CSCE Subcommittee dealt with the political aspects of the negotiations and contained only member state representatives, while the ad hoc Group handled economic issues and included representatives also from the Commission.[71]

That the CSCE's agenda was divided into separate Baskets (one of which was economic cooperation) allowed the member states to try to maintain the division between the economic (EC) and political (EPC) policymaking mechanisms. France resisted the Commission's participation, on the grounds that the CSCE mainly dealt with security issues and was intended to be a conference among states, not blocs.[72] But after much debate, the Commission took part in talks on economic cooperation, expressing the Community view in areas under its competence.[73]

There was to be no separate Community delegation. If the Community had asked to participate in the CSCE, the USSR might have insisted that the CMEA take part as well. Commission representatives joined the delegation of the member state which held the Council presidency. The August 1975 Helsinki Final Act was signed by the Italian prime minister and Council president, on behalf of the Community. That the CMEA accepted this indicated its tacit recognition of the EC's jurisdiction over member states' trade arrangements.[74]

EPC coordination at the CSCE is widely considered to have been successful. The Nine emerged as the most coherent group at the CSCE; the neutral and non-aligned states and often the smaller eastern bloc states, supported EPC positions.[75]

The Final Act was a political statement, rather than a legally binding treaty. In Basket One, the Soviets had to accept that borders were inviolable, not immutable, and that they can be peacefully changed; in return, the principle of non-interference in domestic affairs was declared. Basket Two on economic cooperation contains only vague commitments to liberalize trade (due to Western doubts about achieving mutual reciprocity), while more detailed measures call for better operating conditions for Western businesses. In Basket Three, there are general and specific commitments favouring freer movement and contacts among people.[76]

After Helsinki, the member states continued to coordinate their positions, particularly on economic aspects, at the review conferences (such as Belgrade 1977–8).[77] But by the time of the Madrid Review Conference in 1980–3, East-West relations had deteriorated. NATO began to play a more important role in coordinating Western policy as the follow-up and related conferences (such as the Conference on Disarmament in Europe, 1984–6) dealt more with the military aspects of security.[78]

A more moralistic American foreign policy, beginning with the Carter Administration, emphasized the human rights provisions of the Helsinki Final Act and used the CSCE forum to accuse the Soviet Union of human rights violations. West European countries were uncomfortable with the US approach, but increasingly they too stressed human rights, at least rhetorically.[79] The emphasis, however, was on positive encouragement for liberalization, rather than negative sanctions.

EPC was sidelined as detente deteriorated. The deployment of Cruise and Pershing II missiles after 1979 was not formally touched upon in EPC, given its controversial and military nature. The EPC East European Working Group was only allowed to conduct academic studies, because France, supported by Denmark, wanted to maintain national bilateral policies towards the region.[80] In the early 1980s, however, the member states found themselves in conflict with the US on East-West trade issues and came together to protect their interests in trade with Eastern Europe and the Soviet Union.

2.3 TRADE AND SECURITY

The different US and West European approaches to trade with the Soviet bloc have been termed 'economic containment' and 'interdependence'.[81] The US, primary advocate of the economic containment approach, sought to deny the Soviet Union the benefits of trading with the West; trade would augment its economic and therefore military capability. The 1949 US Export Control Act imposed controls on trade with the Soviet bloc; the same year, those controls were extended on a multilateral basis in the Coordinating Committee for Multilateral Export Controls (COCOM).[82] Under the 1951 US Mutual Defence Assistance Act, the US could deny aid to its allies if they exported certain goods to a communist country.

In contrast, West European states (and West Germany above all) felt that '[p]ositive incentives like trade could draw the Soviet Union into a web of interdependent relationships with the West, and the ties created could reduce the military threat in Europe.'[83] Sanctions would not help create a secure environment in Europe; rather, trade helped to stabilize political relations and could in the long term open up the East European states.[84] Community member states were sceptical of the utility and efficacy of sanctions and export controls (except on military goods and technologies). They also had much stronger economic interests in trade with the East, for obvious geographic and cultural reasons.[85]

By the late 1970s, these two approaches increasingly clashed, as West European countries became more assertive in countering the US. This was evident in the response to the Soviet invasion of Afghanistan in December 1979. The US restricted exports to the USSR and imposed a grain embargo; American allies were then pressed to take similar actions. The initial EPC response to the invasion is notorious for the length of time – nearly three weeks – which it took to be formulated.[86] The Council did agree in January 1980 not to make up for the grain shortfall with its own imports and pledged not to undercut American sanctions, but also expressed its desire to maintain 'traditional' trade flows.[87] The Community was attempting to isolate trade relations with Eastern Europe from the deterioration in political relations between the superpowers.

American dismay with the member states' response to the invasion of Afghanistan caused tensions between the NATO allies. Further disagreements then arose over the appropriate response to the events in Poland.

2.3.1   The Polish Crisis

After Solidarnosc emerged in Poland in August 1980, the West feared a repeat of Hungary in 1956 or Czechoslovakia in 1968.[88] Warnings against Soviet intervention in Poland were coordinated within NATO.[89] The European Council also issued two warnings to the Soviet Union in December 1980 and March 1981.[90]

When martial law was declared in Poland in December 1981 without Soviet military intervention, the allies were caught unprepared. The US imposed economic sanctions on both Poland and the Soviet Union – considered to be responsible for the crisis – and then put heavy pressure on the West Europeans to follow suit. The US sanctions were also aimed at impeding the construction of a natural gas pipeline from the Soviet Union to Western Europe, which depended on Western credits and technology. The Reagan administration objected to the project, on the grounds that the West Europeans would be providing sensitive technology to the Soviets, who would then control a large percentage of Western Europe's gas supply. No US firms could supply equipment for the pipeline; General Electric could not supply components to its licensees in West Germany, Italy and the UK. But the pipeline project continued; a recently nationalized French firm supplied the components.[91]

The West European states used the Community/EPC framework to counter the US pressure. As Peter Marsh noted:

> [T]he member states undoubtedly found it advantageous to use the Community framework to develop a common resistance to American attempts to orchestrate a Western sanctions policy against Poland and the Soviet Union, on the grounds that such a policy threatened the Community's interests in East-West economic relations.[92]

The response to the US demands was the first time Community sanctions were imposed, and followed an EPC discussion. Belgium was Council president during the first half of 1982, and considered that the sanctions question fell under both the EC and EPC frameworks; the barriers between them could thus be reduced.[93]

On 15 December 1981 the foreign ministers, meeting in EPC, called for an end to martial law, but it was clear that this would not meet US demands for sanctions.[94] On 4 January 1982 the foreign ministers played for time, agreeing to consider measures on credit and economic assistance to Poland and on commercial policy towards the USSR.[95] No economic sanctions were actually imposed against Poland, although some member states decided (in NATO) to limit new credits to Poland and not to reschedule Poland's official debts. The Commission and Council also decided that food aid, as well as emergency medical aid, would be delivered through non-governmental organizations (NGOs).[96]

In February the Council discussed restricting some imports from the Soviet Union, although Greece opposed the proposal; the Commission then proposed reducing quotas on eight per cent of Soviet imports. On 15 March, the Council further limited the Commission's proposal, reducing quotas on 1.4 per cent of Soviet imports.[97] The Council regulation contained only a vague reference to the political reasons behind it ('Whereas the interests of the Community require that imports from the USSR be reduced'), so that it could be based on article 113; nonetheless, this was the first time that a Community instrument was used to implement a position first decided in EPC.[98] The use of a Community instrument also proved necessary because Greece still objected to the measure, preventing an EPC consensus. Since EC regulations could be differentiated, Greece could be exempted from it in a separate regulation.[99]

Differences with the US were made clear. In March 1982, the heads of state or government 'recognized the role which economic and commercial contacts and cooperation have played in the stabilisation and the development of East-West relations as a whole and which they wish to see continue on the basis of a genuine mutual interest.'[100]

For the US, the Community's response was inadequate and proof that the member states were dangerously dependent on trade with Eastern Europe (even though trade with the CMEA countries was a very low percentage of their total trade). The matter was discussed in early June 1982 at the Versailles summit of the G-7. Agreement was supposedly reached on improving export controls on strategic goods and on limiting credits to the Soviet Union and Eastern Europe.[101] But the US then forced the issue: on 18 June, it extended the December sanctions to all subsidiaries and licensees of US companies. They were forbidden to export any oil and gas equipment made with American technology or components to the Soviet Union. The sanctions directly affected several West European firms involved in the construction of the gas pipeline.

All of the EC member states immediately protested at this interference in their commercial affairs. In late June, the foreign ministers and the European Council objected to the US decision as an illegal extraterritorial extension of US law.[102] France and the UK ordered their companies to carry out contracts with the Soviet Union; Italy and West Germany strongly encouraged theirs to do the same.[103]

To handle the pipeline dispute with the US, the member states relied on the Community framework rather than EPC, as

Julie Katzman has noted. Member states resisted discussing tensions with the US in EPC as it could send too political a message. The Community's protests to the Americans centered on the economic, trade and legal implications of the US move, not its political ramifications. Community involvement would allow the large member states to avoid direct conflict with the US while increasing their bargaining power, and let the smaller member states play more of a role.[104]

On 14 July, the Community delivered a formal protest to the US; on 12 August, the Commission and Council presidency again presented an official note to the US stating the unanimous position of the member states: the US should withdraw the sanctions.[105] In November 1982, the US backed down and lifted its sanctions, claiming that its allies had agreed on stronger measures regarding trade with the Soviet Union, a view immediately rejected by French President Mitterrand.[106] Between 1982 and 1984, however, a major review of COCOM was undertaken, which resulted in tighter controls on sophisticated computer and telecommunications equipment, and the lifting of controls on some computers.[107] Studies on East-West economic relations were then carried out by various organizations, including NATO; generally they concluded that trade and credit should flow according to market indicators and that governments should not grant preferential treatment to the state-trading countries.[108]

The Community's sanctions against the Soviet Union were not renewed in 1983, since martial law in Poland had been lifted in July 1983 and political prisoners released. Transatlantic tensions subsided, although the US remained wary of close ties between Western and Eastern Europe until 1989. It greeted the EC-CMEA talks that led to mutual recognition in 1988 with caution. The US warned that the deal would be more economically beneficial to the CMEA than to the EC and that it would cause a rift between the EC and the US.[109]

The disputes over the Polish crisis and the pipeline prompted the formulation of a common position on trade relations with Eastern Europe. The member states banded together to counter the US emphasis on the link between trade and military security and to protect their interests in East-West trade. In doing so, they contributed to the Community's development: 'A classic example of an external threat promoting internal solidarity, the pipeline row served, in the final analysis, to strengthen the Community and to increase the credibility of the Commission.'[110]

CONCLUSION

By 1988, the Community/EPC was playing a larger role in Eastern Europe. But the gamut of instruments available to the Community was incomplete, some still being held by member states, and this limited what it could do in the region. The Community/EPC could not have pursued an ambitious, proactive policy in Eastern Europe anyway: not only would member states have objected to the pre-empting of their own prerogatives, but Cold War realities impeded such an independent move. As the Cold War ended, it was not clear that the member states would agree to an active common policy towards Eastern Europe.

The member states had, however, clarified their common interests in maintaining political and economic ties with Eastern Europe, especially in times of tension between the superpowers, and had increasingly asserted those interests. They had agreed that such ties (particularly trade) were important for engendering liberalization and encouraging independence from Moscow. CSCE principles later formed the basis of conditionality in relations with Eastern Europe, which in turn was based on the specificity of relations with the separate CMEA states. The member states had recognized (albeit reluctantly) that lowering the barrier between the separate policy-making mechanisms (external economic relations and foreign policy) was necessary. The Community had established its jurisdiction over trade policy, and the East European states had already turned to it for trade concessions. EC trade agreements (with Romania and Yugoslavia) had been used to reward independence in foreign policy. With the EEC-CMEA agreement, the Commission was in a prime position to increase its involvement in relations with Eastern Europe, as it negotiated trade and cooperation agreements with the separate CMEA members. By 1988, then, the Community/EPC had established a legacy – albeit limited – of cooperation on relations with Eastern Europe and had set precedents which could be expanded upon as communism collapsed.

3 Developing a Common Foreign Policy Towards Eastern Europe, 1988–9

The collapse of communism in the fall of 1989 coincided with a very dynamic period in the Community's history, what with the drive to complete the single European market and plans for an economic and monetary union. The Community manifested a new assertiveness.[1] There was a general expectation, both within the Community and outside it, that the Community would be a 'cornerstone' of the new European architecture. It had the right instruments to match the East European states' priorities of economic reform, trade with the West, and inclusion in 'Europe'. This expectation of Community leadership, however, took time to develop. In the spring of 1989, after months of hesitation, the member states finally agreed that there should be a common, consistent approach to Eastern Europe. The Community was thus in a position to take the lead in responding to the astounding events of autumn 1989.

In the first section of this chapter, the development of a common foreign policy towards Eastern Europe in 1988–9 will be traced. By mid-1989, the main objective of the policy had basically been agreed: encouraging and supporting the reform process. The success of the reforms was considered crucial for ensuring long-term stability and security in Europe, in the belief that capitalist, free-trading, democratic countries make better neighbours because they do not pose a threat to security. To encourage reforms, the Community offered trade concessions and aid conditional on progress towards democracy and the market economy, and the protection of human rights. Applying conditionality[2] clearly links economics and politics.

Conditionality seems to be a reverse of the Community's position during the Cold War, when trade with communist Europe was seen as a way to stabilize political relations: trade could be used as a 'carrot', but the Community hesitated before using it as a 'stick'. At the end of the Cold War, the Community modified its stance, and wielded its economic power to support economic and political reforms in Eastern Europe.[3] Developing closer relations was still seen as a way to promote stability, but conditionality has gradually developed as a norm,[4] or standard, for Community/Union foreign policymaking. Although it competes with other considerations (such as commercial interests), it is now increasingly applied (though not always consistently) in the EU's relations with all third countries.[5]

The second section of this chapter will discuss the policy instrument that the Community initially used to support reform in Eastern Europe: trade and cooperation agreements. After the signing of the EEC-CMEA Joint Declaration, the Community concluded agreements with the separate CMEA members, on a conditional basis. The trade and cooperation agreements became the first stage in the Community's relations with East European countries, but in 'pre-revolutionary' 1988–9, they were really the EC's only policy instruments.

3.1   TOWARDS A COMMUNITY *OSTPOLITIK*

The Community's dynamism of the late 1980s contrasted with the so-called 'Eurosclerosis' (stagnant economic growth, institutional gridlock) of the 1970s and early 1980s. The fast-approaching end of the Cold War freed the Community of the limitations imposed by the highly politicized and militarized bipolar confrontation. It seemed more able to act collectively, and on a wider world stage, than previously. The climate of international relations was more conducive to the exercise of civilian, or 'soft', power and multilateral cooperation.[6] Yet the Community member states still did not agree on a common policy towards Eastern Europe for some time.

Belgium and the Commission were the first to push for a common, consistent policy on Eastern Europe, beginning in 1988. Belgium, traditionally a strong proponent of common, consistent foreign policies, advocated a common stance on East-West relations.[7] Belgian Foreign Minister Leo Tindemans called on the Community/EPC to comply fully with Title III of the SEA: member states should try to act jointly, and EC and EPC policies should be consistent.[8] The Commission, now much more involved in relations with Eastern Europe as it negotiated trade and cooperation agreements with the CMEA members, advocated a more prominent role for the Community. Its active president, Jacques Delors, did not hesitate to become involved in the discussions on a policy towards Eastern Europe.

The Belgians were particularly alarmed by the proliferation of national initiatives towards the Soviet Union: several member states visited Moscow in the autumn of 1988, to strengthen economic co-operation and offer credits. The smaller member states feared that the large states would forego Community solidarity in favour of their own policies. In the month of October alone, the UK, West Germany, France and Italy had approved or signed commercial loan packages of £1 billion, £940 million, £300 million, and £400 million respectively, to the Soviet Union.[9] The large member states were reacting to the new opportunities by trying to secure benefits for themselves, using policy instruments they refused to let the EC control.

On 18 July 1988, a month after the EEC-CMEA declaration, the twelve foreign ministers decided that their October Gymnich meeting would be devoted to a reflection on the future of relations with Eastern Europe (and the Soviet Union) and the formulation of a coherent reaction to the changes in Eastern Europe.[10] At the Gymnich meeting, they asked for two documents to be submitted to the Rhodes European Council on 2 and 3 December 1988. The first, to be drafted by the Political Directors and the EPC Secretariat, would be a general document on the political guidelines that the Twelve should follow in relations with the Soviet Union and Eastern Europe. The Commission would draft the second, on economic relations with the East European states. These requests appear to be an attempt to ensure consistency.

The October Gymnich meeting, however, also exposed divisions over Community relations with Eastern Europe.[11] At this point, developments in Eastern Europe depended on the success of Gorbachev's reforms, and the divisions reflected optimism or pessimism about that prospect. One group, including the UK and Portugal, considered the developments in the Soviet bloc to be positive, but wanted to wait and see how Gorbachev's reforms turned out. West Germany and Italy led the other group, arguing that the Community should not wait to support Gorbachev. Without a common analysis of developments, a common approach was not possible.

In a speech to the EP on 16 November 1988, Delors called for a common approach to Eastern Europe. He wanted the Rhodes European Council to agree on an analysis of East-West relations and on the role to be played by the Community. He also pressed for common rules on export credits, to stem competition over trade credits to the Soviet Union. The Commission needed an idea of the framework within which economic relations should develop.[12]

Delors and the Belgian government in particular wanted the Rhodes European Council to adopt a separate declaration on East-West relations.[13] In the end, the European Council only included a paragraph on East-West relations in its statement on the Community's international role. As Simon Nuttall noted, 'no more prescient than others, the Heads of State and Government had not yet realized the changes in store and the need for a fresh policy'.[14]

The statement on the Community's international role was aimed primarily at reassuring third countries that the single European market would not create a 'Fortress Europe'. It acknowledged that economic and security policies are inseparable, especially in Europe, and that the external policies of the EC and EPC should be closely linked. The leaders welcomed the development of relations with the CMEA members; they would also develop a political dialogue with them (and initial contacts for bilateral political dialogue with the Soviet Union, Poland and Hungary were made the following year). 'The European Council reaffirms its determination to act with renewed hope to overcome the division of our continent and to promote the Western values and principles which Member States have in common.'[15]

The two documents on economic and political relations prepared for the Rhodes summit, however, remained on the table, to the dismay of the Commission and Tindemans.[16] On 17 January 1989, Delors told the EP that at the Rhodes summit he had

> expressed his personal regret that political co-operation was making less headway than economic co-operation and that the Twelve were reluctant to agree on common positions or to take joint initiatives in the East-West dialogue.[17]

Tindemans urged his colleagues to discuss the formulation of a general Community policy on relations with the Soviet Union and Eastern Europe at the 20 February 1989 meeting of the General Affairs Council. Belgium wanted the Community to define common orientations to guide the member states' national policies towards Eastern Europe.[18]

The debate at the General Affairs Council, however, did not satisfy either Belgium or the Commission. The Council could only agree that coordination of economic and political relations with Eastern Europe was desirable. The UK and France were reluctant to set Community procedures that could limit their freedom of action in the region; other member states hesitated to support Belgium and the Commission.[19] The Council did approve the Commission's mandate for negotiating trade and cooperation agreements with Poland and Bulgaria, a measure loaded with political significance (see Section 3.2.2).

By spring 1989, however, the pace of events in Eastern Europe was influencing the member states' attitudes towards cooperation on a common policy. In Poland, the Round Table talks were initiated and concluded; Solidarity was legalized; and open, multiparty legislative elections were to be held in June. In Hungary, laws allowing the freedom of association and the formation of independent political parties were approved in January and February 1989; in May, the government began dismantling the barbed-wire fence on the Austrian border. These were 'refolutions', in Timothy Garton Ash's words: a mixture of reform led from above and popular pressure from below;[20] though the revolutions were yet to come, the changes were still remarkable in context.

After a Gymnich meeting in mid-April, the Spanish foreign minister and Council president, Francisco Fernandes Ordoñez, said that the Twelve would adopt a 'common strategy' in their relations with Eastern Europe. Delors welcomed the debate as the start of deeper reflection on the issue.[21]

At the General Affairs Council meeting on 24 April, a significant step towards a common policy was taken. The Council largely agreed to proposals put forward by Belgium and the Commission. It emphasized the need to follow a more comprehensive, consistent and dynamic approach to Eastern Europe. It insisted on the necessary coherence of the various Community actions and indicated that it would be up to the General Affairs Council to guarantee that coherence. Coherence must be assured at two levels. First, cooperation between the Community and Eastern Europe must complement that of member states. Better coordination between these policies was needed, and the Commission was to prepare a report on this. Second, greater consistency must also be established between Community and EPC policies. Communication between the EC and EPC should be improved and intensified and both should adopt a summary document indicating the initiatives taken at both levels.[22]

Thus after months of quibbling, the Council had agreed that there should be a consistent approach towards Eastern Europe. According to one observer,

> rapid political developments have evidently persuaded countries such as the UK and France of the need for better co-ordination, even if that means some Commission encroachment into the area

of East-West political relations that member states have so far jealously guarded for themselves.[23]

Consistency could be achieved by applying conditionality, although the norm was not yet articulated clearly. Yet, in the Community's relations with East European countries, conditionality was already being applied. The opening of negotiations for, and the specific provisions of, the trade and cooperation agreements depended particularly on respect for human rights. At the 24 April meeting, however, the Council only reaffirmed that agreements with the East European states were to be differentiated according to each state's specific characteristics. Not mentioned in the Council's conclusions was that the 'specificity' of agreements allows conditionality to be applied. But conditionality *was* applied: at the same meeting, the Council suspended negotiations with Romania because of its internal political repression, and called for the rapid conclusion of a generous trade and cooperation agreement with Poland (see Section 3.2.2).

Coreper and the Political Committee jointly prepared a report on the Community's economic and political relations with Eastern Europe for the Madrid European Council, 26–7 June 1989.[24] At the summit, the twelve leaders 'reaffirmed the full validity of the comprehensive approach integrating political, economic and cooperation aspects which the European Community and its Member States follow in their relations with the USSR and with Central and Eastern European countries.' They regretted the violations of human rights still occurring in some East European countries, and 'reaffirmed the determination of the Community and its Member States to play an active role in supporting and encouraging positive changes and reform.'[25]

A few days later, at the G-7 summit in Paris on 14–16 July, the Community emerged as the leading actor in the West's relations with the reforming Eastern Europe. The G-7 agreed to work together, along with other countries and international institutions, to support the reforms in Poland and Hungary. To manage this undertaking, they asked the Commission 'to take the necessary initiatives in agreement with the other Member States of the Community, and to associate, besides the Summit participants, all interested countries.'[26]

The G-7 decision is significant in several respects. Firstly, it signalled a change in the West's attitude towards the reforming East European countries (but not yet towards the USSR). Aid was now considered an appropriate instrument of policy towards Eastern

Europe: Poland and Hungary *were* serious about reforming and needed Western help. Policy towards Eastern Europe from then on had three aims: aid was intended to facilitate economic reforms; reforms would help reintegrate each country into the world economy; and this would help create a new European regional security order.[27]

Secondly, the EC was considered to have a special responsibility for its East European neighbours:

> The practical demonstration of the relevance of the Community to the reconstruction of Europe as a whole facilitated the emergence of a consensus inside the Community, and indeed outside it, that the EC as such was ideally placed to become a cornerstone of the new European construction.[28]

The Community was expected, by its member states and by outsiders, to lead in the region. The Community's dynamism certainly fuelled such expectations, helped of course by the fact that the member states had already agreed that a common approach was needed.

Thirdly, the Commission had been thrust into a highly visible leadership role, not only by third states, but also by the four largest EC member states (G-7 participants); undoubtedly, this would have implications for the Community, both for external policy and for internal developments. 'For the first time, the Commission was a foreign policy actor in its own right.'[29]

After the G-7 summit, history 'accelerated'; in the autumn of 1989, the communist regimes crumbled under the weight of people power. No one anticipated these extraordinary events, but the Community was well-placed to try to respond to them, having already assumed a leadership role in helping the reformist regimes.

This was a historic moment, and there was a general sense that the Community *should* lead, as a 'cornerstone' of the new Europe. All of the member states agreed that collective action would be far more effective than separate national responses to the events in Eastern Europe (the 'politics of scale'). They all agreed that the Community had the appropriate instruments to respond to East European requests for trade concessions, financial help and assistance with economic and political reforms. The so-called 'core' – France and Germany – strongly supported a common policy: Germany preferred not to act alone in Eastern Europe, for primarily political and historical reasons; France advocated an active common *Ostpolitik* to balance a potentially dominating German role in Eastern Europe.

The Community's objectives (support for reform) and means to achieve them (specificity, conditionality) basically remained the same, but further initiatives were launched to try to match the momentous challenges arising from the revolutions in Eastern Europe. Immediate help was needed with economic reforms, although by making assistance conditional on political reform, the Community tried to foster democratic change as well. Many of the policy instruments used to support economic reforms (aid, trade concessions) were either already under EC jurisdiction or had been wielded at the EC level in other circumstances (which put the Community, rather than EPC, in the 'driving seat'). In a sense, then, the Community was relying on 'standard operating procedures', but at a much faster speed than usual and in a region where previously its role had been limited. The Community also extended its jurisdiction and generated new initiatives for Community and Western action to boost the reform process (see Chapter 4).

In the buzz of activity, the Commission played a crucial role. Simon Nuttall notes: 'Everything had to be done by everybody, all at once. The intrinsically economic nature of the problem gave the lead role to the Commission, which did not muff its lines, and was backed up in its rapid and integrated action by the Member States.'[30]

The line between EPC and EC was fading quickly, under the pressure of events. In November 1989, Delors reiterated that relations with Eastern Europe could not be artificially separated into economic and political spheres.[31] EPC and EC business was coordinated in a new procedure. The chairs of the relevant EPC and Council working groups attended each other's group meetings.[32] Closer coordination was evident higher up as well. On 19 September, External Relations Commissioner Frans Andriessen and French Foreign Minister and Council President Roland Dumas visited Warsaw to discuss the changes in Poland and sign the trade and cooperation agreement.[33] From 16 to 18 November, Delors and Dumas visited Warsaw and Budapest to survey the economic and political situation there.[34] The extent of EC–EPC collaboration highlights the exceptional nature of the Community's policy towards Eastern Europe in the pre-Maastricht Treaty era. It also reflects the pressing need for 'everyone to act all at once'.

On 9 November, perhaps the most symbolic event of the revolutions of 1989 occurred: the Berlin Wall fell. France, as Council president, then called a special European Council summit in Paris on 18 November 1989 to discuss the Community/EPC's stance on the developments in Eastern Europe. The leaders only discussed relations with Eastern Europe, not the possibility of German unification,[35] but the events in East Germany certainly rammed home the magnitude of the changes in Eastern Europe. The European Council convened a couple of weeks before a Bush-Gorbachev summit (near Malta), and was thus the first high-level exchange of views on events in Eastern Europe.

The *EC Bulletin* noted that the twelve leaders 'were struck by the convergence of views and the shared concern that there should be a joint reaction from the Twelve.'[36] The summit represented an important step in the Community/EPC's development: political cooperation and Community activities were integrated and guidelines for Community action were drawn up on the basis of a common analysis. The European Council gave high-level political backing to the Community's initiatives, endorsing a number of French and Commission proposals to aid Eastern Europe, including a loan to Hungary, two training programmes and the European Bank for Reconstruction and Development, or EBRD (see Chapter 4).[37]

The regular European Council summit, held in Strasbourg on 8 and 9 December 1989, was primarily devoted to a discussion of internal developments, namely Economic and Monetary Union. This was to ensure that the Community proceeded with integration as Germany moved towards unification (see Chapter 5).[38]

The summit adopted two texts on Eastern Europe, one from EPC on the broad political framework, and the other from the EC on concrete activities. The two documents were consistent in substance, but had not been prepared by a joint drafting body, as had happened at the Rhodes summit.[39] Both show that the member states were aware that this was a turning point in history and agreed that the Community should play a decisive role in it. In the 'EC' document, the leaders reflected:

> The Community's dynamism and influence make it the European entity to which the countries of Central and Eastern Europe now refer, seeking to establish close links. The Community has taken and will take the necessary decision to strengthen its cooperation with peoples aspiring to freedom, democracy and progress and with States which intend their founding principles to be democracy, pluralism and the rule of law.[40]

Strengthening cooperation also entailed association (see Chapter 5); already in the autumn of 1989, the Community had begun to consider a longer-term strategy to support the transformation in Eastern Europe.

The 'EPC' document declared that the Community and its member states were

> fully conscious of the common responsibility which devolves on them in this decisive phase in the history of Europe... . At this time of profound and rapid change, the Community is and must remain a point of reference and influence.[41]

The leaders called for closer political relations with the Soviet Union and East European states, in so far as they were committed to reform. Relations with the Community/EPC were thus emphatically linked to the democratization of its aspiring partners.

In the rest of this chapter the first policy instrument used by the Community, the trade and cooperation agreements, will be examined. Since 1991, they have been supplanted by association agreements (discussed in Chapter 5). The Community's aid initiatives will be covered in Chapter 4.

3.2   TRADE AND COOPERATION AGREEMENTS

From the signing of the Joint Declaration through November 1989, the Community and the CMEA held exploratory talks twice, to discuss cooperation. By the autumn of 1989, the CMEA had identified several areas for cooperation, including energy, transport and technology. The EC, however, felt that cooperation could take place in more appropriate fora, such as the UN Economic Commission for Europe.[42]

EC-CMEA negotiations had proceeded slowly: the Commission wanted to ensure that agreements with the separate CMEA members were concluded first. The Community was certainly not enthusiastic about cooperating with such a Cold War relic, nor did the East European countries encourage it. The Commission noted in January 1990 that the East European states 'look to the Community to take a prudent position, avoiding action which might reinforce outmoded structures while strengthening bilateral links with Comecon members.'[43]

By late 1989, EC-CMEA relations were lost in the Community's intense activity to aid the separate CMEA members. Even before the CMEA was formally dissolved on 28 June 1991, the sticky problem of bloc-to-bloc cooperation had been overcome by basically ignoring it. The CMEA's demise, however, meant that the former Comecon 'partners' were no longer linked in an institutional framework. The Community then encouraged the East European states to cooperate and form a free trade area (see Chapter 7).

From June 1988 to July 1989 (and the launching of aid programmes), the Community was primarily concerned with expanding trade and cooperation with the separate CMEA members. The General Affairs Council on 25 July 1988 'confirmed the importance the Community attaches to developing these relations on the basis of a pragmatic and flexible approach, taking account of the special features of each individual case'.[44] Member states ruled out granting aid to Eastern Europe; in October 1988, UK Foreign Secretary Sir Geoffrey Howe said the Community agreed on 'credits, yes; charity, no'.[45] To a great extent, this was because reforms had not progressed far enough to assuage concerns about the security implications of aiding countries that still belonged to the Warsaw Pact. Yet at the same time member states were competing to provide export credits to the Soviet Union, and still had their own cooperation agreements with East European states. Member states' reluctance to permit greater EC involvement at this stage indicates lingering resistance to any infringement by the Community of their prerogatives in relations with Eastern Europe.

The Community hoped that closer trading relations with the East European states would not only create opportunities for EC businesses, but also contribute to overall security (the classic liberal position). As German Foreign Minister Hans-Dietrich Genscher noted, '[e]conomic cooperation creates trust, common interests and stability.'[46]

The trade and cooperation agreements are significant in several respects. Firstly, in negotiating these agreements, the Community developed the norm of conditionality. Until 1988, specificity did not entail conditionality; the opening of exploratory talks with the CMEA members in the mid-1980s was not made conditional on political reform (rather it depended on whether they were willing to approach the Community). In 1988, however, the sense that things were changing in some CMEA states and the Community's growing assertiveness led it to use conditionality to encourage reform. If a country contravened CSCE human rights provisions, the EC would withhold the prospect of a trade and cooperation agreement. Countries that were further ahead in the reform process would be accorded more beneficial treatment. Only at the end of 1989, however, was the conditionality norm articulated clearly. In 1988–9 the Community was developing a foreign policy towards Eastern Europe, based on the conditional use of the trade and cooperation agreements, without explicit political direction from EPC.

Secondly, the agreements represent an extension of the EC's competences in an area where the member states had previously tried to limit them. As discussed in Chapter 2, the member states had effectively restricted the Community to negotiating trade provisions with the East European countries, while they concluded far-reaching economic cooperation agreements which promoted their industries and firms. In the late 1980s, however, the member states allowed the Community to conclude *cooperation* agreements with the CMEA members.

Thirdly, the member states agreed, at first reluctantly, to eliminate eventually their numerous national QRs on East European imports. Even before autumn 1989 (when all restrictions were lifted immediately), they had agreed to drop their restrictions in stages.

In Section 3.2.1 below, the general features of the trade and cooperation agreements will be outlined; in Section 3.2.2, the separate negotiations on the agreements will be discussed, to illustrate the application of conditionality. Section 3.2.3 will cover the extraordinary measures that the Community took, from the autumn of 1989, to improve market access for the reforming East European countries, even as several agreements were being negotiated.

3.2.1 Provisions of the Agreements

From 1988, the Community negotiated and concluded agreements with Hungary, Poland, Czechoslovakia, Bulgaria, the GDR[47] and Romania. (A trade and cooperation agreement was also signed with the Soviet Union on 18 December 1989.)[48] Table 3.1 summarizes some of the salient features of the agreements.

The agreements do not cover 'sensitive' goods (coal and steel products, textiles and some agricultural products), which are covered by voluntary restraint agreements. The agreements all provide for reciprocal MFN treatment. They contain a territorial clause, the object of so much controversy during the negotiations on the EEC-CMEA declaration.

The agreements altered the Community's 'autonomous policy', the EC label applied to the member states' specific quantitative restrictions on East European imports (see Section 2.1.1). Although

Table 3.1   Trade and Cooperation Agreements, 1988–91

	Date signed	Date of entry into force	Duration	Deadline for removal of QRs	OJ refer.
Hungary	26 Sept 88	1 Dec 88	10 years	31 Dec 95	L327 30 Nov 88
Poland	19 Sept 89	1 Dec 89	5 years	31 Dec 94	L339 22 Nov 89
CSFR	7 May 90	1 Nov 90	10 years	31 Dec 94	L291 23 Oct 90
Bulgaria	8 May 90	1 Nov 90	10 years	31 Dec 95	L291 23 Oct 90
GDR[1]	8 May 90	–	10 years	31 Dec 95	–
Romania	22 Oct 90	1 May 91	10 years	31 Dec 95	L79 26 Mar 91

Sources: *EC Bulletin* and *Official Journal*.
Note: [1] The agreement never entered into force and thus was not published in the Official Journal. See *EC Bulletin* no. 5, 1990, pt. 1.3.10 for a summary of it.

only three to five per cent of EC-East European trade was affected, the restrictions covered goods that are significant for the East European economies such as textiles, glassware, footwear, chemical products and certain agricultural goods.[49] Many quotas still went unfilled, prompting the Commission to assert that East European exports to the Community were not stymied by the restrictions but by their shoddy quality.[50]

These national restrictions on imports were clearly incompatible with the single European market: controls at intra-EC frontiers were to be abolished by 1 January 1993, making it impossible to keep out goods that had been imported into the Community via another member state. Because of the sensitivity of the issue, however, restrictions on imports from third countries were to be eliminated gradually, on a case-by-case basis.[51]

In their negotiations with the Commission, all of the East European states sought the complete elimination of the restrictions. The extent to which the Commission could fulfill these wishes reflects how far national objections could be overcome in the name of a Community endeavour. Discussions on the removal of the quantitative restrictions were the most heated for the first two trade and cooperation agreements, with Hungary and Poland. The Community eventually agreed to lift specific quantitative restrictions in stages, leaving until 1994 or 1995 those on highly sensitive products.[52]

The agreements encourage economic cooperation in a variety of areas, such as industry, agriculture, energy, transport and environmental protection, according to the requests of each East European country.[53] They maintain the practice of 'mixed competence' between member states and the Community. The EC has concluded cooperation agreements with third countries before, but this always raised the thorny problem of respective competences between the Community and the member states. In the East European agreements, the problem was resolved as per usual: member states must substitute the provisions of the agreements for incompatible or identical provisions in any agreements they have concluded with the East European states, but they can still pursue bilateral economic cooperation programmes.[54]

The very inclusion of 'economic cooperation' in these agreements, however, represents a significant extension of the Community's competences, as previously only the member states had negotiated cooperation accords with the East European states. No provisions were made to finance economic cooperation, although that would not have been unprecedented: for example, the 1976 and 1977 cooperation agreements with the Maghreb and Mashreq countries provided for EC grants and European Investment Bank (EIB) loans. That the member states could provide significant funds for economic cooperation with East European states meant that they could upstage the Community. It also meant that the trade and cooperation agreements with East European countries, while providing a rudimentary framework for cooperation, proved inadequate once the Community began actively to support reform.

A joint committee of representatives from both parties was to oversee the functioning of the agreement. This would be another occasion for the Community to extend its control over external economic policy: member states would have to coordinate their positions within the committee, and the Commission would increase its contacts with the East European country.[55] The joint committees met yearly until the trade and cooperation agreements were replaced with association agreements.

3.2.2 Conditionality in Practice

The agreements with each of the East European states reflect the development of political and economic reform in those states. The state of reform in each country also affected the progress of negotiations. At this stage, conditionality was not always stated clearly, as evidenced in the different treatment of Bulgaria and Romania. While the Community's use of conditionality obviously did not cause the 'revolutions of 1989', it did provide a guide for reforms once they had been initiated, and the new regimes seemed eager to prove that they were fulfilling the EC's conditions.

The EC-**Hungary** agreement, signed in September 1988, was the Community's most extensive agreement with any state-trading country at that time, reflecting the more advanced state of Hungary's reforms. The Commission publicly stressed that the agreement did not set a precedent, but effectively it did serve as an example of what other East European states could gain from the EC if they too implemented far-reaching reforms. After partially abandoning the 1968 New Economic Mechanism, the regime had introduced further reforms in the early 1980s; in May 1988, reform-minded Karoly Grosz became Communist Party leader.

Hungary had approached the EC in 1983–4, to discuss extending the sectoral agreements.[56] Hungary demanded several concessions, which the Community refused to grant, because Hungary was not yet a market economy. The talks faltered, and did not revive until mid-1986, after the CMEA and its members had accepted the EC's parallel approach. In April 1987, the Council granted the Commission a mandate to negotiate a trade and cooperation agreement; negotiations began that June.[57]

Disagreements arose primarily over the timetable for the elimination of quantitative restrictions on Hungarian imports. Most EC member states were willing to drop their quantitative restrictions, eventually, as a sign of goodwill towards the fastest reformer in the eastern bloc. Some, like Italy (which had a high number of quotas), were not so ready.[58] Hungary wanted the final deadline for eliminating all quotas to be 1992; the EC first pushed for an indefinite obligation and then tried for 1998.[59] A deal was eventually struck whereby protection against a surge of sensitive Hungarian imports could be implemented until 1998 (the 'super-safeguard' clause), in exchange for dismantling quantitative restrictions by 1995. The foreign ministers apparently – and improbably – promised the Commission that the extension of their quotas until 1995 would not prejudice the single European market.[60] The Commission and the German presidency pushed hard to conclude the agreement before the summer of 1988 (and the end of Germany's presidency); on 30 June, it was initialled by the negotiators (shortly after the EEC-CMEA declaration was signed). The agreement was signed on 26 September and went into force on 1 December.

The first exploratory talks on an agreement with **Poland** were held in July and November 1986.[61] In successive rounds of informal talks, Poland made it clear that it wanted to conclude a trade and economic cooperation agreement. In December 1988, the Commission asked for a mandate to negotiate an agreement based only on article 113, which would cover industrial and agricultural products and encourage cooperation in some areas, but would not set a deadline for the elimination of all quantitative restrictions.[62]

The Council, however, was prepared to go even further, to reflect political developments in Poland. In early February 1989, representatives from the Polish government, Solidarity and the Catholic Church began to discuss reforms at the Round Table talks. The Council's negotiating mandate to the Commission, approved on 20 February, authorized the Commission to discuss a five-year agreement that would set dates for the removal of quantitative restrictions and cover all areas of economic cooperation.[63] Negotiations opened in March.

The successful conclusion of the Round Table discussions in April 1989, which legalized political parties and set a June date for parliamentary elections, was welcomed in Commission and EPC declarations.[64] At its 24 April meeting, the General Affairs Council noted that the events in Poland required a more favourable, flexible stance in negotiations.[65] On 22 May, Andriessen suggested amending the agreement to reflect the EC's approval of the political changes: a deadline could be set for the final removal of all quantitative restrictions; some agricultural products could be included; and EIB loans could be provided. The Council broadly supported the first two proposals, but hesitated over the last.[66] The UK, backed by France and the Netherlands, opposed lending to heavily-indebted Poland: dealing with third countries' debts did not fall under the EC's competence.[67]

Unquestionably, though, Poland hoped the Community would address its massive debt problem. During a visit to Brussels in May, Solidarity leader Lech Walesa appealed to Delors for support. Delors then promised that the EC would launch an initiative in favour of the middle-income indebted countries at the G-7 summit in July.[68]

Negotiations on the trade and cooperation agreement ended on 25 July 1989 and it was signed on 19 September. In the end, the EC only noted a Polish declaration expressing its desire for access to EIB financing.[69] Unlike the agreement with Hungary, in which concessions on agricultural products are to be discussed in the joint committee, Poland and the EC agreed to lower levies and/or duties on about ten agricultural products. The willingness of EC member states to grant such concessions reflected the new attitude towards aiding Eastern Europe and the fact that Poland's economy was in worse shape than Hungary's and was experiencing food shortages.[70] The final deadline for removing all quantitative restrictions was 1994, and Poland did not have to agree to a super-safeguard clause, indications of the EC's more benevolent approach to reforming East European countries, and Poland's less threatening export capacity.

In 1983, talks between **Czechoslovakia** and the Commission began regarding additional sectoral agreements. The Community suggested instead an agreement on industrial goods, like the 1980 agreement with Romania.[71] In November 1986, the Council gave the Commission a mandate to negotiate an agreement on trade in industrial products. In mid-1988, the conclusion of the negotiations was delayed because Czechoslovakia, aware of the EC-Hungarian agreement, asked for a final deadline for the lifting of EC quantitative restrictions. Such a clause would have exceeded the Commission's mandate, however and Czechoslovakia had to retract its request. The Commission reiterated that the EC-Hungary agreement did not set a precedent for other agreements.[72] In 1988, the process of political and economic reform in Czechoslovakia was not nearly as advanced as it was in Hungary.[73]

The four-year agreement on trade in industrial products was signed on 19 December 1988 and went into effect on 1 April 1989.[74] Some quantitative restrictions on Czech goods were to be lifted as soon as the agreement went into effect, but no provisions for removing other restrictions were set. Although the agreement does not include economic cooperation and was based on article 113 only, the EP ratified it because it was considered to be a politically important one.[75]

In December 1989, the 'velvet revolution' swept through Czechoslovakia. Within days of its formation on 8 December, the new government headed by Prime Minister Marian Calfa asked the Commission to begin negotiations on a trade and cooperation agreement.[76] Informal talks began, and Andriessen visited the country in January 1990.[77] On 5 March, the Council approved a negotiating mandate for a trade and cooperation agreement.[78] Negotiations went quickly: the agreement was signed on 7 May and went into force on 1 November. The final deadline for removing quantitative restrictions was 31 December 1994, reflecting the EC's approval of the pace of reform. By the time the agreement had been concluded, however, it was out of date. Extension of aid to Czechoslovakia was soon to come, along with the accelerated removal of quantitative restrictions (see Section 3.2.3). Already in March 1990, Foreign Minister Jiri Dienstbier stated that Czechoslovakia wanted to conclude an association agreement and eventually join the EC.[79]

The first exploratory talks between the Commission and **Bulgaria** were held in October 1986. Bulgaria wanted a trade and economic cooperation agreement; the Commission wanted to limit the agreement to trade, with only general principles established on cooperation.[80] In December 1988, the Commission asked the Council for a negotiating mandate for agreements, based on article 113, with Bulgaria and Poland. The Council wanted to go further and on 20 February 1989 approved a wider negotiating mandate for both agreements. Although Poland's reforms were progressing much faster than Bulgaria's, the agreement with Bulgaria would be part of the same normalization process.[81] In negotiations in April and May, however, Bulgaria demanded immediate trade liberalization measures and a final deadline for the elimination of all quantitative restrictions. The EC was not willing to go that far because Bulgaria was not implementing market economic reforms.[82]

Concerns over the treatment of the Turkish minority in Bulgaria were also increasingly voiced. In 1989, Bulgaria intensified a campaign of forced assimilation of its estimated 800,000 ethnic Turks. In June 1989, Belgium invoked the CSCE mechanism on human rights against Bulgaria, asking for information on the Turkish minority.[83] In October, France, EC Council president, requested information on seven dissidents, on behalf of the Twelve and other Western countries.[84]

In June 1989, the negotiating session between Commission and Bulgarian officials that was to be held at the end of July was postponed and negotiations were suspended. No official reason was given, although later it was acknowledged that the political situation, particularly the treatment of minorities, in Bulgaria had occasioned the rupture.[85]

In November 1989, the velvet revolution began to sweep through Bulgaria, though it did not leave behind such radical changes as elsewhere. The Bulgarian prime minister wrote to Delors on 1 December to inform him of the government's intention to hold free elections and ensure the rights of the Turkish minority, and to ask for the resumption of negotiations. A new cabinet was appointed in February 1990, though still composed entirely of Communists. Negotiations with the EC resumed in March 1990.[86] The trade and cooperation agreement was signed on 8 May 1990 and came into force on 1 November 1990.

Just as the Community's relations improved with the other CMEA members, those with **Romania** – once the West's privileged partner behind the Iron Curtain – deteriorated. In June 1986, the Commission asked for a mandate to negotiate a cooperation agreement with Romania, which was approved in December. The 1980 agreement would be extended to cover agricultural products and economic co-operation. During negotiations in 1987, Romania insisted that the 1980 trade provisions be revised in its favour, but the EC maintained that they were not up for reconsideration.[87]

The EC was concerned with the decline in its trade balance with Romania; in the 1980 accord, Romania had agreed to expand and diversify its imports from the Community, but the EC's exports to Romania were falling (see Table 2.1). More significantly, Romania was showing blatant disregard for the CSCE provisions on human rights. By 1988, Romania's violations of human rights, mistreatment of minorities, and planned destruction of thousands of villages (many of which were inhabited by ethnic Hungarians) in a 'systemization' programme, had sparked outrage in the Community. The Community and the Twelve criticized Romania in EPC declarations and at the CSCE follow-up conference in Vienna (1986–9). On 7 September 1988, the Greek presidency expressed concern to the Romanian authorities over the systemization programme.[88] In February 1989, the Romanian ambassador in Madrid (Spain held the presidency) was summoned to the Spanish foreign ministry and the Spanish ambassador in Bucharest met with a Romanian foreign ministry official, to request information about 24 Romanians who had protested over the destruction of villages.[89] Romania refused to reply to the request and on 28 March the presidency issued a press statement requesting Romania to comply with CSCE commitments.[90]

Romania, alone among its Comecon 'partners', refused to establish formal diplomatic ties with the Communities after the EEC-CMEA agreement.[91] Negotiations on extending the 1980 agreement were blocked at the beginning of 1989.[92] In March 1989, the EP demanded that the Community reexamine relations with Romania. During the

EP debate on the resolution, Andriessen affirmed that given the conditions in Romania, there could be no question of continuing negotiations.[93] On 24 April, the Council and Commission suspended the talks, because of Romania's failure to honour CSCE human rights obligations. They declared further: 'Any resumption of the negotiations will take place only if clear evidence emerges of a significant improvement in Romania's respect for human rights and its observance of the commitments it has entered into through the Helsinki process.'[94] This clear declaration of the reasons for the suspension contrasts with the silence over the suspension of talks with Bulgaria; this indicates that the Community still resisted using the 'stick' except in very blatant cases.

Unrest broke out in Romania in December 1989, which the government attempted to put down with force. An EPC statement on 19 December condemned the regime and its brutal repression of the demonstrations.[95] The 1980 trade agreement was frozen and application of the GSP suspended.[96] On 22 December violence in Bucharest forced the dictator Nicolae Ceausescu and his wife Elena to flee, though they were captured the same day and executed on 25 December. The 'Council of National Salvation', consisting of many former Communists, assumed power and announced its desire to normalize relations with the Community.[97]

In January 1990 Andriessen visited Romania, emphasizing the need to strengthen democracy and hold elections, and affirming that negotiations on a trade and cooperation agreement could begin soon.[98] The conclusion of an agreement was still a long way off. The Commission postponed the resumption of talks until the end of March 1990, because the new government's reform programmes were not very detailed and contacts were difficult.[99] The Romanian authorities then got their act together and provided the Commission with information on political and economic reforms. Diplomatic relations were established in March.[100]

The Council approved the negotiating mandate for a trade and cooperation agreement in May and the agreement was initialled on 8 June 1990.[101] That same month, however, the government allegedly trucked in several thousand miners to battle with student protesters in Bucharest. The Commission announced that as a result it would not proceed to the conclusion of the agreement.[102] An EPC statement deplored the indiscriminate use of force against peaceful demonstrators and reiterated that the Community would only support countries committed to pluralist democracy.[103]

The General Affairs Council, meeting in mid-June, stated that it could not set a date for the signing of the agreement.[104] The decision was not, however, without controversy. At the July Council meeting, some members states (including France and Italy) argued that marginalizing Romania could jeopardize the democratization process, rather than encourage it; others (the UK and Netherlands) disagreed and the matter was left unresolved.[105] On 22 October, though, the Council signed the agreement.[106] The EP then delayed ratification until 22 February 1991.[107] The Council concluded the agreement on 4 March and it entered into force on 1 May 1991.

The difficult process of transformation in Bulgaria and Romania would place those countries in the slow lane in terms of progress towards closer relations with the Community. The wisdom of such an approach would be increasingly doubted. Could strict conditionality backfire? Was the Community – by insisting on the fulfilment of economic and political criteria as a condition of closer relations – generating isolation, economic hardship and the creation of another 'Iron Curtain' in Europe? Would applying conditionality simply drive East European countries back into the Soviet/Russian sphere of influence? Yet grouping Romania and Bulgaria together with countries such as the Czech republic and Poland seems incongruous given the state of reform in the first two countries. Since 1988–9 the debate about the application of conditionality has centered in particular on relations with these two countries.

3.2.3 Further Trade Concessions

The G-7 decision to extend aid to Poland and Hungary in July 1989, and the accelerating collapse of communism throughout Eastern Europe, prompted the Community to reconsider the extent to which it had agreed to open its markets to East European imports. In an action plan for Western and Community aid drawn up in September 1989,[108] the Commission maintained that the trade and cooperation agreements did not remove trade restrictions fast enough. It proposed four measures to improve market access for Poland and Hungary: the accelerated removal of quantitative restrictions; concessions on agricultural imports; tariff concessions; and extension of GSP benefits. The initial reaction of the General Affairs Council on 2 October was favourable; Italian Foreign Minister Gianni De Michelis even proposed that as of 1 January 1990, Italy would eliminate those quantitative restrictions scheduled for removal in 1994 or 1995.[109]

On 6 November 1989, the Council abolished specific quantitative restrictions as of 1 January 1990 for Poland and Hungary.[110] It also asked the Commission to submit a proposal that went even further, by suspending non-specific QRs (that is, on imports from any country) on goods from Poland and Hungary.[111] On 4 December the Council did just that.[112] Thus, the member states agreed to do away with the very restrictions that they had been so obdurate about during the negotiations on the trade and cooperation agreements, one of which had just been signed with Poland in September, plus additional non-specific restrictions. The QRs lifted were those on non-sensitive goods; steel, textiles and agricultural goods were not included. Nonetheless, the measures are significant and reflect the interests of the Community and its member states in supporting reform in Eastern Europe. As other East European countries launched reforms, these benefits were extended: as of 1 October 1990 to Bulgaria and Czechoslovakia and as of 1 May 1991 to Romania (the day the trade and cooperation agreement entered into force).[113]

Tariff preferences under the GSP were granted to Hungary and Poland as of 1 January 1990. The benefits were extended to Bulgaria and Czechoslovakia in January 1991. Romania had obtained some preferences under the GSP in 1974, but from January 1991, those preferences were expanded.

While concessions on agricultural products remained blocked,[114] textile and clothing quotas were increased: in 1990 and 1991 for Czechoslovakia, Hungary and Poland, and in 1991 and 1992 for Bulgaria and Romania.[115] Agreements on ECSC products were signed with Poland and Hungary in October 1991 and with Czechoslovakia in February 1992.[116]

Even with these additional measures, the Community's openness to East European goods was considered inadequate by free traders within the EC and by the East European countries. The new association agreements provided for better market access and replaced the previous agreements and concessions (see Chapter 5).

The trade and cooperation agreements could also not be fully exploited as long as COCOM restrictions on exports to Eastern Europe were still in place. The rules now seemed absurd: how could industry in Eastern Europe be modernized if technology could not be exported there? After the European Council met in November 1989, French European Affairs Minister Edith Cresson revealed that the leaders agreed to try to introduce flexibility into COCOM rules.[117] But in February 1990, the US stalled on West European proposals to loosen some restrictions: Eastern Europe would have to guarantee that goods would not be adapted for military use, or reexported to the Soviet Union.[118] At a COCOM meeting in June 1990, however, restrictions on one-third of the products on the restricted list were dropped (including computers, machine tools and telecommunications) and other restrictions were relaxed.[119] Further restrictions were lifted in 1992. In November 1993, the members agreed to dissolve COCOM.[120]

CONCLUSION

Until the spring of 1989, the member states were reluctant to limit their freedom of manoeuvre in Eastern Europe. It was still considered a sensitive area of primarily national interest, and as the communist regimes liberalized, the member states sought to benefit from strengthening their bilateral relations with them. But following the signs of definite change in Poland and Hungary, the member states agreed to work out a common approach towards Eastern Europe. The basic objectives (support for economic and political reform) and principles/norms (specificity, conditionality) of the common policy were made fairly clear before the revolutions swept through Eastern Europe. The use of trade and cooperation agreements drove this process forward considerably, and placed the Community (more so than EPC) in the 'driving seat' of policymaking.

Once the magnitude of events in Eastern Europe became apparent, the member states supported a leading role for the Community (and the Commission). There was a sense that it was responsible for ensuring that the transformation succeeded. The member states realized that they could not possibly face the challenge posed by the collapse of communism separately; the politics of scale were at work. The Community was the entity to which the reforming East European states turned for assistance and to a remarkable extent, the Community responded collectively (and quickly) to their requests. But the Community also did more than simply respond to East European demands: by applying conditionality, it used its instruments to encourage political and economic reforms. Some of those instruments are discussed in Chapter 4.

4 Aid

While the trade and cooperation agreements may have been appropriate policy instruments in a 'pre-revolutionary' era, they were inadequate for the new circumstances in Eastern Europe. In July 1989, aid became an instrument of Western policy towards Poland and Hungary (the fastest reformers), with the launching of the G-24 aid programme, coordinated by the Commission. When the 'revolutions of 1989' swept through the rest of the region, the Community was 'catapulted' into a leadership role.[1] As communism collapsed in one country after another, the Community led the West's aid initiatives in Eastern Europe. It is one of the largest donors to Eastern Europe.

The Commission's coordination of the G-24 aid programme will be discussed in Section 4.1. The Community also set up its own aid programme, PHARE (Section 4.2), extended loans to the East European countries (Section 4.3) and helped establish the EBRD (Section 4.4).

4.1 THE COMMISSION'S ROLE IN COORDINATING G-24 AID

The G-7 decision to entrust the Commission with the task of coordinating the West's programme to assist the economic reform process in Poland and Hungary, though unprecedented, makes sense.[2] The Twelve had agreed (in April) to coordinate their relations with Eastern Europe and the Commission was in the midst of negotiating trade and cooperation agreements with the East European states. The decision was fostered by Delors' close relationship with three main leaders, German Chancellor Helmut Kohl, French President François Mitterrand, and US President George Bush. In talks with Bush in June, Delors set out his ideas on how reforms in Poland and Hungary could be supported. Bush urged coordination of Western aid, since the US could not provide all the resources itself. Kohl approved of the idea, needing an acceptable international framework for a national effort to aid Eastern Europe. France would not have been averse to Commission leadership, given the close ties between Mitterrand and Delors, and France's desire for the Community to balance German influence in the region.

What caused the most excitement was that the Commission had never been called upon formally to coordinate the actions of non-member states; no provisions in the Rome Treaty provide for such a development. The Commission did not hesitate to seize the opportunity to expand its influence. It reacted quickly to the G-7 invitation, although it had to scramble to find the personnel to do so.[3] A G-24 Coordination Unit was set up within Directorate-General (DG) I for External Economic Relations (now DG IA).

At the General Affairs Council held one day after the G-7 summit, the Commission presented its guidelines and plans for the aid programme, which were approved by the ministers.[4] It also convened a meeting on 1 August, to discuss aid coordination. Invited to the meeting were representatives from the 24 members of the OECD.[5] The programme is thus known as the G-24 aid programme, although international financial institutions (the IMF, World Bank and EBRD) also participate. The G-24 hold regular meetings at senior official and working group levels, and occasionally at ministerial level, to ensure that policy and aims are coherent, discuss possible joint projects, and assess the progress of reforms in each recipient country.

At the 1 August 1989 meeting, the Commission presented its plans and proposals, which the G-24 endorsed. The Commission identified five priority areas for aid: agricultural supplies and restructuring; access to markets; investment promotion; vocational training; and environmental protection. Working groups were set up in each area to coordinate actions and make proposals.[6] Additional working groups were set up in other areas later. On 4 May 1993, G-24 senior officials decided that the working groups would continue in the areas of nuclear safety, macroeconomic assistance and environmental protection, but groups would discuss other sectors on a country-by-country basis. This would ensure that the recipient countries were more integrated into the decisionmaking process.[7]

The Commission's coordination role includes acting as a clearing-house: the G-24 are supposed to inform it about their aid programmes, so as to avoid taking 24 separate but overlapping and therefore inefficient bilateral actions to aid the East European countries. Most G-24 initiatives originate in the Commission. The Commission tries to bring donors together to appraise possible projects and finances some joint projects.[8] Joint projects have been difficult to put together, not least because donors compete to fund visible, prestigious projects.[9] They also favour certain countries, because of geographic proximity and traditional ties. German aid to Poland, for example, is very substantial; Finland and Sweden give a lot to the Baltic states; Italy is the largest single donor to Albania. These national aid programmes coexist with PHARE, the Community's aid programme, which is one of the largest sources of aid to Eastern Europe.[10]

It has been much easier for the Commission to attract donors to projects under PHARE. According to one official, PHARE (with its large resources) has become the '25th member' of the G-24 and its officials have great influence on G-24 activities.

International financial institutions have become integrated within the G-24 process. There is a great deal of coordination between the Commission, IMF, World Bank and EBRD. PHARE, for example, finances technical assistance and feasibility studies, which permit the EIB and EBRD to make loans for investment projects.[11]

Table 4.1 illustrates G-24 assistance to all East European recipients from 1990 to 1996. The EU and its member states accounted for 53.76 per cent of total G-24 aid. Germany was the largest single donor, with 17.77 per cent of the total, while EU programmes (including PHARE and macro-financial assistance), plus EIB and ECSC loans, account for 16.31 per cent of assistance. The G-24 assistance includes aid for debt reorganization (13.5 per cent of sector aid) and export credits (almost 20 per cent of total assistance), neither of which the Community itself provides. The EU provides the most grant aid.

The G-24 have coordinated their views regarding which countries should receive aid, based on conditionality. After the events of late 1989, the G-24 considered extending the programme. The Community's position on conditionality became G-24 policy: 'The pre-eminently political task of establishing and verifying conditionality was thus carried out on the Community side.'[12] The Commission played a significant role in this, in close contact with the member states: on G-24 conditionality (and other political issues), the Commission and national officials worked together in the informal advisers' group, which met weekly in Brussels.[13]

At the December 1989 G-24 meeting of foreign ministers, four countries were considered for aid: Bulgaria, Czechoslovakia, GDR and Yugoslavia. Romania was added to the list in February 1990. Several Commission missions were sent to the candidate countries; in January 1990, Commissioner Andriessen visited Czechoslovakia, Bulgaria and Romania, to gather information on their economic and political reforms.[14]

In February 1990, the Commission proposed to the Council that potential aid recipients must fulfill five conditions: they must be

Table 4.1   G-24 Assistance Commitments, 1990–6
(to all recipients)

	Total Assistance Committed (ECU million)	of which grants (ECU million)	Donors' percentage of total aid
Austria	3975.31	965.33	4.05
Belgium	271.27	89.27	0.28
Denmark	1470.43	823.93	1.50
Finland	758.63	232.29	0.77
France	6565.46	2311.57	6.69
Germany	17 436.73	4115.38	17.77
Greece	87.22	66.49	0.09
Ireland	3.38	2.04	0.00
Italy	1601.42	605.49	1.63
Luxembourg	32.79	10.29	0.03
Netherlands	1371.84	695.53	1.4
Portugal	3.95	0.01	0.00
Spain	713.22	13.23	0.73
Sweden	1557.39	405.45	1.59
UK	884.11	206.73	0.90
Total EU Member States	36 733.16	10 543.04	37.44
EU Programmes	11 051.43	8288.63	11.26
EIB	4761.00		4.85
ECSC	200.00		0.20
EU Total (including member states)	52 745.59	18 831.67	53.76
Iceland	5.62	4.09	0.01
Norway	581.62	164.26	0.59
Switzerland	1017.87	508.16	1.04
EFTA Secretariat	1.68	1.68	0.00
Australia	131.68	8.77	0.13
Canada	1828.42	1297.32	1.86
Japan	5270.31	1215.01	5.37
New Zealand	232.76	1.00	0.24
Turkey	471.23	80.21	0.48
US	11 126.39	6422.53	11.34
EBRD	5016.99		5.11
World Bank	9356.90		9.54
IMF	10 322.27		10.52
Grand Total	98 109.34	28 534.70	100

Source: G-24 Scoreboard, 9 September 1997.

committed to the rule of law, respect for human rights, the establishment of multiparty systems, the holding of free elections in 1990 and economic liberalization. The countries concerned would not have to demonstrate success in implementing such reforms, but would have to be committed to achieving them.[15] The General Affairs Council on 5 February approved the Commission's report: 'This co-ordinated assistance should be provided on the basis of commitments from the countries concerned to political and economic reform. In addition, the programme of assistance should be adapted to each country's own situation, specific requirements and absorption capacity.'[16]

Once the Commission determined progress had been made, the European Council in April 1990 agreed that G-24 aid should be extended to the five countries.[17] In June, however, the situation in Romania deteriorated. The foreign ministers (meeting as the General Affairs Council and in EPC) and Commission expressed doubts about extending aid. The foreign ministers sent the troika of political directors to Romania, to gather information on the situation there.[18] The Commission did not invite Romanian representatives to a G-24 ministerial meeting in July.[19]

On 4 July, G-24 foreign ministers decided to extend aid to Bulgaria, Czechoslovakia, the GDR and Yugoslavia. The G-24 determined that Romania did not qualify for assistance, but stated that aid could be extended once Romania met the five conditions.[20] G-24 aid was not extended to that country until 30 January 1991. The Soviet Union and its successor states (with the exception of the Baltic republics) are excluded from the programme.[21]

4.2 PHARE

PHARE is the framework within which most of the Community's initiatives to assist the reform process in Eastern Europe have been taken.[22] While the Community had prior experience in development aid programmes, what was significant was that now the Community was acting – and leading – in a region from where it had previously been excluded and for predominately political reasons. PHARE's size and importance have placed the Community – and especially the Commission – in an extraordinary position of influence. The member states, however, have tried to set limits on PHARE.

While PHARE primarily supports the economic transformation in Eastern Europe, its objective is, in the end, political: in doing so, it will 'help to establish democratic societies based on individual rights.'[23] PHARE 'supports the development of a larger democratic family of nations within a prosperous and stable Europe.'[24]

The General Affairs Council approved the legal framework for PHARE in December 1989.[25] PHARE became operational at the start of 1990 for Poland and Hungary; the programme was extended as the G-24 extended aid to other East European states, on the basis of conditionality (although conditionality is not mentioned in the PHARE regulations). On 17 September 1990, five more beneficiaries were added: Bulgaria, Czechoslovakia, the GDR, Romania and Yugoslavia.[26] The Council, however, only finalized the extension of PHARE aid to Romania at the end of January 1991, after the G-24 had decided that the political and economic situation in the country was satisfactory.[27] (In 1991, the Community set up a separate programme, TACIS, to aid the Commonwealth of Independent States.)

PHARE's initial budget (for 1990) was 300 million ECUs, but with the extension of the programme to other East European countries, it was increased by 200 million ECUs in 1990. By 1992, PHARE's budget had more than doubled (see Table 4.2). In July 1994, the Commission suggested that 7.072 billion ECUs be allocated to PHARE for 1995–9.[28] PHARE's tasks were increasing since the June 1993 European Council decided to consider enlargement to the East European countries: PHARE was to help prepare them for eventual membership (see Chapter 6). But some southern member states were concerned that aid to Eastern Europe was draining resources from Mediterranean countries.[29] The Essen European Council in December 1994 could only agree that the 1995 PHARE budget (1.1 billion ECUs) would be the

Table 4.2   PHARE Funds Committed, 1990–5
(in ECU million)

1990	495.1
1991	773.6
1992	1012.3
1993	1007.9
1994	973.3
1995	1154.7
Total	5416.9

Source: European Commission, 'The PHARE Programme Annual Report 1995', COM (96) 360 final, 23 July 1996, p. 3.

minimum budget for each year until 1999 (5.5 billion ECUs for 1995–9).[30] At Cannes in June 1995, however, the European Council agreed to provide 6.693 billion ECUs for PHARE for 1995–9. The amount allocated would increase yearly, to 1.634 billion ECUs in 1999.[31]

The member states have tried to increase their control over PHARE by specifying that aid must be used for specific programmes. They have been 'jealous' of PHARE, because its resources and importance dwarf their own aid programmes, with the exception of Germany's, and have thus tried to reduce PHARE's effective budget.[32] For example, PHARE has provided humanitarian aid for refugees in the former Yugoslavia; up to 0.5 million ECUs was even contributed to the EC's monitoring mission there.[33] PHARE funds are being used to develop the regions along the East European states' borders with the Community, an initiative backed by Germany, which was seeking help for its own similar projects. But the member states cannot significantly challenge PHARE's importance and the Commission's influence.

The Commission's DG IA (originally DG I) manages PHARE. The service had been organized on a sectoral basis, but in 1995, the Commission reorganized it on a country by country basis so as to better focus aid on each country's pre-accession programme, preparing them for eventual EU membership.[34] The PHARE service is short-staffed, and has had to rely on personnel on short-term contracts – an indication of the Council's unwillingness to budget extra funds for permanent staff.[35] Staff in the Commission's delegations in the recipient countries help administer PHARE.[36]

PHARE is demand-driven. The recipient countries reach agreement on annual (increasingly multiannual) indicative programmes with the Commission; within the areas indicated specific projects are identified by the recipient country and funded. Consultants are then hired to manage or carry out each project.[37]

The demand-led approach has been problematic: sometimes resources are not efficiently used.[38] Bulgaria and Romania in particular have often left PHARE aid unused, reflecting governmental confusion and internal conflicts over reform. Some conditionality has been introduced at the disbursement level: in 1994, a programme involving the Romanian Ministry of Health was terminated on the ground of non-performance.[39]

Funding decisions must be approved by a management committee of the member states' representatives. The Commission proposes measures and the committee approves them by a qualified majority vote: one way in which member states have tried to limit the Commission's influence within PHARE.[40]

Initially, funds had to be committed within the year.[41] As early as January 1990, the Commission urged the Council to allow 'adequate multiannual budgetary provisions'.[42] In November 1992, the Council agreed that there should be a multiannual approach to programming.[43] In 1993, the Commission began adopting a multiannual approach in several indicative programmes.[44] But implementation of the multiannual indicative programmes is still subject to the annual budgetary procedure, so that funds allocated in the programmes can only be indicative.[45]

PHARE has been criticized for not disbursing enough funds, cumbersome and slow bureaucratic procedures, centralized management and a reliance on expensive EC consultants who do not know local conditions.[46] In July 1993, Sir Leon Brittan, the Commissioner for External Economic Relations (1993–4), announced that PHARE would be decentralized and streamlined.[47] The 1993–7 PHARE guidelines state that projects would be more differentiated between the beneficiary countries. Special fast-track decisionmaking procedures for small projects were introduced. A 'decentralized implementation system' has been increasingly used, whereby an agency in the recipient country is responsible for executing individual PHARE programmes.[48] The disbursement of PHARE funds (initially very low) has since risen: almost all of the 1995 committed funds were contracted, for example.[49]

PHARE is the largest single source of grant financing for the East European countries. Aid is directed to several priority sectors, including privatization and private sector development, agricultural restructuring, environment and nuclear safety, infrastructure, education and training, and humanitarian and food aid (Tables 4.3 and 4.4 list the distribution of PHARE funds, by country and by sector). Aid is given to provide essential imports of equipment and inputs, but most aid has been concentrated on providing know-how, or technical assistance, to help the recipients draft legislation, design policy and build institutions. Under the PHARE 'umbrella', several framework programmes have been established, including the Trans-European mobility scheme for university studies (Tempus)[50] and the Joint Venture PHARE Programme (JOPP), which helps EC firms set up joint ventures in the recipient countries.

PHARE has evolved to reflect the changes in Eastern Europe and changes in the Community's priorities. For example, aid has been

Table 4.3   PHARE Funds Committed by Country, 1990–5
(in ECU million)

Albania		Lithuania	
1990	0	1990	0
1991	10	1991	0
1992	110	1992	20
1993	75	1993	25
1994	49	1994	39
1995	88	1995	42
Bulgaria		**Poland**	
1990	24.5	1990	180.8
1991	106.5	1991	197
1992	87.5	1992	200
1993	90	1993	225
1994	85	1994	208.8
1995	83	1995	174
Czech Republic		**Romania**	
1990	0	1990	15.5
1991	0	1991	134.3
1992	0	1992	152
1993	60	1993	139.9
1994	60	1994	100
1995	110	1995	66
Czechoslovakia		**Slovakia**	
1990	34	1990	0
1991	99	1991	0
1992	100	1992	0
1993	0	1993	40
1994	0	1994	40
1995	0	1995	46
Estonia		**Slovenia**	
1990	0	1990	0
1991	0	1991	0
1992	10	1992	9
1993	12	1993	11
1994	22.5	1994	24
1995	24	1995	25
GDR		**Former Yugoslavia**	
1990	35	1990	30.2
1991	0	1991	13.1
1992	0	1992	47.7
1993	0	1993	25
1994	0	1994	25
1995	0	1995	25

Table 4.3 *(Continued)*

Hungary		Multi-country Programmes	
1990	89.3	1990	72.3
1991	115	1991	88.4
1992	101.5	1992	116
1993	100	1993	112.3
1994	85	1994	86
1995	92	1995	104
Latvia		**Other Programmes**	
1990	0	1990	13.4
1991	0	1991	10.4
1992	15	1992	43.6
1993	18	1993	74.8
1994	29.5	1994	119.5
1995	32.5	1995	243.2

Source: European Commission, 'The Phare Programme Annual Report 1995', COM (96) 360 final, 23 July 1996, pp. 30–1.

increasingly channelled to regional cooperation projects and to projects to foster democratization (see Chapter 7).

The 1993–7 guidelines stated that PHARE would move from technical assistance to investment support measures in sectors such as environment, energy, job creation, research and infrastructure. This was supposed to reflect the progression of economic reforms. Initially, countries need help establishing the regulatory and institutional framework for a market economy and devising a reform programme. Later, they need direct support for long-term restructuring, in the form of investment and financing.[51]

But several member states were not enthusiastic about the changes. At a General Affairs Council meeting in May 1993, the UK contested a Commission proposal to finance infrastructure projects.[52] A month later, the UK, Ireland and the Netherlands tried to limit funds for infrastructure development to ten per cent of the PHARE budget; the Commission and other member states pushed for a limit of 15 per cent.[53] The European Council in Copenhagen on 21–2 June 1993, agreed on 15 per cent to be used to facilitate infrastructure improvements in recipient countries.[54]

In July 1994, the Commission suggested that the limit on infrastructure spending be lifted.[55] Some member states were concerned that this

Table 4.4 PHARE Funds Committed by Sector, 1990–5
(in ECU million)

Agricultural Restructuring		**Public Health**	
1990	136	1990	0
1991	89	1991	45
1992	80	1992	15
1993	78.5	1993	26.5
1994	17	1994	13
1995	40.6	1995	2
Civil Society and Democratization		**Public Institutions/ Administrative**	
1990	0	**Reform**	
1991	0	1990	10
1992	9	1991	26.5
1993	10	1992	25.1
1994	16.2	1993	65.7
1995	10.5	1994	81.9
Critical Aid		1995	24.6
1990	101.7	**Social Development and**	
1991	71.4	**Employment**	
1992	119.7	1990	3
1993	44.9	1991	35.5
1994	30	1992	48.2
1995	25	1993	15
		1994	28.5
Education, Training and Research		1995	47.3
1990	36.6		
1991	90	**Approximation of Legislation**	
1992	140.5	1990	0
1993	162.2	1991	0
1994	169.9	1992	0
1995	147.1	1993	0
		1994	0
Environment and Nuclear Safety		1995	2
1990	102.5		
1991	92.5	**Consumer Protection**	
1992	90	1990	0
1993	38.9	1991	0
1994	77.5	1992	0
1995	82	1993	5
		1994	4
Infrastructure (energy, transport,		1995	2
telecommunications)			
1990	6.8	**Financial Sector**	
1991	42.5	1990	7
1992	96.8	1991	40
1993	114.9	1992	44.7
1994	326.4	1993	61
1995	457.2		

Table 4.4   *(Continued)*

Private Sector Development and Enterprise Support		1994	56
		1995	40.5
1990	64	**Integrated Regional Measures**	
1991	180.5	1990	0
1992	191.5	1991	4.3
1993	194.5	1992	16.5
1994	93.4	1993	10
1995	139.2	1994	4
		1995	47
		Other Sectors	
		1990	27.4
		1991	56.5
		1992	135.2
		1993	180.9
		1994	55.5
		1995	87.6

Source: European Commission, 'The Phare Programme Annual Report 1995', COM (96) 360 final, 23 July 1996, pp. 32–3.

confused the roles of PHARE and the EBRD.[56] The European Council in Essen, 9–10 December 1994, though, did raise the limit: 25 per cent of PHARE financing could be used to help develop infrastructure, including building links with the EU's trans-European networks.[57] PHARE acts as a bridge between the contributions of international financial institutions, private operators and national efforts.

In March 1997, the Commission adopted new PHARE guidelines for those recipient countries preparing for eventual EU membership. PHARE would have two main priorities: institution building (for which 30 per cent of PHARE funds would be earmarked) and financing investment (allocated 70 per cent of funds). To help the recipients adopt the *acquis communautaire*, PHARE would help strengthen democratic institutions and administrations, and finance investment and infrastructure projects in areas such as transport and environment.[58]

4.3   LOANS

In addition to PHARE, the Community has extended loans to the East European countries. In September 1989, the Commission proposed making Poland and Hungary eligible for EIB loans.[59] In a change from the reluctance of member states to contemplate EIB loans to Poland just a few months earlier (see Section 3.2.2), the economic and finance ministers ('Ecofin Council') approved the proposal on 9 October 1989. The EIB's Board of Governors then authorized loans of up to 1 billion ECUs to Poland and Hungary.[60] EIB loans have since been extended to other East European countries, as they implemented reforms (see Table 4.5).[61] The loans help renew and develop infrastructure, contribute to energy, telecommunications, and environment projects and support small- and medium-sized enterprises.

ECSC loans have also been extended: on 7 May 1990, the General Affairs Council agreed to lend up to 200 million ECUs to Poland and Hungary to improve the environment and work safety record of coal mines and to increase steel consumption, but not production (given the 'sensitivity' of steel imports in the Community).[62] In November 1991, the Council agreed to extend ECSC loans to Czechoslovakia, Bulgaria and Romania.[63] In addition, in March 1994, the Council decided that Euratom could lend up to 1.115 billion ECUs to East European countries (and Russia and Ukraine as well), to help improve nuclear safety.[64]

The Community has also granted medium-term loans for macroeconomic stabilization for the reforming East European states, basically to

Table 4.5   EIB Lending to Eastern Europe, 1990–6
(in ECU million)

Albania	46
Bulgaria	286
Czech Republic	992
Estonia	68
Latvia	31
Lithuania	101
Hungary	872
Poland	1406
Romania	475
Slovakia	353
Slovenia	150
Total	4780

Source: European Investment Bank, 'EIB Financing in Central and Eastern Europe', February 1997.

cover balance of payments deficits or support structural reform programmes. The first loan, 870 million ECUs for Hungary (agreed by the Ecofin Council in February 1990), was the first Community macro-financial operation for a third country. Since then, loans have been extended to several other East European countries (see Table 4.6).

The other G-24 donors are supposed to contribute as well, but they have been less willing to do so.[65] EU assistance is to be discontinued when the recipient can fully rely on financing from international financial institutions and private capital.[66]

Disbursement of the loans depends on IMF approval of the recipient's structural reforms and fulfilment of economic criteria set by the Commission. A loan to Bulgaria was approved in October 1992, but not released until May 1994 because of the slow progress of reform there; disbursement of assistance to Albania and Romania was also held up in 1994 and 1995.[67] The Ecofin Council reactivated the loan to Romania in March 1997, backing the new Romanian government which had just adopted a reform programme.[68] In 1996, the decision

Table 4.6 EC Macro-Financial Assistance to Eastern Europe, 1990–6 (in ECU million)

Hungary	870	(1990)
CSFR	375	(1991)
Hungary	180	(1991)
Bulgaria	290	(1991)
Romania	375	(1991)
Albania	70	(1992)
Estonia	40	(1992)
Latvia	80	(1992)
Lithuania	100	(1992)
Romania	80	(1992)
Bulgaria	110	(1992/1994)
Romania	125	(1994/1997)
Albania	35	(1994)
Slovakia	130	(1994/repealed)
Total	2860	

Sources: European Commission, 'Report from the Commission to the Council and the European Parliament on the Implementation of Macro-Financial Assistance to Third Countries in 1995', COM (96) 695 final, 8 January 1997; *EU Bulletin*.

Note: date on which maximum amount was authorized is in parenthesis.

to grant assistance to Slovakia was repealed because Slovakia's economic situation improved and because the Commission's conditions had not been met.[69]

In providing macro-financial assistance, the Community has extended its competence. It has been *too* successful for some member states: some economic and finance ministers have complained that the EC is doing the work of the IMF and World Bank.[70] The Community, however, continues to provide such assistance.

Member states have resolutely retained competence in the area of export credits. The Commission has repeatedly proposed setting up Community export credit instruments. In July 1994, the Commission proposed a directive establishing common principles for credit guarantees to promote national exports, but it sparked opposition.[71] Export credits are a major part of the member states' assistance to Eastern Europe.

4.4   THE COMMUNITY'S ROLE IN ESTABLISHING THE EBRD

The EBRD has often been touted as a Community project: 'The creation of the EBRD is the Community's main multilateral initiative for Central and Eastern Europe.'[72] The reality is a bit different, although the Community – a multilateral organization – did play a major role in setting up another multilateral organization. The initiative forms part of the effort to promote private investment in Eastern Europe.

French President Mitterrand launched the idea of creating a development bank for Europe in October 1989, without consulting his EC partners beforehand.[73] Many have claimed intellectual ownership of the EBRD idea and a number of related proposals were made public before Mitterrand's speech.[74] Nonetheless, France held the Council presidency and so was in a prime position to propel the idea forward. In fact, France's possessive hold on the project sparked opposition from other member states.

Not all of the member states were as enthusiastic; for example, Italy, the Netherlands, the UK and West Germany did not see the need to create a new institution.[75] The EIB could just as well lend to investment projects in Eastern Europe.

Mitterrand, however, dismissed these objections. The EIB should stick to financing projects primarily within the Community.[76] The

EBRD could help Gorbachev's Soviet Union, which was not a member of the IMF or World Bank. Perhaps more importantly, France wanted to lead a high-profile initiative and counter West German influence in the region.

France put the EBRD proposal on the agenda for the informal European Council summit in Paris in November 1989, and the twelve leaders agreed to study it.[77] On 29 November, senior officials agreed that the Community plus the twelve member states would hold the majority of shares, but other states would join too. West Germany successfully pushed for participation to be open to the US, although France had originally wanted to limit membership to European states.[78] The Strasbourg European Council in December 1989 then called for negotiations to begin in January 1990.[79]

France convened the constitutive conference. On 15 and 16 January, the first meeting was held in Paris (not in Dublin, even though Ireland was Council president) and was chaired by Jacques Attali, an advisor to Mitterrand. Those attending were all the G-24 countries, seven East European states and the Soviet Union, Cyprus and Malta.[80] France had drafted a statute (based on the Community's proposals) and circulated it to non-EC members before an EC position had been reached. Arguably it seemed more a French than a Community project and several member states accordingly objected.[81]

Throughout the negotiations, frequently no agreement could be reached to present a common EC position. Some member states, including Italy and the smaller states, pushed for a common stand; others, including the UK, felt the G-24 should coordinate their position.[82] The most controversial decisions were those on the location of the headquarters and the appointment of the president. The G-7 apparently decided among themselves that the headquarters would be in London and the president would be Attali (the large member states thus winning the two biggest prizes), a decision then endorsed by the founding conference in May 1990.[83] Belgium, Luxembourg and the Netherlands then protested the fact 'that certain decisions on fundamental questions were taken or strongly influenced through the use of arbitration in non-Community fora, and without taking account of Community procedures'.[84]

The member states also disagreed over the extent of the EC's participation as a shareholder. Most member states favoured an EC share equal to that of the larger states; the UK, West Germany and the Netherlands did not.[85] In the end, the Community and the member states together were the main shareholders, with 51 per cent of the

capital of 10 billion ECUs: the Commission and the EIB had three
per cent each; the four large member states, 8.5 per cent each.[86]

In July 1994, the Commission suggested that all EU directors in the
EBRD uphold a previously agreed common position.[87] The proposal
has not been approved, an indication of the limits placed by the
member states on common EU action and their attempts to retain
some freedom of manoeuvre in relations with Eastern Europe.

The EBRD is the first multilateral organization *obliged* to link loans
to political conditionality.[88] Only countries that are committed to *and
applying* the principles of multiparty democracy, pluralism, and market
economics are eligible for loans.[89] The EBRD's loans mostly finance
private sector investment (while other regional banks lend mostly to
the state sector).

CONCLUSION

The Community's aid and loan programmes make manifest its importance in Eastern Europe. The Community (and Commission) has
effectively extended its competence – to coordinating non-member
state aid programmes, managing a large aid programme in a region
previously 'off-limits', and extending macro-financial assistance.
Externalization seems to apply here: external demands for Community
action led to an extension of the Community's powers and a new role
for the Commission. While the member states have not been entirely
comfortable with the extent to which the Community (and the
Commission in particular) has been active in the region, they have not
tried, or been able, to limit fundamentally its role: the politics (and
economies) of scale necessitated collective action to assist the transformation process and the East Europeans expected the Community to
deliver assistance.

As the revolutionary dust settled in Eastern Europe, it was clear
that the myriad initiatives launched in late 1989 were insufficient.
Europe had changed fundamentally and its institutional architecture
would have to adapt. Enlargement of the Community became a key
issue.

5 Association

Already in the autumn of 1989, it became apparent that the policy instruments discussed in Chapters 3 and 4 – the trade arrangements, PHARE, and so on – would be insufficient for reaching the Community/EPC's objectives in Eastern Europe. The East European countries were demanding closer relations and most of all, eventual Community membership. Many in Western and Eastern Europe argued that the reform efforts would continue, even as they caused hardship, only if the Community promised that the East European states could eventually become members and established closer, more formal ties with them. The Community thus had to decide to tighten its links with countries whose democratic and capitalist credentials were still uncertain, yet the success of the reforms was perceived to depend on such a decision.

The debate over enlargement began virtually from the moment communism fell in Eastern Europe and was heavily influenced by the incorporation of East Germany into the Community, discussed in Section 5.1. East European demands for Community membership had particular resonance because East Germany had been swept quickly into the Community as part of unified Germany: why then could not the other East European countries join? Section 5.2 will introduce the 'widening versus deepening' debate, which was initially resolved by deciding to conclude association agreements with the East European countries. In Section 5.3, the negotiations with the East European states on association agreements will be discussed. This solution to the widening versus deepening debate, however, proved to be a temporary one.

5.1   EAST GERMANY'S INCORPORATION INTO THE COMMUNITY

The Community/EPC had little or no influence over the process of German unification. The external dimension of German unity was handled in the 2+4 framework, consisting of the four World War II allies (France, the Soviet Union, the UK and the US) and the two Germanies. Neither EPC nor the EC was involved (even though three

83

member states, France, the UK and, naturally, West Germany were). It was in the 2+4 forum that crucial Soviet acceptance of German unification and German membership of NATO was obtained. But early on, the Community accepted the prospect of German unification, thus sending an important signal that the GDR could join the Community. In addition, '[t]here seems little doubt that the USSR (and Germany's other neighbours) would not have been as willing to allow unification to proceed had it not taken place within the context of the EC.'[1]

The full story of German unification has been told elsewhere; the process will only be briefly reviewed here. Section 5.1.1 will discuss the Community's policy towards East Germany; Section 5.1.2 will review the GDR's incorporation into the Community.

5.1.1 Community Policy Towards The GDR

The GDR had always been a 'special case' in the Community's relations with third states. Of the CMEA states, it had been one of the most antagonistic towards the Community, yet its goods could be exported to West Germany without being subject to EC customs regulations. In June 1988 (when the EEC-CMEA agreement was signed), the GDR expressed interest in reaching a trade agreement with the Community that would not interfere with the protocol on inter-German trade.[2] But the East German government was resisting pressures for reform, and by the time the Berlin Wall fell on 9 November 1989, the Commission had not even asked for a negotiating mandate.

Immediately after the Wall fell, the Community concentrated on concluding an agreement with the GDR and extending PHARE aid, just as it was doing with the other East European states. On 17 November, the GDR requested that negotiations begin on a trade and cooperation agreement; on 21 December, the Council gave the Commission a mandate to negotiate an agreement.[3] It was similar to the other East European agreements: a ten-year agreement providing for the lifting of all quantitative restrictions by 1995 and cooperation in several areas. Negotiations went quickly: the agreement was initialled on 13 March 1990.[4] The Council concluded it on 8 May, but it never entered into effect because in the meantime, Germany was unified.

In July 1990, the G-24 voted to extend aid to the GDR and in September PHARE aid was also extended. Upon unification, the former GDR became ineligible for PHARE and G-24 assistance.[5]

5.1.2   Widening the Community

The fall of the Berlin Wall posed a particular challenge because it immediately raised the question of German unification and therefore the inclusion of the East German Länder in the Community. After long proclaiming its desire to overcome the division of Europe, the Community could hardly oppose unification. Several member states, however, were less than enthusiastic about the prospect. But the Commission very early on realized unification was likely and acted to control the implications for the Community.

Less than a month before the Wall came down, Delors had argued that the right of self-determination applied to everyone. The 'German question' could be resolved by strengthening the federalist features of the Community.[6] In late 1989 and early 1990, the Commission's stance on unification remained constant, while several member states vacillated.[7]

The Commission reacted quite quickly to the fall of the Berlin Wall. After a special meeting on 10 and 11 November, it acknowledged that the GDR was a special case and that there were essentially two prospects: either the GDR would join the Community as the 13th member state, or it would join as part of the Federal Republic.[8] This differed from the position of some member states; at that time, Thatcher was only envisaging an association agreement with the GDR.[9] France was also initially uncertain about the prospect of unification.[10]

The extraordinary European Council summit in Paris on 18 November 1989 did not discuss German unification. Kohl apparently reassured the other leaders that West Germany was not being distracted by events in the east from its commitment to West European integration.[11] But Kohl then appeared inclined to act unilaterally: on 28 November, he announced a ten-point plan, without consulting any of his neighbours or EC partners first, which envisioned a confederation of the two Germanies in the medium term.[12]

Kohl's move dismayed many, but particularly France, Germany's supposedly closest partner. France, however, took advantage of the row to push Germany into agreeing to convene an IGC on the Economic and Monetary Union (EMU), one of France's goals for its Council presidency. At the Strasbourg European Council on 8 and 9 December, Germany agreed that the IGC would begin in December 1990, in exchange for France's agreement on the principle of German unification.[13] The European Council then accepted the prospect of German unification, under certain conditions, indicating implicitly that the GDR could be integrated into the Community. It declared:

> We seek the strengthening of the state of peace in Europe in which the German people will regain its unity through free self-determination. This process should take place peacefully and democratically, in full respect of the relevant agreements and treaties and of all the principles defined by the Helsinki Final Act, in a context of dialogue and East/West cooperation. It also has to be placed in the perspective of European integration.[14]

Explicit acceptance of the GDR's incorporation into the Community still took some time. In January 1990, Delors stated that 'there is a place for East Germany in the Community should it so wish', provided the conditions set in the Strasbourg European Council's declaration were met.[15] But at an informal foreign ministers' meeting on 20 January 1990, some member states, including the Netherlands and Belgium, felt that the GDR should be treated like the other East European states. Even if the GDR's particularity was acknowledged, there was a general reluctance to contemplate German unification in the short run.[16] Events, however, conspired otherwise.

An alliance advocating rapid unification won the East German elections on 18 March 1990. Both German governments agreed to achieve German economic and monetary union on 1 July 1990, without consulting the Community first.[17] Kohl then met with the Commission on 23 March to discuss the implications of unification for the EC and agreed to liaise with it on the unification negotiations.[18]

The increasingly dominant view in the Community favoured integrating East Germany via unification with West Germany: '[i]t was politically more expedient to treat German unification not as an accession, but as an expansion of the territory of an existing member state.'[19] In March, French Foreign Minister Roland Dumas noted that it would be easier to integrate East Germany in that way than to allow it to join as the 13th member state.[20]

The Commission's report on the effects of German unification on the Community, presented on 18 April, reflected this.[21] It would not be necessary to revise the Community treaties or to conduct formal membership negotiations if East and West Germany were to unite. The Commission foresaw a three-stage process of integrating East Germany into the Community, beginning with German economic and monetary union on 1 July 1990[22] and ending with the full application of all EC laws on the former GDR territory. In the transition period, the East German Länder would enjoy a derogation from certain laws until the end of 1992 (and the entry into force of the single European market). The Commission fudged on the issue of how much unification would cost the Community.

The report was adopted by the extraordinary European Council in Dublin on 28 April 1990, convened specifically to discuss German unification and relations with Eastern Europe. The Community thus accepted that no changes would be made to the treaties to incorporate the former GDR.[23]

The two Germanies held negotiations on the unification treaty from 6 July to 31 August 1990. The head of the Commission's special task force on unification took part in the talks.[24] Since the 2+4 talks were to end on 12 September,[25] Bonn decided to accelerate unification, bringing the date forward from 1 January 1991 to 3 October 1990. As a result, the EC's legislative process had to be speeded up. On 6 September, the trio of EC presidents – EP President Enrique Baron Crespo, Delors and Italian Foreign Minister and Council President Gianni De Michelis – set a timetable to push through several extraordinary provisional measures. By 17 September, the special measures were approved by both the EP and Council. The final legislative package for integrating the GDR into the Community was adopted on 4 December and entered into force on 1 January 1991.[26]

German unification had an important implication for the Community's policy towards Eastern Europe: it represented the logical end-point of the attempts to encourage reform in Eastern Europe – enlargement of the Community. Timothy Garton Ash asked the obvious question: 'if East Germany can join, why, in logic or justice, should not Czechoslovakia?'[27] The former East Germany fulfilled an aspiration repeatedly expressed by the other East European states, Community membership and moreover, did so quickly. 'This was a fascinating example of the Community's ability to act effectively and rapidly, provided that the political will to do so exists.'[28] In this case, the political will arose to prevent German unification from wrecking the Community and the Western security order. But because the event was so exceptional, it was questionable whether the political will would be found to integrate the other East European states. A debate over 'widening versus deepening' has since dominated the formulation of policy towards Eastern Europe.

5.2   WIDENING VERSUS DEEPENING: ROUND ONE

Article 237 of the Rome Treaty (later replaced by article 0 of the Maastricht Treaty) states that any European state may apply to become a member of the Community. During the Cold War, eligibility was not such a troublesome issue: 'As long as the Soviet Union drew the line between Eastern and Western Europe, the question of Europe's institutional limits was containable.'[29] Where the Community's boundaries should lie in the post-Cold War era has been much more difficult to establish.

Soon after they came into power, the new leaders of most of the East European states declared that their number one foreign policy priority was to 'rejoin Europe', and membership in the Community was the most sought-after prize. In May 1990, Czechoslovak Prime Minister Marian Calfa said he hoped that his country would be a full EC member by 2000.[30] Two months later, Hungary's prime minister, Jozsef Antall, announced that his country wanted to join by 1995.[31]

The East European countries argued that they should be allowed to join the European integration process from which they had been forcefully excluded.[32] Community membership had helped to consolidate democracy in Greece, Spain and Portugal, so it could be expected to do the same in Eastern Europe. The prospect of membership would help alleviate 'internal' security threats – particularly the social pressures stemming from the costs of the economic transition. Czechoslovak Foreign Minister Jiri Dienstbier asserted that 'association with and eventual full membership in the EC of Czechoslovakia, Hungary, (in quotation) and Poland is a basic precondition for stability and security in Central Europe.'[33]

In the near future, however, Community membership for the East European states could not possibly be an option. Even the three fastest reformers, Czechoslovakia, Hungary and Poland, would encounter enormous problems. Their economies were too weak to be able to compete within the EC. In eastern Germany, economic activity had collapsed after unification. 'The process of German reunification provides considerable evidence that in their own interests, East European States require a long transitional period before acceding to the EC.'[34]

The former GDR even benefited from substantial help from Western Germany; such resources were not available for the other East European states. In January 1990, Delors pointed out that if the

East European states were eligible for EC structural funds, they would receive 14 billion ECUs a year, plus 5 billion ECUs in EIB loans. This indicated not only the scale of assistance needed by the East European states (compare this to the 1990 PHARE budget of 500 million ECUs and to total Community expenditure in 1990 of 45.6 billion ECUs) but also the impracticality of enlargement before their economies were in better shape.[35]

Further enlargement raised much more serious difficulties than past enlargements. The queue of membership aspirants was growing, such that the Community could easily double its membership. The Community's institutions and decisionmaking procedures would have to be reformed; the CAP and structural funds would need to be rehauled if poorer states were to join (much of the Community's budget funds these two policies).[36] Otherwise, the Community risked ineffectiveness, decreasing legitimacy, and possible irrelevancy.

It was feared that even accession of the richer EFTA members would impede the completion of the single European market. In January 1989, Delors had tried to preempt membership applications from the 'EFTAns' by proposing the European Economic Area (EEA), a formal partnership between the Community and the EFTAns, which eventually entered into force on 1 January 1994.[37] But several EFTAns still pursued the membership option, and thus preceded the East European countries in the accession queue.[38]

Within the Community, the virtually intractable internal issues were initially pushed aside. Instead, in 1989–90, the debate took place between 'wideners' and 'deepeners'. On one side were those who argued that deepening must occur before widening to Eastern Europe. Deepening was clearly linked to German unification: the right response to a more powerful united Germany was further deepening and specifically political union.[39] In addition, without a common foreign, security and defence policy, the Community would be unable to influence the course of events in Eastern Europe. French and Italian leaders and Commission officials were among those making these arguments. In a 1990 New Year's address, French President François Mitterrand proposed setting up a European confederation: the Community should first reinforce its structures; *then* a confederation linking all European states should be built.[40] Eastern enlargement was too distant a prospect to be considered. For France, a more integrated Community could conduct a more active *Ostpolitik*; enlargement to the east would shift the Community's balance further in united Germany's direction.[41]

On the other side were those who argued that deepening could effectively exclude East European countries for decades, as they would have to reach higher economic and political objectives before joining. 'Widening' the Community to include the East European states should occur before further integration took place. The UK's more enthusiastic reception of East European membership demands was seen as a strategy for delaying – or blocking – deepening.[42] Germany straddled both positions: it strongly supported further integration, but also supported eventual membership for the new democracies.[43]

In 1990, this first round of the widening versus deepening debate was resolved by proceeding with deepening and associating the East European countries to the Community. In addition to the IGC on EMU (already agreed to in December 1989), the European Council in April 1990 agreed to convene an IGC on political union. The IGCs concluded in December 1991 with agreement on the Maastricht Treaty.[44]

The Community also decided to conclude association agreements with the reforming East European countries. In the fall of 1989, Genscher in particular pushed for association. On 14–15 October 1989, the foreign ministers and the Commission held a special meeting during which the new political architecture of Europe was discussed. Genscher called for new models of association with Eastern Europe to be devised; Delors suggested that the same kind of close links being forged with EFTA could be forged with Poland and Hungary.[45]

At the Paris summit of Community leaders on 18 November 1989, Delors presented the Commission's proposals for the Community's new *Ostpolitik*.[46] It would be based on three concentric circles: the EC, EFTA (linked by the EEA) and Eastern Europe (the Soviet Union remained outside of this scheme). The Community, at the centre, would be strongly integrated. A new kind of association agreement would be concluded with the reforming East European states, even if they remained members of the Warsaw Pact.[47] The European Council in Strasbourg the following month agreed that the association concept should be studied further.[48]

Association agreements were more than a defensive response to East European demands for better market access and closer ties with the Community. Concentric circles would resolve the widening versus deepening dilemma, at least in the short run. In fact, David Allen maintains that Genscher developed the concentric circle concept 'in a bid to meet the demands of many of his EC partners that Germany pushes ahead with integration while at the same time not closing the EC off from the states in the East.'[49] Other observers argued that '[c]oncentric circles is a compromise in the sense that it includes Eastern Europe in Europe, but it retains a major difference between the EC as a core actor and those who are led and helped by it.'[50] France and the Commission favoured a strong Community conducting an active *Ostpolitik*; Germany wanted to erase the border between Eastern and Western Europe as soon as possible.

Association could be considered in two ways: as a stepping-stone to EC membership, or as a long-term solution for the future architecture of Europe, a way to stem enlargement. The new associates clearly believed the former proposition; France clearly supported the latter.[51] Only the association agreements with Greece and Turkey had mentioned the possibility of membership[52] (and only Greece eventually became a member), while the other states that have joined the Community since the 1970s did not conclude association agreements beforehand. Genscher, however, had envisaged the possibility that states could move from one concentric circle to another, as they met basic conditions for Community membership.[53]

Association has been criticized as essentially aimed at avoiding the membership question.[54] But it can be seen more positively than a stance to put off enlargement, which in 1990–1, was much too early to consider seriously anyway. Françoise de La Serre viewed it as a 'model capable of overcoming the dilemma of broadening versus deepening of the Community... . [It] is the first step toward a reorganization of the European space around the EC.'[55] Enlargement in the near future was not realistic; in the meantime, the Community had to draw the East European states closer, to address their demands for closer ties and ensure their reforms succeeded. Concentric circles was an innovative way to address the many internal and external exigencies facing the Community in the immediate post-Cold War period.

5.3   THE EUROPE AGREEMENTS

5.3.1   Developing the Association Concept

In January 1990, the incoming Council president, Irish Foreign Minister Gerard Collins, stated:

the Twelve intend to develop with the countries of Eastern Europe, in so far as they are committed to the path of democratic change, closer and more substantial relations, based upon an intensification of political dialogue and increased cooperation in all areas. A major aim of this policy is support and encouragement for the establishment of free, open and democratic societies in which the full enjoyment of human rights is guaranteed by the rule of law.[56]

The 'closer and more substantial relations' entailed association. In a series of reports in 1990, the Commission developed the association idea. It pushed for further steps to be taken due to the pace of change in Eastern Europe, the expectations of East Europeans, and 'the Community's own interests in the political and economic future of Europe'.[57] It advocated moving quickly to association: 'Early approval of the goal of association will contribute to political stability, encourage the development of new instruments for cooperation and strengthen confidence on the part of economic operators.'[58]

At its extraordinary summit on 28 April, the European Council affirmed the Commission's proposal for three stages of Community policy towards Eastern Europe: the PHARE and G-24 aid programmes; the trade and cooperation agreements; and association.[59] Future associates would have to fulfill basic economic and political conditions: democratization and transition towards a market economy.[60]

In late August 1990, the Commission presented a detailed report on 'second-generation' association agreements. The agreements were to be called Europe agreements, 'to mark the importance of the political initiative which they represent.'[61] The Europe agreements were to be much more overtly political than previous association agreements. They were to: create a climate of confidence and stability favouring reform and allowing the development of close political relations; strengthen the foundations of the new European architecture; improve the climate for trade and investment; and help the East European countries better manage the transition process. Membership was *not* an objective.

Each association agreement would be adjusted for each country, thus maintaining specificity and privileging the development of bilateral relations with each East European country. An institutional framework for political dialogue would be set up (the first time association agreements would include such provisions). This would strengthen and institutionalize the low-level bilateral political dialogues with Czechoslovakia, Hungary and Poland that began in

1990.[62] A free trade area would be established, but the Community would open up first. Financial support would be provided on a multi-annual basis, in a mix of grants and loans.

Prospective associates would have to give 'practical evidence of their commitment' to five conditions: the rule of law, human rights, a multi-party system, free and fair elections and a market economy. Only Czechoslovakia, Hungary and Poland initially met the requirements.[63]

5.3.2 Negotiating the Europe Agreements

Implementing the association decision was not a smooth process, hampered by the member states' protectionism. The negotiations on Europe agreements all encountered numerous difficulties. The member states were very reticent to make concessions, especially on trade; the East European states, after all, were still developing free market economies. Domestic economic interest groups seemed to be able to block liberalization. But eventually the member states did make some concessions, after much prodding by the Commission and free-trade advocates, including of course, the East European states.

Czechoslovakia, Hungary, and Poland
Negotiations with Czechoslovakia, Hungary and Poland opened on 20, 21 and 22 December 1990.[64] The Commission negotiated the agreements, but because they were 'mixed', the presidency sat beside the Commission negotiators.[65]

During the protracted negotiations, several problems arose over market access, especially for the sensitive products: agricultural, steel and textile products. The three East European states maintained that the proposed agreements differed little from the trade and cooperation agreements.[66] The attempt to keep association separate from membership also blocked agreement. The East Europeans demanded persistently that a reference be made in the agreements to their future accession to the EC.[67] This was the problem with the concentric circles idea: most states sought to join the inner-most circle as soon as possible. After three rounds of talks, the negotiations were deadlocked.

To jumpstart the negotiations, the Commission proposed revising the negotiating mandates. On 15 April 1991, the General Affairs Council agreed, probably because the member states were aware that otherwise the talks could fail, and with them, a pillar of the

Table 5.1   Europe Agreements, 1991–3

	Europe agreement signed	Europe agreement concluded	In force	Official Journal ref.	Interim agreement in force (OJ ref.)
Poland	16 Dec 91	13 Dec 93	1 Feb 94	L348 31 Dec 93	1 Mar 92 (L114 30 Apr 92)
Hungary	16 Dec 91	13 Dec 93	1 Feb 94	L347 31 Dec 93	1 Mar 92 (L116 30 Apr 92)
CSFR[1]	16 Dec 91	–	–	–	1 Mar 92 (L115 30 Apr 92)
Czech Republic	4 Oct 93	19 Dec 94	1 Feb 95	L360 31 Dec 94	
Slovakia	4 Oct 93	19 Dec 94	1 Feb 95	L359 31 Dec 94	
Romania	1 Feb 93	19 Dec 94	1 Feb 95	L357 31 Dec 94	1 May 93 (L81 2 Apr 93)
Bulgaria	8 Mar 93	19 Dec 94	1 Feb 95	L358 31 Dec 94	31 Dec 93 (L323 23 Dec 93)

Sources: *EC Bulletin*, Official Journal
Note: [1]The interim trade agreement with Czechoslovakia continued to regulate trade relations between the Community and the Czech Republic and Slovakia after the split.

Community's policy towards Eastern Europe. The most important change was that the preamble could mention that the ultimate, but not automatic, goal of the associated states (not of the Community) is accession to the Community; Germany and the UK in particular pushed for this. The Community would offer somewhat better market access for some agricultural products, textiles and steel.[68]

The Council's concessions were not enough. In mid-May, the Polish deputy prime minister charged that EC protectionism was harming Poland's comparative advantage in the sensitive goods.[69] The sixth round of talks between the EC and Poland, in July, was particularly contentious.[70] Although the Commission then indicated that it would probably be necessary to change the mandate, the General Affairs Council on 29 July put off a decision on revisions.[71]

The attempted coup in Moscow of 19–22 August 1991 jolted the member states. It confirmed the precariousness of the democratic transformation in the Soviet Union and raised fears of a return to authoritarianism or nationalism. A more nationalistic Soviet Union could try to reassert its influence over Eastern Europe; the Community should thus draw the East European countries closer.

An EPC statement condemned the coup attempt, and stated that the Community and its member states wanted to conclude the association agreements in the near future.[72] The Commission took advantage of the widespread shock and urged the Council to make further trade concessions and strengthen the political dialogue provisions.[73] The extraordinary General Affairs Council meeting on 27 August, however, postponed a decision until 6 September.[74]

On 6 September, the Council considered the Commission's proposals. Portugal objected to liberalizing textile trade, but would drop its reservations in exchange for Community aid to its textile producers. France, backed by Ireland and Portugal, however, would not agree to concessions on meat products. The meeting broke up abruptly, having reached no decisions and with all in a bad mood.[75]

French farmers had regularly protested against concessions for East European imports.[76] The bovine meat market was depressed; France suffered because it is a big meat producer. The EC-level interest groups, the COPA and COGECA also objected to the proposed concessions.[77]

But France came under much public pressure to back down. At a press conference after the meeting, Hans van den Broek, the Dutch foreign minister and Council president, complained about the attitude of one member state. A vital national interest could not possibly be at stake when the quantity of meat in question was so small.[78] Further public criticism of the French move came from the Danish and UK prime ministers and German president.[79] Poland announced that negotiations could only continue on the basis of an enlarged Commission mandate; the next session would not be a formal one, but merely an expert-level working meeting.[80]

On 30 September, the Council met again and this time reached a compromise, which was virtually the same one discussed at the earlier meeting. Restrictions on textile imports would be dropped within six years and Portugal would get EC aid. Triangular agreements would resolve the problem of meat exports: any meat exports to the EC over and above a ten per cent increase per year would be paid for with EC aid but given to the Soviet Union, Romania and Albania.[81]

However, a final difficulty remained: Spain, among others, called for the associates to agree to voluntary export restrictions on steel. The Commission opposed this, and in the end, Coreper worked out a compromise: the Commission would monitor steel imports to ensure that state aids were not distorting competition; no additional safeguard clause for steel was included in the agreements.[82]

The Commission's mediation role was instrumental in improving the Community's trade concessions. Charles Grant notes that Delors managed to persuade the French to make concessions. In May 1991, for example, he appeared on French television to argue for more trade with Eastern Europe. His constant lobbying eventually led to improved EC concessions and allowed the conclusion of the agreements. The Danish foreign minister, Uffe Ellemann-Jensen, maintained that 'Delors deserves credit for getting the French on board for the Europe agreements.'[83]

The three Europe agreements were signed on 16 December 1991. Because they are mixed agreements, containing provisions which do not fall under the Community's competence, each member state had to approve them.[84] Pending this, interim trade arrangements – consisting of the trade provisions only and based on article 113 – entered into force on 1 March 1992.[85]

On 16 September 1992, the EP gave its assent to the Europe agreements with Hungary and Poland.[86] The member states did not, however, approve them quickly. Only on 13 December 1993 did the Council conclude the two agreements; they entered into force on 1 February 1994.

The breakup of Czechoslovakia on 1 January 1993 complicated matters. In September 1992, the EP refused to assent to the agreement with Czechoslovakia due to the country's impending division.[87] In April 1993, negotiations on separate Europe agreements with the Czech Republic and Slovakia began. The agreements were signed on 4 October 1993 and the EP assented to both on 27 October.[88] They entered into force on 1 February 1995.

Bulgaria and Romania

Bulgaria and Romania had again been left in the slow lane, because they did not meet the conditions for closer relations with the

Community. The EPC statement during the August 1991 attempted coup in the Soviet Union, however, declared that the Commission would explore ways to expand cooperation with Bulgaria and Romania. The Commission proposed negotiating Europe agreements with Romania and Bulgaria.[89] Geopolitical concerns seem more important in this decision than a positive appraisal of Bulgaria's and Romania's fulfilment of the criteria for concluding Europe agreements.[90]

On 30 September 1991, the Council agreed that exploratory talks with Bulgaria could begin, but that talks with Romania could begin once the political situation was 'normalized'.[91] In late September, violent demonstrations broke out in Romania, provoking an EPC statement that condemned the violence and reiterated that economic and political reforms were indispensable for the full development of relations with the Community.[92] On 16 December, the foreign ministers agreed that initial talks could begin with Romania.[93]

In April 1992, the Commission asked the Council to approve the negotiating mandates. It proposed that the agreements contain a reference to human rights and democracy. The proposal follows two declarations, by the European Council in June 1991 and the Development Council in November 1991, in which the intention to include clauses on human rights in Community agreements with third countries is stated.[94]

The first three Europe agreements did not contain such a clause, though, and Bulgaria and Romania objected to their different treatment, considering it a sign that the Community did not 'trust' them.[95] They were probably right: while the proposed clause crowns a policy already based on conditionality, it could indicate that Bulgaria and Romania did not fully meet the established criteria for Europe agreements and thus the Community had to retain some leverage to encourage political and economic reforms.

At its meetings on 7 and 21 April 1992, the Council could not agree on the Commission's proposals, mostly because of concerns about offending Bulgaria and Romania.[96] Finally, on 11 May, the Council approved the mandates. It decided that the two Europe agreements were to be conditional on respect for human rights, democratic principles and the principles of the market economy.[97] This was the first time that such a clause was to be included in a legal instrument with third countries. The Council further declared: 'respect for democratic principles and human rights ... and the principles of the market economy are essential components of cooperation or association agreements between the Community and its CSCE partners.'[98] All the

Europe agreements (and interim agreements) signed after May 1992 –
including with the Czech Republic and Slovakia – contain a clause
permitting appropriate measures to be taken if human rights, democratic principles and principles of the market economy are not
respected.[99]

The Commission's mandates were restrictive with respect to steel, a
result of successful lobbying by Spain and a reflection of growing
concern about East European steel imports.[100] The Commission also
unsuccessfully argued for further concessions in textiles and agricultural trade: Commissioner Andriessen even publicly chastised the
Council for making inadequate concessions.[101] Bulgaria in particular
was unhappy with the Community's protectionism.[102]

The negotiations ended with Romania in November and with
Bulgaria in December 1992.[103] The Europe agreement with Romania
was signed on 1 February 1993 and with Bulgaria on 8 March 1993.[104]
A lengthy ratification process and internal disagreements over the
Community's trade protection measures followed. Both agreements
entered into force on 1 February 1995.

Interim trade agreements were signed at the same time as the
Europe agreements and were supposed to enter into force quickly.
Romania's interim trade measures applied from 1 May 1993.
Conclusion of the interim agreement with Bulgaria, however, was
delayed by the Council because of a prolonged dispute about the
Community's decisionmaking procedure for trade protection
measures.[105] The interim agreement remained blocked until
December 1993, even after the June 1993 European Council had
approved further trade concessions, the EP had condemned the
Council and Bulgaria had demanded compensation.[106] It finally
entered into force on 31 December.

5.3.3   Content of the Europe Agreements

All six Europe agreements are broadly similar.[107] The preambles note
that the agreements are important for building a stable Europe, of
which the Community is a 'cornerstone'. They stress a commitment to
pluralist democracy, based on the rule of law, human rights, a multiparty system and free and democratic elections. The preambles in the
agreements with Bulgaria, the Czech Republic, Romania and Slovakia
also mention respect for the rights of minorities, indicating growing
concern about minority rights. Each preamble mentions that the
associate's final objective is Community membership and that the

Europe agreement will help achieve that objective. The aims of the association (in article 1) are notably political: the association is to provide a framework for political relations, promote trade, economic and cultural cooperation, and assist the associate's integration into the Community.

As is the case in other association agreements, an Association Council, consisting of the EC Council, Commission representatives, and representatives from the associate's government, meets at least once a year to examine any major issues arising within the framework of the agreement.[108] It is assisted by an Association Committee, composed of senior civil servants. Members of the EP and the associate's parliament exchange views in an Association Parliamentary Committee.

The agreements include provisions for a political dialogue, the first time such provisions have been included in a Community agreement based on article 238 (and again indicating a blurring of the EC-EPC dividing line). The dialogue, on international issues of mutual interest, is intended to facilitate the associate's integration into 'the community of democratic nations' and to enhance security and stability throughout Europe. It is to take place 'as appropriate' at the highest level between the presidents of the European Council and the Commission and the associate's president. At ministerial level, the dialogue takes place within the Association Council. Senior officials from the associate, Council presidency and the Commission are to meet regularly. These provisions establish a formal political dialogue which is more intense than most other bilateral dialogues and the dialogues with regional groupings, but not as intense as the framework for consultations with the US provided for in the November 1990 transatlantic declaration.[109]

The agreements provide a framework for integrating the associates into the Community. The four freedoms of movement, for goods, capital, services and labour, are to be extended gradually between the Community and the associate. A free trade area will be established over a period of ten years: the Community will open its markets sooner, while the associates will not open their markets until the end of this period. The main provisions for the associates' goods are listed in Table 5.2. National treatment will be extended for the establishment and operation of all firms and professions. Workers from the associates who are legally employed in the Community are to be ensured non-discriminatory treatment, but further measures on the free movement of workers are only to be discussed in the Association Council.[110]

Table 5.2 Europe Agreement Trade Provisions

	Industrial products	Textiles	ECSC products	Agricultural products
Interim agreements with CSFR, Hungary, Poland	Duties eliminated for some goods immediately; others more gradually; all to be eliminated in 5 years (by 1 January 1997) All QRs removed immediately	All duties eliminated in 6 years (by 1 January 1998) All QRs removed in 5 years at earliest	**Steel:** All duties eliminated by 1 January 1997; all QRs removed immediately **Coal:** All duties eliminated in 1 year (for Hungary, by 31 December 1995); QRs removed in 1 year (derogations for Germany and Spain)	Schedule of annual reductions of levies and duties, and increases in quotas, depending on product
Interim agreement with Romania	Same as above; final deadline is 1 January 1998	Same as above (by 1 January 1999 for duties)	**Steel:** same as above (by 1 January 1998 for duties) **Coal:** all duties removed by 31 December 1995; QRs same as above	Same as above

Table 5.2 *(Continued)*

	Industrial products	Textiles	ECSC products	Agricultural products
Interim agreement with Bulgaria	Same as above; final deadline is 1 January 1998	Same as above	**Steel:** all duties eliminated by 1 January 1997 **Coal:** all duties removed by 31 December 1995; QRs same as above	Same as above

Source: Official Journal.

Furthermore, the associates' legislation is to be progressively approximated to the *acquis communautaire*. Provisions for economic cooperation are spelled out in a wide variety of areas, including industry, science and technology, education and training, energy and environment. Associates could participate in some Community programmes in those areas and in cultural programmes.[111] No financial protocols are attached to the agreements (although other association accords have them). The Community resisted giving specific figures for assistance, so it would retain the flexibility to allocate aid as conditions require.[112] The agreements state that the associates are eligible for PHARE funds, EIB loans and eventual balance of payments or currency stabilization assistance.

CONCLUSION

The widening versus deepening debate was initially resolved with the concentric circles idea, which entailed concluding Europe agreements with the East European countries. Concentric circles satisfied both internal and external exigencies. It responded to East European calls for closer relations and was an attempt to restructure the new European architecture in the Community's interests.

Implementing the association decision was contentious and for the East European states, the association circle did not offer enough. The member states proved very reluctant to make compromises to satisfy the demands of the East European countries for better market access and a promise on enlargement. The influence of domestic interests in the sensitive sectors was strong. Prodded by the Commission and aware of the greater issues at stake, the member states eventually agreed to some limited concessions. Still, some 'pay-offs' were needed for an agreement to be reached: EC aid for Portuguese textile producers and triangular arrangements for meat exports. These concessions would prove to be too limited and the Community came under renewed pressure to revise the Europe agreements, as discussed in the next chapter.

The Europe agreement framework has nonetheless turned out to be a dynamic one, providing for the integration of the associates into the EU. The agreements remain the primary link between the EU and the East European countries and have paved the way for a decision on enlargement and the preparation of the associates for accession.

6 Integration

The Europe agreements did not resolve the questions of whether and when the East European states should join the Community, but the associates continued to demand answers and the member states had to come up with a collective response. After much prevarication, in June 1993, the European Council agreed that the East European associates could join, provided certain membership conditions were met. The EU then devised an innovative and extensive pre-accession strategy, to integrate gradually the associates into the Union. Several key steps towards enlargement were taken in 1997, the most important being the decision to open membership negotiations with some of the associates.

Enlargement was agreed to because it should help spread stability and security to Eastern Europe. It has become, along with Economic and Monetary Union, the biggest challenge facing the EU at the turn of the 21st century. But while much emphasis has been placed on preparing the associates for eventual membership, the member states have not agreed on how to prepare the Union itself for a successful enlargement. Widening and deepening are not alternative options.

The first section of this chapter will cover the debate over how to answer the East European demands for better market access and a clear perspective on enlargement. Section 6.2 will discuss the pre-accession strategy, endorsed by the Essen European Council in December 1994. The final section (6.3) will review the enlargement process since Essen, including the December 1997 decision on opening membership negotiations.

6.1   TOWARDS COPENHAGEN

The Europe agreements provide the associates with a framework for political and economic cooperation, gradual integration into the Community and greater access to the EC market. But the associates have made two criticisms about the agreements: the trade concessions were not enough and no dates or conditions for eventual EC membership were set.

The Community did not immediately answer their criticisms. From early 1992 to the June 1993 Copenhagen European Council, the Community skirted round the enlargement issue and put off decisions on improving market access. In general, it was not a propitious period for Community-East European relations. The Community was distracted by numerous other dilemmas: salvaging the Maastricht Treaty after the Danish 'no' in the June 1992 referendum; concluding the GATT Uruguay Round; dampening volatility in the Exchange Rate Mechanism (ERM); trying to resolve the Yugoslav crisis; and enlarging to the EFTAns. Germany, a key actor in Community-East European relations, was preoccupied with unification and might have been shying away from major foreign policy initiatives after the debacle of the recognition of Slovenia and Croatia in December 1991. Nonetheless, at Copenhagen, the European Council reached several important decisions, on trade, enlargement and closer ties with the East European associates. The next two sections will discuss the run-up to Copenhagen: Section 6.1.1 will cover trade and Section 6.1.2 will review the enlargement issue and the development of a political dialogue with the associates.

6.1.1 Improving Market Access

The trade provisions of the Europe agreements, reproduced in the interim agreements, entered into force much earlier (1992–3) than the Europe agreements themselves, so the associates benefited from the liberalization of trade almost immediately. But since 1992, the EC has been running a trade surplus with its eastern neighbours (see Table 6.1). To some extent this was to be expected given their need for Western technology and the recession in Western Europe, which stemmed demand for East European exports. Eastern Europe, however, has suffered a much worse economic slow-down, raising serious questions about the Community's growing surplus. EC-East European trade is also much more significant for the East European countries than for the Community (see Table 6.2). In early 1994, imports from the East European countries amounted to 4.4 per cent of the EU's total imports and exports to the region were 5.3 per cent of all EU exports.[1] Thus the extent to which the Community market is open to East European products is important and the associates were far from satisfied with the market access provided by the Europe agreements.

Table 6.1 EC Trade with Eastern Europe, 1988–96
(in billion ECU)

Country	1988	1989	1990	1991	1992	1993	1994	1995	1996
Poland									
Exports	2.75	3.94	4.93	7.88	8.15	11.11	12.32	15.29	19.83
Imports	3.36	3.86	5.28	6.21	7.08	8.46	10.13	12.25	12.24
Balance	-0.61	0.08	-0.34	1.66	1.07	2.66	2.19	3.04	7.58
CSFR						**Czech Rep.**			
Exports	2.17	2.38	2.91	3.82	6.26	7.08	9.22	11.65	13.96
Imports	2.21	2.56	2.79	4.06	5.53	5.64	7.38	8.99	9.75
Balance	-0.04	-0.17	0.12	-0.24	0.73	1.45	1.85	2.66	4.21
						Slovakia			
Exports						1.58	2.19	3.19	3.99
Imports						1.42	2.24	3.09	3.42
Balance						0.16	-0.45	0.10	0.58
Hungary									
Exports	2.35	2.99	3.22	3.49	4.06	6.44	8.06	8.73	9.99
Imports	2.16	2.59	3.00	3.62	3.99	4.88	6.06	7.61	8.81
Balance	0.19	0.40	0.22	-0.13	0.07	1.57	2.01	1.12	1.18
Romania									
Exports	0.61	0.69	1.41	1.33	1.85	2.51	2.89	3.79	4.44
Imports	2.23	2.55	1.62	1.47	1.40	1.80	2.79	3.40	3.59
Balance	-1.62	-1.86	-0.20	-0.14	0.45	0.72	0.10	0.40	0.85
Bulgaria									
Exports	1.41	1.48	1.03	1.03	1.11	1.48	1.75	2.05	1.69
Imports	0.46	0.53	0.59	0.75	0.89	1.01	1.42	1.84	1.70
Balance	0.94	0.95	0.44	0.28	0.21	0.47	0.33	0.22	-0.05

Source: Eurostat.

Table 6.2   Eastern Europe's Trade Flows, 1989–94
(% of total)

	Exports 1989	1991	1993	1994	Imports 1989	1991	1993	1994
To/From the EU								
Czech and								
Slovak Republics	29.7	45.6	57.7	62.3	30.2	42.4	56.3	60.7
Hungary	33.8	58.6	58.1	63.7	39.7	56.7	54.4	61.1
Poland	35.5	64.3	69.2	69.2	37.4	59.1	64.7	65.3
Bulgaria	14.6	17.4	30.0	35.5	25.8	26.4	33.5	38.9
Romania	35.8	38.0	40.8	48.2	9.4	30.9	44.7	48.2
To/From the East European region (same six countries)								
Czech and								
Slovak Republics	14.4	13.2	8.5	9.9	15.1	7.4	5.0	5.2
Hungary	10.4	5.8	7.5	7.4	10.9	6.9	6.0	7.1
Poland	11.5	5.8	5.3	5.2	11.3	4.9	3.8	4.4
Bulgaria	8.8	5.2	4.4	3.2	8.3	5.7	4.3	5.4
Romania	6.7	5.7	5.2	5.9	10.3	6.9	4.9	4.8

Source: United Nations Economic Commission for Europe, *Economic Bulletin
for Europe*, vol. 48, 1996, p. 77.

The Commission generally agreed with the associates and con-
tinuously urged the member states to offer further trade concessions.
In two reports on relations with Eastern Europe, one to the Lisbon
European Council of June 1992[2] and the other to the Edinburgh
European Council of December 1992,[3] it argued strongly in favour of
improving the trade provisions in the Europe agreements.

Neither European Council, however, took any decisions on the
Commission's proposals. The southern member states in particular
objected to them.[4] The Edinburgh European Council asked the
Commission to prepare another report on relations with Eastern
Europe and promised to reach decisions on it at its Copenhagen
meeting.[5] The member states, however, then warned the Commission
not to propose any substantial trade liberalization measures.[6]

In May 1993, the Commission presented its report to the
Copenhagen European Council detailing how relations with the East

European associates could be strengthened.[7] The proposals for improving access to the EC market went much further than some member states had expected, and reflected an alliance between External Economic Relations Commissioner Sir Leon Brittan (a strong proponent of free trade) and External Political Relations Commissioner Hans van den Broek, who had dropped their rivalry to push for freer trade.[8] The Commission proposed speeding up the timetable in the Europe agreements for increasing quotas and cutting tariffs on industrial and sensitive products.

The Commission's report included several other proposals on dialogue with the associates and enlargement (see Section 6.1.2), as well as on PHARE. The Danish presidency was determined to keep all of the proposals together in one package, to be decided on by the foreign ministers (and officials in the Council's East European Working Group), who had the larger foreign policy picture in mind; this would prevent officials from economic ministries from blocking the trade concessions.[9] The growing trade surplus with Eastern Europe also helped curb member states' protectionism.

On 10 May, the foreign ministers welcomed the proposals in a preliminary discussion on them, although the French foreign minister called for a study to be done on the impact of the market access proposals.[10] At a foreign ministers' meeting on 8 June, a free-trade coalition including the UK, Germany, the Netherlands and Denmark ensured acceptance of the Commission's proposals.[11] The European Council in Copenhagen on 21–2 June 1993 endorsed the proposals (see the concessions listed in Table 6.3).[12] The Commission and Danish presidency had succeeded in 'upgrading the common interest'.

6.1.2   Widening versus Deepening: Round Two

The Europe agreements did not acknowledge that the *Community's* objective was enlargement to the associates. For Anna Michalski and Helen Wallace, this could be because the member states did not want 'to repeat mistakes of the past in giving promises which have proved difficult to honour' (a reference to the case of Turkey).[13] But the associates persistently demanded that the Community set out a timetable and conditions for enlargement.

The demands for a clear stance on enlargement became ever more compelling as turmoil spread throughout the former Yugoslavia and Soviet Union in 1992 and 1993. The popularity of nationalist

108 The Making of EU Foreign Policy

Table 6.3   Copenhagen European Council Concessions

Industrial products	Textiles	ECSC products	Agricultural products
Duties removed in 4 years will be removed in 2 All duties to be removed in 3 years (by 1 January 1995 for Visegrad group; by 1 January 1996 for Bulgaria and Romania)	Duties to be eliminated one year earlier (for Visegrad group, by 1 January 1997; for Bulgaria and Romania, by 1 January 1998)	Steel: duties to be removed one year earlier	Levies to be reduced by 60% 6 months earlier than in interim agreement 10% increase in quotas applied 6 months earlier

movements in Russia and a more assertive Russian policy towards the former Soviet republics also sparked fears that Russia might try to re-establish a sphere of influence in Eastern Europe.[14] The disappearance of the old bloc system left the East Europeans feeling exposed. They feared they would fall into an insecure 'grey zone' and needed a framework for integration into Western security organizations.[15] Integration would also help reduce internal security threats, stemming from social tensions and inter-ethnic disputes. There was thus pressure on the member states to respond positively to the membership demands, to help consolidate the transformation in Eastern Europe and ensure security in Europe.

To a certain extent the internal Community debate on enlargement took place on the same terms, between wideners and deepeners.[16] But that debate (first one, then maybe the other) was increasingly out of date. Widening and deepening would have to occur simultaneously. Most member states accepted the potential security benefits of enlarging to Eastern Europe, both for the East Europeans and for the Community, because enlargement could ensure a stable, secure and prosperous Eastern Europe. In addition, the 'European identity' of the East European states could not be disputed, especially as they implemented political and economic reforms along Western lines. The option of actually *denying* membership to the East European countries was never considered seriously in the Community. Association and

membership *were* ruled out (in March 1992) for the former Soviet republics (with the exception of the three Baltic states).[17]
Enlargement, however, posed many problems. Even if several rich EFTAns joined, the Community could not afford to extend CAP and the structural funds to the much poorer and more rural East European countries (see Table 6.4).[18] Yet CAP reform faced opposition from farmers and France in particular, and the poorer member states were concerned about losing EC funds. France and other southern member states were concerned that enlargement to Eastern Europe would alter the balance of power within the Community in favour of Germany.[19]

The Maastricht Treaty reforms were not enough to allow an extensive enlargement. For an EU of 20 or more member states to function

Table 6.4 GDP and Agriculture in East European Countries and Poorest EU Member States, 1995

	GDP (ECU billion)	GDP per head in ECU (% of EU average)	GDP per head in ECU at purchasing power standards (% of EU average)	Agric. % of value added	Agric. % of employment
Bulgaria	9.9	1180 (7)	4210 (24)	13.9	23.2
Czech Rep.	36.1	3490 (20)	9410 (55)	5.2	6.3
Estonia	2.8	1850 (11)	3920 (23)	8.1	13.1
Hungary	33.4	3340 (19)	6310 (37)	6.2	8.0
Latvia	3.4	1370 (8)	3160 (18)	9.9	18.5
Lithuania	3.5	930 (5)	4130 (24)	9.3	23.8
Poland	90.2	2360 (14)	5320 (31)	7.6	26.9
Romania	27.3	1200 (7)	4060 (23)	20.5	34.4
Slovakia	13.3	2470 (14)	7120 (41)	6.3	9.7
Slovenia	14.2	7240 (42)	10 110 (59)	5.0	7.1
Greece	87.4	8360 (48)	11 320 (66)	14.7	20.4
Ireland	49.2	13 740 (80)	16 020 (93)	7.5	12
Portugal	77.1	7770 (45)	11 620 (67)	5.1	11.5
Spain	428.1	10 920 (63)	13 230 (77)	3.7	9.3

Source: European Commission, 'Agenda 2000: 2. The Challenge of Enlargement', COM (97) 2000 final, 15 July 1997, p. 62.

effectively, the EU's institutions and decisionmaking procedures would have to be further altered. More qualified majority voting in the Council was called for, to prevent blocked decisionmaking. The weighting of votes would have to be reassessed to correct the bias towards small states (which would worsen with enlargement to the small and medium-sized East European associates) and because with enlargement to just five East European states, the poor member states could muster more than a blocking minority in the Council (providing they vote together), which could lead to strife over finances.[20] Member states would hold the rotating presidency less frequently, and even the troika would be perceived as weak if the presidency were held by a succession of small states. The number of MEPs, Commissioners and ECJ judges would have to be cut if the institutions were not to become too large. With enlargement, the number of official languages would rise (as would translating and interpreting costs) unless other arrangements were made, such as adopting working languages.

The 1996 IGC (provided for in the Maastricht Treaty) would have to address these issues, yet the European public did not seem enthusiastic about further integration (the ratification of the Maastricht Treaty was not proceeding smoothly), and several member states opposed several of the reforms, such as reducing the use of the national veto.

Formulating a response to the East European demands for concrete decisions on enlargement was therefore extremely difficult. In an attempt to address the demands for widening and reduce the need for internal institutional and policy reform, several alternatives were advanced, some of which have been incorporated into the Union's policy.

Mitterrand periodically reproposed his confederation idea.[21] In June 1991, he suggested that the East European states would be in no condition to join the Community for decades, so the confederation would launch trans-European cooperation in areas such as environmental protection and telecommunications.[22] The East Europeans were suspicious that it would delay their entry into the Community. Czech President Havel commented:

> I believe it would not be right, and perhaps even harmful to European stability, if the creation of the confederation curbs in any way the rapprochement between the democracies of central and eastern Europe and the European Communities, or if it perpetuates their position as second-class countries.[23]

Along similar lines, in May 1992 the EP Committee on Institutional Affairs proposed creating a system of ad hoc associations for cooperation on pan-European problems.[24]

Several outside observers suggested that the East European states first join EFTA or the EEA (moving from one concentric circle to the next, rather than straight to the centre).[25] This of course would still be economically difficult and the East Europeans suspected that joining EFTA or the EEA would delay Community membership. Neither framework seemed particularly attractive even to the EFTAns, as they lined up to join the Community.

The above proposals maintain a clear difference between Community member states and non-member states. That distinction is blurred in proposals for different forms of 'partial membership'. In 1991, Volker Rühe, then Secretary-General of the German Christian Democrat Party, advocated involving the East European countries in EPC before they acceded to the Community.[26] This would include the associates in a security framework, while excluding them from expensive policies (namely the CAP and structural funds).

On 19 April 1991, Commissioner Andriessen suggested that the Community create an affiliate membership category. This would allow the Community to offer the benefits of membership, and therefore stability, to those European countries that wanted to participate in European integration but were not ready to accept all of the membership commitments. Affiliate members would have 'a seat at the Council table on a par with full members in specified areas, together with appropriate representation in other institutions, such as the Parliament.'[27] The areas included foreign policy, monetary affairs, transport, environment, research and energy.

Andriessen's idea was greeted sceptically within the Community: affiliate membership would complicate Community procedures and be very difficult to realize.[28] Achieving consistency between the Community's external relations and EPC would become even more difficult if the membership of those frameworks differed. If partial members were allowed to vote, they could block proposals in an attempt to influence policies in which they were not included (such as CAP). Partial membership would be unworkable in practice.[29] It could be seen as 'second-class' membership by the associates, and thus would still not satisfy their membership aspirations.

This reception is somewhat curious given the rash of proposals on differentiated integration which followed the rejection of the Maastricht Treaty in a Danish referendum in June 1992 and the UK's reluctance to proceed with ratification. Most of these envisaged a 'two-speed' Europe, in which a 'hard core' of select member states would proceed with integration, leaving unwilling member states (such as Denmark and the UK) in a series of less integrated concentric circles on the outside.[30]

There are already precedents for differentiated integration: optional participation in the ERM of the European Monetary System; the long 'grace' periods allowed Spain and Portugal before they had to comply with all Community laws; and the UK and Danish opt-outs from the Maastricht Treaty. The WEU had limited membership, and then introduced various levels of membership beginning in 1992. The Eurocorps and the Schengen agreement on open borders signalled further differentiation.[31]

But differentiated integration risks breaking up the Community/ Union. The hard core proposals were shelved (for the while) once they were no longer needed to threaten to leave the UK behind unless it ratified the Maastricht Treaty. The Community even seemed to rule out further opt-outs (by choice or necessity), in insisting that future members accept the entire *acquis communautaire*. John Redmond charges that the unwillingness to consider drastically reforming an enlarged Community meant that the Community could not formulate a coherent policy towards aspiring member states.[32] That is too harsh, particularly given that nothing less than the reinvention of the Community was at issue, when it was not even certain that the limited reforms in the Maastricht Treaty would go ahead.

It took time, but by mid-1993, the Community had laid out its position on enlargement and indicated how relations with the associates should develop until then. The Community/EPC initially moved to strengthen relations with the associates by instituting a multilateral political dialogue with them. An agreement on enlargement was finally reached at the June 1993 European Council.

In 1992 and 1993, the Community/EPC gradually developed a framework for multilateral political relations with the associates. The Europe agreements provided for a bilateral political dialogue with each associate, but this did not begin until they entered into force. Instead of further developing bilateral relations with each associate, however, EPC developed an ad hoc *multilateral* political dialogue with the associates.[33]

The multilateral dialogue met both internal and external exigencies. As the number of associates rose, all of whom demanded closer relations, it was the most practical way to strengthen political ties with them. The dialogue would help build a common European approach to international issues – the situation in Russia in particular – and 'train' the associates in EPC's mode of operation. It would also encourage the East Europeans to cooperate with each other (see Chapter 7).

The dialogue began in May 1992 with a meeting between the troika and the Visegrad group (Czechoslovakia, Hungary and Poland),[34] at the joint request of the Visegrad countries.[35] They discussed the Yugoslav crisis and relations with the former Soviet republics.[36] (Bulgaria and Romania were not included in the dialogue until later in 1993, because they had not yet concluded Europe agreements.)

Development of the dialogue, however, was closely connected to the enlargement issue. Until the Copenhagen European Council, the enlargement question impeded the institutionalization of the dialogue; relations developed instead on an ad hoc basis.

The European Council in Lisbon, 26–7 June 1992, discussed a Commission report on enlargement, which it had requested in December 1991 because of the growing interest of non-members in joining the Community.[37] The report suggested several membership conditions, in addition to the three basic ones set out in the Maastricht Treaty (European identity, democratic status and respect of human rights).[38] Applicants must accept the rights and obligations of the entire *acquis communautaire* and the CFSP, and be able to fulfill all the necessary obligations. Some countries (the EFTAns) were already well-prepared for membership, others (including the East European states) were not.

Because the East European countries wanted to strengthen their political links with Western Europe, the Commission suggested creating a European Political Area. European leaders could meet regularly within the framework of a confederation or in a conference convened by the European Council (a clear echo of Mitterrand's confederation proposal). East European countries could be associated with specific EC policies and participate in meetings on subjects of trans-European interest (a fainter echo of Andriessen's affiliate membership idea).

The Lisbon European Council did not take up the proposals. France, Italy, Spain and Portugal stressed the difficulties the East European states would experience if they joined the Community and viewed the Europe agreements as a framework for preparing the associates for accession. Germany and the UK, however, wanted the associates and particularly the Visegrad group, to be more closely integrated with the Community sooner rather than later.[39] As a compromise, the European Council insisted that relations with the East European countries would develop within the framework of the Europe agreements. This was the path of least resistance, already cleared. The multilateral political dialogue would be intensified and extended to include meetings at the highest political level.[40]

The reluctance of the Lisbon European Council to go beyond the Europe agreement framework is clearly connected to the enlargement question. On the same occasion, the European Council approved a report by the foreign ministers on possible areas for CFSP joint actions. The foreign ministers suggested that the EU could take joint action to establish political frameworks to foster cooperation in Eastern Europe, reinforce EU-East European relations, and develop links between the East European states and other European organizations.[41]

Granted, the Maastricht Treaty was not yet in force, so a joint action to reinforce relations with East European countries could not be taken. The need to do so was nonetheless clearly recognized. But the member states had not yet decided how to respond to the continuing demands from the associates for a clear perspective on membership, plus the Maastricht Treaty was itself in doubt; this uncertainty affected the development of closer relations with the associates.[42] To go so far as to create a European Political Area could propel the Community towards enlargement. By strengthening relations within the Europe agreement framework and continuing the ad hoc multilateral political dialogue, the associates could be kept in the 'association circle', which might or might not be eventually included in the Community itself. The Community's options were left open.

The incoming British presidency sought to implement the Lisbon conclusions on the political dialogue with the Visegrad group. It announced that it would hold two meetings with Czechoslovakia, Hungary and Poland, one at ministerial level on 5 October 1992 (with all the member states present) and the other at head-of-state level on 28 October (with just the Council and Commission presidents there). The exclusion of Bulgaria and Romania did not please several member states, including France, nor Commissioner Andriessen. But the Council then agreed that relations with Romania and Bulgaria had not yet progressed enough to include them.[43] This debate again reflects the tension between applying conditionality and the view that stability is best ensured by inclusion in Western cooperation frameworks.

Prior to the meetings, on 11 September 1992, the Visegrad countries called on the Community to state that their membership was a

Community aim: 'This simple, but historic statement would provide the anchor we need.'[44]

The member states, however, could not reach agreement on the membership issue.[45] So on 5 October, when the twelve foreign ministers and Andriessen met the Visegrad foreign ministers, no timetable for membership negotiations was drawn up, nor were any conditions set. Instead, they all reaffirmed that the Europe agreements would help the Visegrad countries achieve their final objective of membership. Political dialogue would be strengthened because it fosters 'political convergence, a better mutual understanding and enhanced security and stability throughout Europe'.[46]

On 28 October, UK Prime Minister John Major and Delors met in London with the four Visegrad prime ministers (Czechoslovakia – soon to be no longer – was represented by both the Czech and Slovak prime ministers).[47] The Visegrad leaders again pressed for better access to the EC market, closer political ties and a timetable for entry into the Community. Both Delors and Major declared that they favoured enlarging the Community to include the Visegrad group, but that a timetable for membership could not be set. They promised that the Community would draw up a list of membership criteria before the Edinburgh European Council in December.[48]

The leaders agreed to establish a regular political dialogue. Consultations 'as appropriate' would take place at the highest level between the Visegrad group and the Council and Commission presidents. Meetings 'as appropriate' would be held between the Visegrad ministers and either all twelve EC foreign ministers, the troika, or the presidency (in all cases, the Commission would be present). Senior officials from the Visegrad group and the troika would also meet regularly.[49] As a schedule of meetings was not specified, the multilateral political dialogue was still more ad hoc than institutionalized.

In early December 1992, the Commission added its voice to those pressing for a statement on membership. In a report on relations with Eastern Europe, it urged the Edinburgh European Council to accept the East European countries' objective of EU membership, once they could meet the necessary conditions:

> By offering this perspective, the Community will provide encouragement to those pursuing reform and make the short term economic and social consequences of adjustment easier to bear. This perspective will also provide a stimulus to investment and discourage excessive nationalism.[50]

To be eligible for membership, candidates must: be able to assume membership obligations (the *acquis communautaire*); have stable institutions guaranteeing democracy, the rule of law, human rights and respect for minorities; have a functioning market economy; endorse the objectives of political, economic and monetary union; and be able to cope with competitive pressure and market forces within the Union. In addition, the Community would have to be able to absorb new members while maintaining the momentum of European integration.

The Commission suggested that the associates could be more closely involved in EPC, sitting in on certain expert meetings. This would 'help overcome political barriers and pave the way for the involvement of partner countries in political cooperation'.[51] The Community could also establish a European Political Area. Regular enlarged Council meetings with the associates could be held in areas of trans-European interest (such as energy and the environment).

On 8 December the foreign ministers (meeting informally) discussed the Commission's proposals. Disagreements among the ministers made it impossible for them to pass the report on to the Edinburgh summit. Germany, the UK and Denmark favoured a formal statement confirming the aim of enlargement; the majority, however, thought the Commission's guidelines still needed to be analyzed.[52] The Edinburgh European Council only encouraged the full implementation of the Europe agreements and the extension of the political dialogue.[53] Other difficult issues dominated the Edinburgh summit: agreements enabling Denmark and the UK to ratify the Maastricht Treaty, increasing funds for the poorer member states, and launching accession negotiations with the EFTAns.[54] These decisions had to be taken before the Community could consider enlargement to Eastern Europe: the further development of relations with the associates was 'hostage' not only to internal disagreements over enlargement but to the numerous other items on the Community's agenda.

The Community's reluctance to indicate a possible date and conditions for accession was fuelling much discontent in Eastern Europe. A Czech official complained: 'We fought hard to have the possibility of membership included in the [Europe] Agreement and now it appears that the Community is reneging on its commitment in this domain.'[55] Polish Prime Minister Hanna Suchocka called on the Copenhagen European Council to confirm 'the will of the Community to see Poland and the other associated states as future members of the European Union.'[56]

Nor were the Visegrad countries happy with the political dialogue. They charged that meetings were not well prepared, they were not consulted on the agendas, and they were not treated as equal partners.[57] At a meeting of the Visegrad foreign ministers and the EC troika (plus Commissioners Brittan and van den Broek) on 8 March 1993, the four associates called for an institutionalized political dialogue. Because the member states had not yet agreed on the Commission's report on relations with Eastern Europe, the troika could not respond to the request.[58]

In May 1993, the Commission presented another report detailing how relations with the East European associates could be strengthened, which was very similar to its December 1992 report. It argued that 'the European Council should confirm, in a clear political message, its commitment to membership of the Union for Europe agreements signatories when they are able to satisfy the conditions required.'[59] (The conditions were those noted in the earlier report.) The East European countries needed a clear perspective of their membership prospects because it would strengthen their determination to continue with reforms, provide an element of stability against the background of turbulence in the former Soviet Union and Yugoslavia and 'diminish tension in a region where confidence and stability are suffering from the absence of a viable security structure'.[60]

The Commission once again pushed for the development of a European Political Area, through an intensive multilateral political dialogue. These closer links would foster a 'greater sense of belonging to the process of European integration' which would 'reduce feelings of insecurity and consequent tensions in the region, with gains for overall security and cooperation in Europe.'[61] In addition, there should be enlarged meetings of the European Council, Council and subordinate bodies on specific issues, including justice and home affairs.

On 8 June, the General Affairs Council approved the package, although it dropped the term 'European Political Area'.[62] Just before the Copenhagen European Council, in a clear attempt to put off enlargement, France submitted its own set of stricter membership criteria, which included GNP-per-capita level, degree of privatization, level of social protection, inflation levels and public deficit size. Several member states objected, pointing out that it would be unfair to demand that some applicants, but not others (the EFTAns), fulfill such conditions.[63] France also presented a proposal for a Pact on Stability in Europe (see Section 7.3.4), which some suspected was an attempt to set obstacles in the way of enlargement.

In the event, however, France did not block the enlargement decision; it would have to go along with the decision or risk losing influence in the Community (soon to be Union). By accepting enlargement, France could hope to influence the process to a much greater extent and continue to lead an active EU *Ostpolitik*. French concerns about German power were evidently stifled.[64]

The European Council in Copenhagen on 21–2 June 1993 finally agreed on a membership perspective for the associated East European countries: 'Accession will take place as soon as an associated country is able to assume the obligations of membership by satisfying the economic and political conditions required.' Candidate countries must:

- have achieved stability of institutions guaranteeing democracy, the rule of law, human rights, and respect for and protection of minorities;
- have a functioning market economy;
- be able to cope with competitive pressure and market forces within the Union; and
- be able to take on the obligations of membership including adherence to the aims of political, economic and monetary union.

The EU would have to be able to absorb new members, while maintaining the momentum of European integration.[65] This last condition is very ambiguous; the member states must first agree on where European integration is heading and what an enlarged Union should look like.[66]

No timetable for membership was set out; that would depend on progress in meeting the conditions. The EU has used the conditionality of membership (a very powerful lever) to try to influence the reform process and prevent conflicts in Eastern Europe (see Chapter 7).

The European Council also agreed to set up a 'structured relationship' between the Community and the East European associates, thus formalizing the ad hoc arrangements for political dialogue and extending them further (but stopping well short of partial membership). In addition to regular meetings between the presidents of the European Council and Commission and the associates' presidents, joint meetings of all the heads of state and government would be held to discuss specific issues, where appropriate. Advisory meetings would be held between the Council and all associated countries on matters of common interest (energy, environment, transport and so on), the CFSP and judicial affairs. No decisions would be taken at the meetings. A more intense dialogue on CFSP matters was also set out. There would be:

- one troika meeting at foreign minister level and one at the level of political directors during each presidency;
- briefings after each General Affairs Council meeting and each political directors meeting;
- one troika meeting at working group level per presidency;
- regular troika consultations with the associates ahead of important UN General Assembly and CSCE meetings.

In June 1993, the Community thus accepted the prospect of enlargement and agreed to intensify its relations with the associates, to integrate them gradually into the Community. This would further the Community's support of the reform process, on which 'peace and security in Europe' depended.[67] To reach these decisions, the member states made significant compromises, considering their initial reluctance. Several factors made this possible: the Danish 'yes' to the Maastricht Treaty in May 1993 (and the prior decision to allow Denmark to opt out of some parts of the Treaty), which meant that at least some institutional reform could go through; the agreement to proceed with enlargement to the EFTAns (which logically had to precede any agreement to enlarge to Eastern Europe); and the growing realization that East European demands for membership and closer relations had to be answered, in the Community's own interest. To ensure Europe's security, the EU would have to enlarge. It also helped that the transformation in several East European countries had proceeded so rapidly that the prospect of enlargement seemed more 'natural'.

The decision on enlargement was taken under much pressure from the East European countries, yet the Community also set conditions which reflect its own identity and experiences. There was strong pressure from *within* the Community (namely from Germany, the UK and the Commission) for enlargement. Likewise, although the associates demanded closer political ties with the Community, the structured relationship sets out a unique path for integration, with the emphasis on multilateralism and cooperation.

Péter Balázs asserts that the decision to accept the eventual membership of all of the associates and establish a structured relationship with them represents the 'homogenization' of the Union's relations with the East European countries.[68] All of the associates were treated similarly, without differentiating between slower and faster reformers (as the norm of conditionality would prescribe). The emphasis in this period fell more on developing an inclusive approach than on applying conditionality; differentiation has reappeared since, however, as discussed in Section 6.3.

6.2 PREPARING FOR ACCESSION

With the European Council's acceptance of the associates' eventual membership, pressures to provide a prospective timeframe grew. On 31 March 1994, Hungary applied to join; Poland did likewise on 5 April. They applied partly to force the issue onto the agenda of the 1996 IGC, but also to make sure the EU would have to deal with the applications before the mythical date, 2000.[69] Other applications from the East European countries have followed (see Table 6.5). All were forwarded by the Council to the Commission for its opinion.

Within the Union, Germany and the UK in particular pushed for enlargement preparations to proceed quickly. The foreign ministers, Douglas Hurd and Klaus Kinkel, cited three reasons why the EU (and NATO) should enlarge: 'security, prosperity and shared values'.[70] UK Prime Minister John Major argued:

> Through Community membership we can consolidate democracy and prosperity across our continent. Without it, we risk turmoil among neighbours in Eastern and Central Europe and endanger our own long-term prosperity and stability.[71]

Table 6.5 Applications for EU Membership

Hungary	31 March 1994
Poland	5 April 1994
Romania	22 June 1995
Slovakia	27 June 1995
Latvia	27 October 1995
Estonia	24 November 1995
Lithuania	8 December 1995
Bulgaria	14 December 1995
Czech Republic	17 January 1996
Slovenia	10 June 1996

Source: European Commission, 'Agenda 2000: Part 3. The Opinions of the European Commission on the Applications for Accession: Summaries and Conclusions', COM (97) 2000 final, 15 July 1997.

A priority of Germany's presidency from July to December 1994 was the adoption of a strategy to prepare the East European countries for accession.[72] To a certain extent, the rest of the EU agreed. There were widespread concerns that failure to give a concrete perspective on membership might intensify economic and political problems in Eastern Europe and spark a return to nationalism or authoritarianism, particularly with the continuing disarray in Russia.[73] Commissioner Brittan warned that without a firm membership promise, the associates could come under Russian influence.[74] While the risks of driving the disappointed associates into Russia's arms are exaggerated, considering East European suspicion of Russia, those of destabilization are more serious.

But as Germany continued to insist, others, France in particular, increasingly voiced their concerns about the implications of enlargement for the EU. France and the Commission reiterated that before enlargement could occur, the EU would have to carry out sweeping institutional reforms.[75] Enlargement could not dilute the EU. France and several other Mediterranean member states were also worried about an eastward shift in the EU's centre of gravity.[76] All were concerned about the probable cost of enlargement. In July 1995, a Spanish official warned that several member states could block EU treaty amendments if they were going to lose EU subsidies to Eastern Europe.[77]

Ideas for differentiated integration again appeared. These can be loosely grouped into two categories. 'Variable geometry' allows the member states to choose whether to proceed with deeper integration; there are objectives and goals that are not shared by all. In a 'multi-speed' Union, the member states share the same, higher objectives, but will proceed with deeper integration when they are ready and able to do so. A hard core would lead the way.[78]

In the autumn of 1993, Italian Foreign Minister Beniamino Andreatta proposed that enlargement take place as soon as possible, but that a hard federal core should also be created to counter the inevitable slowing down of integration.[79] In late August and early September 1994, both French Prime Minister Edouard Balladur and the German CDU parliamentary group proposed a hard core Europe. On 7 September, John Major proposed a Europe à la carte, allowing member states to pick and choose the policies they wanted to take part in.[80] Major's proposal was largely ignored; the hard-core proposals were harshly criticized, particularly in those countries excluded from the core.[81]

Such ideas were not accepted because 'people have become more conscious of the risks of splitting the Union or weakening the *acquis communautaire*'.[82] The Corfu European Council, 24–5 June 1994, stated that the institutional conditions for ensuring the proper functioning of the EU must be created at the 1996 IGC, which must therefore take place before any accession negotiations begin.[83] The Essen European Council, 9–10 December 1994, requested that the Commission analyze the effects of enlargement on the EU's policies (see Section 6.3). While the debate over institutional and policy reform continued, work progressed on preparing the associates for membership.

6.2.1   The Pre-Accession Strategy

Beginning in the spring of 1994, the Commission put together a pre-accession strategy, to help the associates satisfy the Copenhagen membership criteria and to implement the decisions on EU-associate relations. The Commission's reports were released in July 1994.[84] The pre-accession strategy is unique; no previous membership applicants had the path to membership so clearly indicated.

The strategy was based on initiatives in five areas (using instruments from all three pillars): strengthening the structured relationship (see Section 6.2.2); creating the legal environment for integration (approximation of laws); enhancing trade opportunities; promoting cooperation in areas such as energy, transport and the environment; and assistance for integration and reform (with PHARE and EC loans).

Trade was not such an important part of the strategy, even though the Copenhagen trade concessions did not stem the associates' disappointment.[85] But the Union was reluctant to go further. As the Commission argued, in a vigorous defence of trade policy towards Eastern Europe, by 1993, 60 per cent of the Visegrad countries' total exports entered the EC free of duties and quantitative restrictions; by 1998, the percentage would be 85 per cent, the remainder being agricultural products.[86] Instead, the emphasis would be on integrating the associates into the EU and particularly, into the single European market – an enormous task. To incorporate the *acquis*, the associates must implement over 100,000 pages of Community legislation.[87]

On 28 November 1994, the General Affairs Council approved a report on the pre-accession strategy, based on the Commission's proposals.[88] The Essen European Council endorsed it, and declared that by preparing for the accession of the associates, the EU would help ensure 'the lasting peace and stability of the European continent and neighbouring regions'.[89] This meant that regardless of the acknowledged difficulties of enlargement, the EU was prepared to take significant steps to implement the Copenhagen decision: the acceptance of enlargement was not merely a symbolic decision. The pre-accession strategy is an important watershed: EU-East European relations would from then on be focused on preparing for enlargement.

Furthermore, the European Council affirmed that Europe agreements would be concluded with the three Baltic states and Slovenia and that they would be included in the pre-accession strategy.[90] This is again an example of the uniform treatment of an ever-growing number of East European associates.[91] What is surprising is that the already difficult decision on eastern enlargement was extended and the list of membership candidates expanded (having already been lengthened to include Cyprus and Malta). The four countries met the criteria for Europe agreements, but this raises the question of whether the EU will eventually decide that other European countries also meet the conditions. The credibility of the EU's membership promises would decline if it proves unable to digest the already long queue of applicants. The EU's borders need not be definitively decided, as its leverage over other aspiring members would thus be lost; in return for flexibility, however, the EU would be unable to formulate a long-term strategy on Europe's future shape. This may be an untenable arrangement, as excluded states (such as Turkey and Ukraine) demand hard answers on enlargement.

As to the pre-accession strategy, the Essen summit agreed to align the timetables for trade liberalization in the Europe agreements with Bulgaria and Romania with those of the other associates (again placing the associates on the same footing), since the Copenhagen European Council had accepted the possibility of membership for *all* the associates.

The European Council approved a variety of measures to help the associates integrate into the single market. The Commission had suggested that the EU help the associates implement competition and state aid policies that were compatible with EU policies, so that safeguard measures would not be needed. While protective measures have been rarely used, the continuing threat that they could be used could hinder investment and trade.[92] The European Council stated that once adequate competition rules were implemented, the EU would 'consider refraining from using commercial defence instruments for industrial products' (not exactly a firm promise). The Commission was to offer information to the associates before initiating proceedings on safeguard and anti-dumping measures.

The leaders agreed some measures to encourage regional economic cooperation, with EU help for export promotion.[93] But the European Council hesitated over a Commission proposal to introduce full cumulation of origin in EU-East European trade; the consequences would first have to be studied.[94]

The Essen European Council asked the Commission to produce a White Paper of all the internal market legislation that needed to be adopted by the associates, and to report annually on its implementation.[95] The Commission set up a Technical Information Exchange Office to help the associates comply with the White Paper. PHARE also provides technical and legal assistance to help the associates adopt the *acquis communautaire*.

6.2.2   Consolidating the Structured Relationship

By the end of 1994, the EU had set up remarkable and unprecedented mechanisms for dialogue with all the associates, in all three pillars, before there is even a firm date for beginning accession negotiations. This is the 'structured relationship', an important part of the pre-accession strategy, which builds on the Copenhagen framework and the earlier proposals for East European participation in EU affairs. The structured relationship is unusual: 'never before have applicant countries been invited to participate on a regular basis in joint meetings with the institutions of the Union, until just before accession'.[96]

All of the associates, even those whose membership prospects are doubtful in the medium term, were included. The EU thus apparently played down the importance of conditionality to try to spread the 'Community method' of inter-state relations, hopefully contributing to stability and security in Europe. It is another example of the privileging of the multilateral over the bilateral approach.

The consolidation of the structured relationship took time. The delay in moving forward reflected lingering resistance to an institutionalized relationship with the associates. There were worries about the legal implications of allowing the associates in on Council meetings and the maintenance of the Council's autonomous decision-making capacity.[97]

In the year following the Copenhagen European Council, the dialogue was not fully implemented. Only two informal meetings were held between the Council and the associates on 'sectoral' matters:

transport (30 November 1993) and economic development (5 June 1994).[98] The first ministerial meeting within the political dialogue framework took place on 21 September 1993, when the troika and a Commission representative met with the foreign ministers of all six associates.[99]

To take the Copenhagen conclusions further, Italy and the UK launched an initiative to link the associates with the two intergovernmental pillars of the Maastricht Treaty, the CFSP and cooperation in justice and home affairs. In November 1993, Italian Foreign Minister Andreatta proposed the joint initiative to Douglas Hurd.[100] Andreatta felt that the East Europeans needed to be included in political discussions, not least because it would be a visible sign of their participation in the EU and could thus increase the legitimacy of the governments in the eyes of their electorates. The initiative would involve the UK in a European project, boost Italy's role in the EU and in Eastern Europe, balance the Franco-German axis and respond to East European requests for greater security.[101]

In early December, Hurd agreed with the initiative. The two foreign ministers then wrote to Willy Claes, Belgian foreign minister and Council president, to propose developing new links between the six associates and the EU on the two intergovernmental pillars. Relations with the associates tended to be dominated by economic issues, but the associates desired a closer political relationship which would allow them 'to anchor their societies and institutions to well-established democracies and to a common system of values.'[102]

The joint proposal was presented to the General Affairs Council on 20 December 1993. Claes noted it was timely, given the political turmoil in Russia and Ukraine and the consequent growing anxiety in Eastern Europe.[103] France was not so enthusiastic, because Italy and the UK had taken the initiative in a region where it was supposed to exercise more influence. Delors supported it, as did the associates: they wanted to take part in CFSP meetings.[104]

Less than three months later, on 7 March 1994, the Council agreed to reinforce the political dialogue with the six associated countries.[105] The Council would make provisions for:

- an annual summit of the European Council president, the Commission president and the heads of state or government of the associated countries;
- special joint Councils on CFSP matters during each presidency with the associates' foreign ministers;

- political directors' meetings during each presidency; and
- meetings of experts, in the form of working parties on security, terrorism and human rights, based on the troika or participation by all partners.

The presidency would brief the associates' ambassadors after each European Council and could organize troika meetings of the foreign ministers. Troika meetings of the political directors could discuss urgent matters.

The associates could also back troika démarches and EU statements, participate in certain joint actions and could be invited to coordinate their positions with the EU's position in international organizations and conferences.[106]

The Council decision clearly implements the early proposals for East European participation in CFSP, and even moves closer to a form of affiliate membership. Undoubtedly, many member states agreed to set up such a framework because it would include the associates in a security framework, as the situation in Russia and turmoil elsewhere in the former Soviet Union and Yugoslavia provoked so much concern.

In July 1994, however, the Commission noted that neither the framework agreed at Copenhagen nor the 7 March Council decisions had been fully implemented. The political dialogue, which had so far taken place mainly in troika format,[107] did not sufficiently address key foreign policy and security issues, yet it was 'especially important as a means for overcoming the widespread sense of insecurity in central and eastern Europe.'[108] Joint meetings of the EU and associates should replace the troika format (as the Council had already decided in March). Joint 'sectoral' meetings should be held on matters of common interest, including environment, transport, internal market and social policy.[109]

The German presidency (second half of 1994) then weighed in with its strong support for the structured relationship. It organized more joint sectoral meetings, including one on organized trans-border crime on 8 September and one on the environment on 5 October.[110] The political dialogue provisions were also more fully implemented. On 31 October, the foreign ministers from the EU, associates and four EFTAns met, along with Delors, Brittan and van den Broek, to discuss the pre-accession strategy, regional cooperation and closer links. The framework of the meeting was more official and formal than previous meetings and was extensively prepared in Coreper.[111]

Germany also put forward a paper on the arrangements for joint meetings between the EU ministers and their counterparts from the six associates. The meetings would parallel those of the Council, and be held once or twice a year, on foreign affairs, internal affairs, the environment, economy, agriculture and transport. The proposals were intended to be 'practical guidelines' for implementing the Copenhagen European Council decisions.[112] The German input was crucial in moving implementation forward.

At a Council meeting on 4 October, the German plan was basically approved, although the schedule of the meetings would be decided by each presidency, rather than be established in advance. Five members states, including France, Spain and Belgium, objected to institutionalizing regular meetings and insisted that no decisions could be made at them.[113] French Foreign Minister Alain Juppé argued that there should not be a proliferation of meetings and that the EU's independence of decision must be respected.[114]

The provisions on the structured dialogue were approved by the General Affairs Council on 28 November 1994 and then by the Essen European Council.[115] Each year the heads of state would meet on the margins of the European Council. The foreign ministers would meet biannually, to discuss the full scope of relations with associates. Ministers responsible for internal market development, transport, research, environment, telecommunications, cultural affairs and education would meet once a year, in connection with regular Council meetings. Justice and home affairs ministers would meet twice a year.[116] These meetings are additional to the 'enhanced' political dialogue, as set out in the 7 March 1994 Council decision, which is much more intense.

Each presidency should arrange meetings for that year according to the above schedule and identify priority themes at the beginning of the presidency. The associates will *not* participate in decisionmaking. Launching the structured relationship, the East European leaders were invited to the Essen European Council meeting.[117]

The structured relationship has in practice been more intense than originally provided for: EU and East European leaders have usually met 'on the margins' of the European Council twice a year, and the foreign ministers have met up to four times a year.[118]

The structured relationship was supposed to help integrate the associates into the EU, particularly by socializing the associates into the process of consensus-building in the EU and acquainting them with EU procedures and dossiers. Integration into the CFSP was also to help the associates develop a coordination reflex and avoid some of the dangers that enlargement poses for foreign policy cooperation, notably the disruption of discipline.[119]

But numerous problems with the structured relationship have become evident. Some associates are still 'putting their houses in order': finding interlocutors on the associates' side can be difficult. The structured relationship is burdensome, and often EU ministers send their deputies to meetings. There have been criticisms that the meetings are ill-prepared (by all parties) and lack substance.[120] Assessment of the enhanced political dialogue is more positive, as cooperation has become well established and the meetings at lower levels allow ministerial meetings to be better prepared.[121]

6.3   WHO JOINS FIRST?

The Essen European Council asked the Commission to report on the implications of enlargement for the EU's policies, including CAP, the policy area posing the most difficulties for integration of the associates. The potential costs of enlargement were clearly causing concern, particularly at a time when member states were trimming budgets to meet the criteria for participation in EMU. But the Commission's reports (presented to the Madrid European Council, 15–16 December 1995) did *not* estimate the costs of enlargement, due to uncertainty about economic growth, possible reforms of EU policies (especially the CAP) and the number of acceding countries.[122]

Despite the presumed but uncertain costs, the Union seemed willing to push ahead. Not only had the 'point of no return' long since passed, but a certain momentum was building behind enlargement. In July 1995, Kohl promised the Polish parliament that Poland would join the EU in 2000.[123] On a visit to Poland in September 1996, French President Jacques Chirac gave the strongest endorsement of enlargement yet by a French leader. He declared that Poland should enter the Union from 2000.[124] This illustrates the extent to which the French position on enlargement has shifted from reluctant acceptance to an attempt to lead the process.

The Madrid European Council strongly declared:

> Enlargement is both a political necessity and a historic opportunity for Europe. It will ensure the stability and security of the continent and will thus offer both the applicant States and the current

members of the Union new prospects for economic growth and general well-being.[125]

Significantly, the European Council asked the Commission to speed up preparation on its opinions of the East European membership applications so that they could be forwarded to the Council as soon as possible after the 1996 IGC concluded.[126] The Commission was also to present a composite paper on enlargement, analyze its effects on the Union's policies and propose a future financial framework. These four sets of documents were termed 'Agenda 2000', symbolizing an attempt to set out a long-term strategy for an enlarged Union.

The Florence European Council, 21–2 June 1996, stated that the initial phase of membership talks with the East European countries could coincide with the beginning of negotiations with Cyprus and Malta, six months after the end of the IGC.[127] Since the IGC ended in June 1997, the Luxembourg European Council in December 1997 would choose to begin talks with appropriate applicant countries.

Accelerating the enlargement process, however, meant that two major issues had to be dealt with all the more urgently. One of these reflects the tension between 'homogenization' and the application of conditionality. Because not all the applicant countries would meet the membership conditions at the same time and because the Union could not handle an extensive enlargement, all ten East European applicant countries will not accede to the EU at the same time. Each associate would be judged separately as to whether it met the conditions. Differentiation among the associates was thus assured and in principle would spur further progress with reforms and the adoption of the *acquis*. The associates had long been troubled by the EU's multilateral approach to Eastern Europe, which treated them equally (see Chapter 7).[128]

But differentiation means that some applicant countries will be left out of a first, or even second, round of enlargement. This would have economic, political and security implications for the 'excluded' East European countries.[129] The new member states will enjoy the economic advantages associated with EU membership (including financial assistance and participation in the single European market). The excluded countries could feel isolated and marginalized, which could have destabilizing political effects. These effects could be magnified if there have been tensions between the new member states and the excluded countries. The new member states could veto further enlargements or take an aggressive attitude towards non-members. If accession appears to be a too distant prospect, then support for membership could decline in the excluded states and the EU could lose leverage for encouraging reforms.[130]

The parallel process of NATO enlargement risks aggravating these implications, as some countries will be excluded from both organizations. Being included in one organization but not the other could, however, mitigate any negative effects. Some European NATO members (in particular France) thus proposed (unsuccessfully) including Romania in the first round of NATO enlargement, since it was unlikely to be included first in the EU. Estonia was often mentioned (particularly by the Scandinavian member states and the US) as a possible candidate for the first round of EU enlargement, since none of the Baltic states would join NATO in the near future (due to the risks of offending Russia and the difficulties of defending them).[131] Italy has backed Slovenia's entry into one or both organizations (in a striking reversal of its initial policy). In Madrid in July 1997, a NATO summit decided to enlarge first to the Czech Republic, Hungary and Poland. This put pressure on the EU to widen the first intake of new East European member states, to ensure geopolitical stability.

Several other options were proposed to try to reduce the negative implications of being left out of the first stage of EU enlargement. Negotiations could open with all ten applicants (the 'regatta option' – all 'boats' at the starting line together), thus postponing differentiation. Some form of partial membership could be offered to those left out. A framework encompassing the enlarged EU and the excluded countries could be devised.[132]

In March 1997, the foreign ministers endorsed a French idea to create a permanent European Conference (which resembles Mitterrand's confederation idea).[133] The Conference would be a forum for discussion between the EU member states and all applicant countries (including, perhaps, Turkey) on issues of foreign policy and internal affairs such as immigration. German Foreign Minister Kinkel maintained this would 'give those who aren't in the first wave the feeling that they are not being ignored'.[134] But the European Conference may also be seen as another 'talking shop', a forum for discussion and not for decisionmaking and would thus not sufficiently address the problem. The Commission's 'Agenda 2000' communication suggested other ways of diminishing the negative implications (see below).

The other major issue demanding attention as enlargement loomed was Union reform.[135] The Amsterdam European Council in June

1997, which concluded the IGC, largely put off tough decisions. Under the Amsterdam Treaty, qualified majority voting was extended to a few more areas within the first pillar. Qualified majority voting can be used to implement CFSP decisions, although a member state can raise objections to its use. Some member states may proceed with closer cooperation (using EU institutions and procedures), but a member state can oppose Council authorization of such cooperation for important reasons of national policy.

Under a separate protocol, the large member states will nominate only one Commissioner each from the date of the next enlargement, providing that the weighting of votes in the Council is readjusted in their favour beforehand. A year before the EU's membership exceeds 20, another review of the treaties will take place.

The Amsterdam European Council dodged the hard questions, and thus raised doubts about whether the EU would be able to enlarge successfully, or at all.[136] But the heads of state or government still declared that the IGC concluded successfully: 'the way is now open for launching the enlargement process'.[137] In accordance with this, on 16 July 1997, the Commission presented 'Agenda 2000' to the EP.[138] As a rebuke to the European Council, the Commission suggested convening another IGC as soon as possible after 2000 to reform thoroughly the Union's institutions.[139] Belgium, France and Italy have also demanded that further reform precede enlargement.[140]

The Commission proposed that membership negotiations be opened with the Czech Republic, Estonia, Hungary, Poland and Slovenia (in addition to Cyprus).[141] These five came closest to meeting all the Copenhagen conditions, although they all had work to do to meet the economic conditions and adopt the *acquis*.[142] The inclusion of Estonia and Slovenia seems to take into account geopolitical considerations.

As for paying for enlargement, the Commission assumed that the budgetary ceiling would remain at 1.27 per cent of the Union's GNP from 1999 (as there is little support for increasing member state contributions). But with economic growth and policy reform, the Commission argued optimistically that the structural policies and the CAP could still be extended to the East European applicants. CAP would further shift from price support to direct payments to farmers; support prices for beef, cereals and dairy products would be reduced. The structural funds would be simplified and limited. The Commission estimated that there would be about 275 billion ECUs (1997 prices) for structural and cohesion funds in the period 2000–6. Of this,

45 billion ECUs would be reserved for the new member states (including 7 billion ECUs for pre-accession aid). Transfers to any new member state would not exceed four per cent of its GDP. The Commission proposed rehauling the pre-accession strategy. The EU would conclude 'Accession Partnerships' with each applicant country, which would contain a precise national programme for the adoption of the *acquis* within a set timetable. Aid would be conditional on the applicant country achieving the objectives. Annual reviews would mark progress; membership negotiations could even be opened with applicant countries that had caught up to the front-runners. From 2000, in addition to PHARE, the East European applicant countries would receive 500 million ECUs a year for agricultural development, and structural aid worth 1 billion ECUs a year (out of the 7 billion ECUs pre-accession aid set aside). The Accession Partnerships would assure all of the applicant countries that their membership prospects were still being taken seriously.

The Commission proposed abolishing the structured relationship, because relations would be primarily conducted bilaterally, although there could be ad hoc multilateral meetings on some issues in addition to the European Conference. This renewed emphasis on bilateral relations reduces the previous emphasis on regional cooperation and multilateralism.

The Commission's proposals sparked immediate opposition. Almost all of the agriculture ministers (except Britain's and Sweden's) attacked the CAP reform proposals, and Spain warned that it would not support a reduction in the cohesion fund. A German call for a reduction in its contributions to the EU budget considerably complicated the debate.[143]

The recommendation to begin negotiations with only five of the applicant countries came under fire. Italy, Denmark and Sweden argued that talks should begin with all the countries (the regatta option), to avoid the destabilizing effects of excluding some of them.[144] Several MEPs warned that the EU would create a dangerous division if some countries joined before others.[145] These considerations swept aside earlier arguments (particularly German) for limiting the first intake to less than five East European newcomers, and thus reducing the need for institutional and policy reforms.

The Luxembourg European Council, 12–13 December 1997, agreed to the Commission's proposals for a new pre-accession framework, but called it an 'accession process' involving all ten East European countries on 'an equal footing'.[146] This partially answered the demands that the EU avoid creating a division between the applicant states. Membership negotiations would, however, begin with just five of them: the Czech Republic, Estonia, Hungary, Poland and Slovenia (as well as Cyprus).

To launch the accession process, all of the EU and East European foreign ministers met in March 1998. Accession Partnerships (including additional aid, the amount of which was unspecified) have been concluded with the ten East European countries. Membership talks with the five frontrunners began in spring 1998; the excluded countries could join them, if they make substantial progress in fulfilling the Copenhagen criteria, as tracked in annual reviews. Each country will accede only when it and the EU are ready (although enlargement will most likely occur in stages, with several countries joining at the same time).

Occasional ad hoc meetings of the foreign ministers (and possibly other ministers) will replace the structured relationship. In addition, the European Conference first convened in March 1998.

The European Council did not decide on policy reform (CAP and structural funds), and only declared that the EU's institutions must be strengthened before enlargement, in keeping with the Amsterdam Treaty. The hardest decisions thus remain to be taken.

CONCLUSION

The Community/Union has set up a remarkable structure for the gradual integration of the East European associates into the EU, based on the Europe agreements and the pre-accession strategy. Again and again, reticent member states made concessions, on trade, on the structured relationship and, above all, on enlargement. The process was less one of bargaining (with pay-offs and threatened sanctions) than of convincing reluctant member states to make concessions. Several member states and the Commission pushed through initiatives, successfully upgrading the common interest. The Council presidency was also fundamental in shaping these decisions.

External pressures were significant. The constant East European demands for action at the Community/Union level with regards to trade, dialogue, and enlargement forced the member states to respond jointly. But the collective response (conditionality of membership, structured relationship) has also been unique, reflecting the Community/Union's principles, goals and experiences.

The most significant decision was that on enlargement. The EU moved from the 'politics of exclusion' to the 'politics of inclusion' with respect to its East European neighbours.[147] No doubt several member states would have preferred to postpone a decision to enlarge, but the demands of the East European states (supported by Germany, the UK, Denmark and the Commission, in particular), combined with security concerns and an awareness of the EU's role as a stabilizing force in Europe, eventually obliged those states to agree to enlarge the EU.

Enlargement has become the biggest challenge facing the EU. The member states have proved willing to make many compromises to bring the East European countries closer to the Union. Whether they will now make compromises that enable an enlarged Union to function effectively is an open question.

7 Conflict Prevention

The end of the Cold War was supposed to bring peace to Europe. The euphoria did not last long. Ethnic nationalism exploded in many parts of Eastern Europe. War erupted in the former Yugoslavia in mid-1991. Then violent conflicts and civil war broke out in the disintegrating Soviet Union. Tensions developed between other states in the region, often over the treatment of ethnic minorities.

The evolution of the Union's policy towards Eastern Europe reflects these changing circumstances. In 1988–90, the Community had concentrated on aiding economic reforms; supporting economic reform was also considered necessary for the democratic transition. By extending aid and trade concessions on a conditional basis, the Community hoped to encourage political reform. By 1990, the Community agreed that more had to be done to consolidate the transformation and the East European states became associates. By 1993, eventual integration with the Community was considered to be the best way to spread security and stability in Eastern Europe, but in a longer-term perspective. In the shorter term, the Community would have to take other measures to ensure the success of the transformation, given the worrisome developments in Eastern Europe. The strengthening of ties with the associates and the acceptance of their eventual membership also meant that the Union would be that much 'closer' to instability. Conflict prevention measures, which 'aim at preventing disputes from arising and preventing existing disputes from deteriorating into armed conflict',[1] would have to be implemented.

Until the end of the Cold War, the Community was better known for preventing conflicts between its own member states.[2] The EU's involvement in conflict prevention has since expanded, as a result of its increasing foreign policy responsibilities and external exigencies. The Yugoslav war made manifest the EU's severe shortcomings in dealing with violent conflicts; the EU is much better equipped to try to prevent conflicts from erupting in the first place. In using its civilian instruments to try to prevent conflicts in Eastern Europe, the EU has also been more proactive than reactive.

Conflict prevention is one of those areas where spillover between external economic relations and security is quite evident. Consistent with this, the Commission has been very involved in implementing conflict prevention measures.

In Section 7.1, the perceived threats to security in Eastern Europe will be discussed. Section 7.2 will examine the measures that the Community has taken to try to reduce 'internal' threats to security. Section 7.3 will then survey the measures taken to address 'external' threats to security.

7.1   THREATS TO SECURITY IN EASTERN EUROPE

The sources of insecurity in Eastern Europe can be divided into internal and external sources, although such a division is fairly arbitrary, since intra-state ethnic conflicts or internal instability can spread across borders, or can be exacerbated or even fomented by groups or governments in other states. Internal sources of insecurity arising within states include: economic and political instability resulting from a failure of reforms; the risk that a population disillusioned with reforms could elect authoritarian and/or nationalist rulers; and disputes between ethnic groups. Jan Zielonka has argued that the most acute source of instability in the region emerges 'from the possible failure of economic reforms and democracy-building in the region.'[3] Such a failure could produce economic chaos and political anarchy, which could result in aggressive populism, hyper-nationalism, militarism and economic demagoguery, or even foreign intervention.[4] Ethnic disputes are another internal source of insecurity. In November 1991, the Community/EPC and the US proclaimed that one of the greatest challenges to democracy and prosperity in Eastern Europe was 'dealing with ethnic diversity and the rights of persons belonging to national minorities.'[5]

External sources of insecurity include concerns about Soviet (then Russian) foreign policy intentions: Russia could try to re-establish a sphere of influence in Eastern Europe. Other external sources are inter-state disputes over ethnic minorities and boundaries. Jenonne Walker has warned that the most likely source of conflicts between states in Eastern Europe stems from one state's concern over the treatment of ethnic minorities in a neighbouring state. Territorial disputes also arise in part from minority grievances – states might want to change their boundaries to include more of their dominant ethnic group within their state.[6]

Clearly, conflicts in potential EU members in Eastern Europe could adversely affect the EU's security. The EU has thus tried to prevent violent conflicts arising from these internal and external sources, using its civilian instruments. '[A]s many conflicts and tensions are rooted in political, social and economic instabilities, the Union is much better equipped than any other international organisation to address related problems.'[7] Commission President Delors asserted that

> [t]he European Community has a special responsibility not only because of its importance as a pole of stability and prosperity, but also because it has an armory of instruments to deal with the most pressing problems in the East and in the South. Never has the link between economic stability and security been so obvious.[8]

PHARE, the Europe agreements, the structured relationship, all support the political and economic reforms in Eastern Europe and thus help engender security. Delors stated, however, that the EU's priority would be 'to promote stability on the eastern and southern borders by paying more attention to preventive diplomacy.'[9] One of the specific aims for the CFSP suggested by EC foreign ministers in June 1992 was 'contributing to the prevention and settlement of conflicts'.[10]

This chapter will examine how the Community, then Union, has tried to prevent conflicts in Eastern Europe, particularly since 1991, when the issue became more pressing. 'Conflict prevention' will be interpreted fairly widely, to include not only mediation or economic and diplomatic pressure on disputants, but also attempts to reduce the internal and external sources of insecurity (beyond integrating the associates in the EU and providing aid for economic reforms). The Community/Union has used conditionality to foster democratization and respect for human and minority rights; provided aid specifically for democratization; and encouraged regional cooperation. The WEU, linked to the EU under the Maastricht Treaty, has reached out to the associates. These measures are not solely aimed at preventing conflict, but are expected to achieve that objective, and so will be covered here. The Community also, however, stepped in directly to mediate a dispute between Slovakia and Hungary. The Pact on Stability in Europe was the EU's foremost effort to prevent conflict, and was developed specifically for that aim.

The Community/Union's efforts to eradicate or mitigate the perceived causes of instability and insecurity in Europe have taken place alongside similar efforts by other organizations, namely, the CSCE, Council of Europe and NATO.[11] Those efforts cannot be discussed here, except insofar as they have been linked to the Community's measures.

7.2 THE UNION'S RESPONSE TO INTERNAL THREATS

The measures taken by the Community/Union to address the internal sources of conflict reflect very 'liberal' ideas. Democracy, respect for human and minority rights, economic growth and integration would lead to stability and peace. A debate about whether democracy actually engenders peace has raged among international relations theorists, but not, it seems, among policymakers who appear to be convinced that it does. The June 1991 Luxembourg European Council, for example, declared that respect for human rights was necessary for peace and lasting security.[12]

Reinhardt Rummel has noted that the EU is applying its own experiences with regards to Eastern Europe. Democracy and integration had created peace in Western Europe; '[d]eveloping democracy within the states of Eastern Central Europe and the CIS as well as integration among these states is therefore also regarded as a road to peace in this region.'[13]

Several observers have warned that democratization could exacerbate ethnic tension; new political parties could reflect ethnic divisions, for example.[14] But in their November 1991 joint declaration, the Community/EPC and the US stated: 'We specifically want to underline that political freedom is not the cause of such problems [ethnic tensions and nationalism] but is the necessary pre-condition for achieving durable solutions in the spirit of compromise and mutual tolerance.'[15] Gabriel Munuera agrees: 'Ultimately, the basis for stability is well-known: democracy and socio-economic development provide the greatest hope for managing the problems of Central and Eastern Europe, particularly inter-ethnic relations.'[16]

To encourage democratization and respect for human and minority rights, the Community adopted two main approaches: it set political conditions for closer relations and eventual membership and it extended aid and technical assistance to help build democracy.

7.2.1 Conditionality

Political conditionality has been a guiding norm of the Community/ Union's policy. Trade and cooperation agreements, aid and association agreements were promised to countries that met political conditions. But conditionality appeared in agreements only after the May 1992 decision on the 'human rights clause' (see Chapter 5); this also made it clear that Community 'rewards' could be cut off. Since the outbreak of war in the former Yugoslavia, minority rights have been included in the conditions.[17]

The Copenhagen European Council's membership conditions, which include the achievement of democracy and respect for human and minority rights, are the EU's most powerful instrument for influencing the transformation of Eastern Europe. Mathias Jopp has argued that 'conditions for accession, together with a realistic perspective for membership, are the most effective lever for the Union to influence developments in Central and Eastern Europe.'[18] No dates have been indicated for enlargement, as this depends on fulfilment of the conditions; providing a date could be counterproductive. The promise of membership is a 'consumable power resource'; once fulfilled, the EU's leverage will be exhausted.

To what extent applying conditionality will allow the EU to influence the development of democracy and respect for human rights – and therefore, in the liberal view, the potential for conflicts – is still an open question. Some of the associates have been irritated by conditionality: Hungary once described it as 'patronizing', while Poland argued it was not necessary since it had already demonstrated its commitment to democracy.[19] The success of democratization in a particular state may have more to do with domestic factors, including a general consensus favouring democratization, or with the actions of other international actors. But where democratic reforms are more contested, the EU's conditions could be influential, although it would be difficult to impose democracy or human rights protection against a government's will.[20] Conditionality could help to dissuade governments from human rights abuse, or to discourage a return to authoritarian rule.[21] Setting conditions provides a guide for governments pursuing the rewards on offer and gives them an excuse for launching unpopular reforms.

The leverage provided by (tacit) membership conditions did support the democratization process in Greece, Spain and Portugal, which had been excluded from the Community because they were not liberal democracies.[22] As democratization was launched in the three countries, the EC responded by holding out the prospect of membership and promising more trade and aid. But Geoffrey Pridham argues that domestic developments were still the primary influence on democratization, and the Community could not have prevented a disruption or reversal of the transition process.[23]

There are several problems with conditionality. Which democratic principles and human rights are considered more important?[24] How would the EU determine whether associates are fulfilling the conditions? What would be considered violations of the conditions? Any such judgment is bound to be highly subjective.

There are problems with insisting on the protection of minority rights. By granting substantial autonomy to minorities, states could create a precedent for separation and perpetuate divisions. Member states themselves are divided over the concept of minority rights, with France and the UK in particular more inclined to emphasize individual rights. Insisting on guarantees for minority rights is only one conflict prevention measure, and should be emphasized along with democratic practices and economic stability.[25] The progressive reduction in the importance of borders, by regional integration, would also help prevent disputes over minorities.

Several members states have argued that it is more important for the EU to strengthen relations with the East European states than to apply conditionality.[26] A strict application of conditionality would only isolate those states that most need aid and ties with the Community and generate instability. As discussed in Section 6.3, applying the membership conditions may prove particularly troublesome. Stability could be undermined if it appears that Europe is being divided again.

There is still a reluctance (as there was during the Cold War) to use trade and relations with Eastern Europe as a stick, rather than as a carrot. This has been evident in discussions about relations with Bulgaria and Romania, generally less advanced in their reforms. The extension of the structured relationship to all the associates, irrespective of their progress in political and economic reforms, reflects the view that integration is crucial for maintaining stability.

The EU has become increasingly aware that applying conditionality could turn the 'targeted' state back to Moscow. (States could even use the threat of an alliance with Russia to press for closer relations with the EU.) Of course, this risk should not be exaggerated, given the state of the Russian economy (and general suspicions about Russia) and the pull of the 'West' in general. Geopolitical considerations influenced the decisions to negotiate Europe agreements with Bulgaria and Romania and to strengthen relations with the Baltic states. And for a while there were concerns that Russia would pressure Bulgaria to join a 'counter-alliance'.[27] Slovakia, reprimanded several times by the EU for its poor democratic record, has been cozying up to Russia. The exclusion of some associates from the first round of enlargement could exacerbate this risk.

The application of conditionality in practice makes manifest these various problems. The state of democracy in Slovakia and Romania in particular has raised concerns. Because of their large Hungarian minorities (600,000 in Slovakia; 1.6 to 2 million in Romania), internal developments in those two countries could have negative implications for their relations with Hungary.[28]

In July 1992 (as Czechoslovakia began to split), the Community inquired about the future status of Slovakia's minorities. The new prime minister, Vladimir Meciar, refused to consider legislating minority rights guarantees.[29] He also refused to consider reaching a treaty with Hungary which included provisions on minority rights, fearing that the Hungarian minority would try to secede from Slovakia and reunite with Hungary.[30]

Since autumn 1994, the EU has been very concerned that democratization is being undermined in Slovakia and that Slovak-Hungarian relations have been negatively affected (already strained by the Gabcikovo dam dispute, discussed in Section 7.3.3). After expressing concern through less visible channels of communication, the EU publicly presented a démarche to the Slovak government on 23 November 1994, reiterating that the strengthening of relations between Slovakia and the EU would depend on the new government's policies.[31] On 25 October 1995, the troika presented the Slovak prime minister with another démarche emphasizing that Slovakia must meet democratic norms before it can join the EU.[32] In November 1995, the EP threatened to suspend aid to Slovakia because of violations of human and minority rights and disregard for the rule of law.[33] Numerous other warnings (in public, and through channels such as the association council) have followed.[34] The EU also put much pressure on Slovakia and Hungary to sign a good-neighbourly agreement within the framework of the Stability Pact (see Section 7.3.4). Although an agreement was signed, relations remain tense, especially over the issue of Slovakia's treatment of its Hungarian minority.[35]

The EU has not considered suspending the Europe agreement with Slovakia: it is too blunt a weapon. Slovakia was included in the structured relationship and the WEU's associate partnership scheme (see Section 7.3.2). But in July 1997, the Commission considered Slovakia to be the only East European applicant state that did not meet the political conditions set by the Copenhagen European Council.[36] That membership talks opened with Hungary and not with Slovakia could contribute to a feeling of isolation in Slovakia (compounded by NATO's decision to embrace Hungary and exclude Slovakia). Slovakia does seem to be turning to Russia for security and aid.[37] The tensions between conditionality and stability (which could presumably be provided by closer relations with the EU) are evident here, but rewarding the Slovak government for disregarding democratic principles and refusing to protect minority rights is not an ideal alternative solution, nor would it necessarily trigger a change.

Developments in Romania were also worrying, but they did not prompt as much concern.[38] In August 1994, an extreme anti-Hungarian party, the Romanian National Unity Party, joined the cabinet. In January 1995, ruling Social Democrats signed an agreement with the anti-Semitic and racist Great Romania Party. Western diplomats had pointed out beforehand that such alliances would not improve Romania's image or prepare the way for EU membership.[39] In summer 1995, there were signs that the Romanian government was contributing to anti-Hungarian sentiment.[40]

At a meeting of the French, German and Romanian foreign ministers on 17 July 1995, less than a month after Romania applied to join the EU, Hervé de Charette and Klaus Kinkel reminded Teodor Melascanu that economic reform and democracy were necessary conditions for EU membership and pushed for agreement between Romania and Hungary on minority rights.[41] But the EU did not present Romania with a démarche; concern was instead expressed in the context of the association council.

The warnings seemed to have an effect. In mid-1995, President Ion Iliescu launched an initiative for reconciliation with Hungary. In October 1995, the Social Democrats broke with the Great Romania Party; in August 1996, they broke with the National Unity Party (over a soon-to-be-signed treaty with Hungary). A reformist government then took office in November 1996, which included a minister from the Hungarian Democratic Union in Romania party.

These changes led to an improvement in Romania's relations with the EU: EU macro-financial aid was unblocked in March 1997 (see Section 4.4). France could also gather more support for Romania's early entry into NATO. While the EU cannot claim sole responsibility for the positive turn of events in Romania, its relations with Romania show other countries that there are benefits to be gained by following a reform path. But here again, there could be negative implications of excluding Romania from the first round of enlargement.

7.2.2 Aid for Democratization

Although conditionality has been the primary way in which the Community tries to influence the democratization process, PHARE aid has been increasingly directed to helping the political transformation. To develop civil society, assistance has been given to NGOs. In 1994, the Link Inter-European NGO Programme (LIEN) was set up (and allocated 10 million ECUs) to support NGO initiatives that help provide social safety nets.[42]

In 1993, the PHARE Partnership and Institution Building Programme was launched and allocated 10 million ECUs. Funds were given to support the development of partnerships between non-profit organizations in the Community and Eastern Europe, in sectors such as local and regional government, community development and worker and consumer interests.[43] In 1995, the programme became the Partnership Programme; aid could also be granted to support cooperation among non-profit organizations in the recipient countries.[44]

In July 1992, a trial PHARE democracy programme was launched, with a budget of 5 million ECUs, after the EP insisted that such a sum be allocated for aid for democratization. In 1993, the programme was formally adopted, with a budget of 10 million ECUs. Projects involving East European and EU NGOs are to help develop parliamentary practices, promote and monitor human and minority rights, establish an independent media, encourage local democracy and educate. A September 1997 evaluation of the PHARE Democracy Programme reported that it had had a positive impact on the development of democracy in several East European countries, notably by creating a 'lively' NGO sector.[45]

Funds for strengthening institutions and administrations will be increased with the new 1997 PHARE guidelines although this is separate from the Democracy Programme (see Chapter 4). But the amount of aid targeted specifically to support democratic reforms is still dwarfed by that to help the economic transition. The prevailing view was and is that by supporting the transition to a market economy, the Community helps the transition to democracy. Aid to help build democracy has also been given by the member states and national and transnational organizations (such as political parties), and foundations. The UK's Know How Fund and the Westminster Fund for Democracy are two such aid programmes.

7.3   THE UNION'S RESPONSE TO EXTERNAL THREATS

To address the various threats to security that stem from external sources (a potentially threatening Russia; disputes with neighbours over minorities and borders), several measures have been taken. The Community/Union has encouraged regional cooperation; the WEU has strengthened its ties with the EU's associates; the Commission mediated in the Gabcikovo dam dispute; and the EU launched the Pact on Stability in Europe.

7.3.1   Encouraging Regional Cooperation

Encouraging regional cooperation was long a Community goal, the 'export' of the Community model of multilateral, inter-state relations. '[I]ntegration was not seen as something for Western Europe alone but as a process which serves as an example for the rest of the world to build on and emulate.'[46] Integration is considered a stabilizing factor.[47]

The exception to the Community's support for regional cooperation was, of course, the CMEA. The Community wanted to limit the Soviet Union's control over the East European states' trade relations and so insisted on concluding trade agreements with the separate CMEA member countries rather than the CMEA itself (see Chapter 2). After the CMEA had agreed to this, the Community negotiated trade and cooperation agreements with the East European states on the basis of specificity and conditionality. Applying conditionality, in fact, required the differentiation of relations with the East European states. This meant that the development of bilateral ties between the Community and each CMEA member was privileged over the development of bloc-to-bloc cooperation. The conclusion of the Europe agreements with separate East European countries further developed these bilateral ties and responded to the wishes of the East European countries.

To try to balance this bilateralism, the Community has encouraged the East European states to replace the CMEA with a regional organization or framework for cooperation. Regional cooperation would stimulate economic growth, but more importantly would contribute to political stability and the establishment of good-neighbourly relations, thereby reducing the chances of inter-state conflict.

The East European states, however, have been reluctant to cooperate with each other, wary of any attempt to revive the CMEA. Some have claimed that the encouragement of regional cooperation is an attempt to block their accession to the EU because a separate regional grouping could serve as an alternative to EU membership.[48] Czechoslovakia, Hungary and Poland, for example, rejected the Commission's initial suggestion that the Community conclude only one Europe agreement with all three countries.

Cooperation among the Visegrad countries was adversely affected by tensions over minorities and the Gabcikovo dam (see Section 7.3.3), and by first Hungarian and then Czech reluctance to bind itself too tightly to countries whose prospects of joining the EU seemed less bright.[49] The Visegrad four have also hesitated to cooperate with Bulgaria and Romania (slower reformers) for fear that might delay their own accession to the EU.

Nonetheless, the Community/Union persisted in its encouragement of regional cooperation. All of the Europe agreements mention the importance of measures to foster cooperation among the East European countries. The 1991–2 PHARE general guidelines specified that ten to 15 per cent of PHARE resources would be reserved for cross-national or regional projects involving two or more PHARE countries.[50] Between 1990 and 1995, 579 million ECUs was allocated to multi-country programmes in areas such as infrastructure, environment and education (see Table 4.3). In 1994, a cross-border programme was developed (and allocated 150 million ECUs) to aid cooperation between border regions in PHARE countries and in EU member states and eliminate bottlenecks at border crossings between PHARE countries.[51] PHARE funds are used for regional cooperation projects within the framework of the Stability Pact. The Commission has boasted that PHARE regional cooperation programmes have played a major role in stimulating regional cooperation.[52]

The Community encouraged the Visegrad group to form a free trade area. While it did sign a free trade agreement on 21 December 1992, the group's primary purpose still seemed to be that of pressing for integration into the Community. The Central European Free Trade Agreement (CEFTA) aimed to create a free trade zone by 2000 or 2002, but tariffs among the CEFTA states remain high.[53] Slovenia joined CEFTA in January 1996, Romania became an associate in mid-1997 and Bulgaria and Lithuania are also candidates.

Intra-regional trade is still low, although it has been picking up recently (see Table 6.2).

The multilateral political dialogue, initiated in 1992, clearly sought to spur regional cooperation, in contrast to the framework for bilateral relations set up by the Europe agreements. Commissioner Andriessen commented:

> Already a process has begun between the Community and the three Visegrad countries which points towards a multilateralisation of relations between the parties involved. This could provide a valuable model for other countries in the future.[54]

The multilateral dialogue developed into the structured relationship, which, as the Commission notes, 'also strengthens intra-regional cooperation among the CEEC's themselves when dealing with the Institutions of the Union.'[55] The associates were not entirely pleased with the multilateral approach. The multilateral dialogue 'aims to further regionalism in political dialogue rather than to intensify bilateralism between individual countries and the EU, as many Central Europeans wish.'[56] At a troika-associates meeting in April 1994, the troika emphasized the innovative nature of the multilateral dialogue, while the associates' ministers stated that they preferred the bilateral approach.[57]

The EU tried to encourage the associates to set up a 'rotating presidency', to lead on contacts with the EU in the structured relationship, but they refused to do so. The EU also proposed that the associates participate as a group in CFSP joint actions and declarations, but had to drop the proposal when they objected (the associates sign up individually).[58]

In their June 1992 report on possible CFSP joint actions, the foreign ministers declared that in Eastern Europe, the EU will 'promote political stability and contribute to the creation of political and/or economic frameworks that encourage regional cooperation or moves towards regional or sub-regional integration.'[59] The Pact on Stability in Europe (a joint action) has been by far the EU's most important initiative to encourage regional cooperation. Promoting intra-regional cooperation is also part of the pre-accession strategy.[60]

Although the willingness of the associates to cooperate with each other is not an official membership condition, the Commission's opinions on their membership applications note the state of their relations with each other. All border disputes are to be resolved before accession; the associates should agree to refer disputes to the

International Court of Justice, as eventually occurred in the Gabcikovo dam dispute (see Section 7.3.3).[61]

The Community has used conditionality directly to influence relations between the associates. Thus, it encouraged a resolution of the Gabcikovo dam dispute between Slovakia and Hungary, and urged Hungary, Romania and Slovakia to conclude treaties within the framework of the Stability Pact (see Sections 7.3.3 and 7.3.4).

The Community's response to the Czechoslovak split illustrates a subtle use of conditionality. While the risk of a conflict between the two successor states was very unlikely, here was an opportunity to demonstrate that disputes between states could be handled peacefully and to encourage cooperation between the Czech Republic and Slovakia.

The immediate reactions of several EC officials to the prospect of a division of Czechoslovakia were not positive. The EC tried to indicate that the reasons for a division of the country were by no means clear to outsiders. On 21 June 1992, Council President Joao de Deus Pinheiro said that the division of the CSFR was a mistake and would make things more difficult for them. Delors publicly agreed with him. Andriessen indicated that the Europe agreement would have to be reexamined in the event of a split.[62] The Lisbon European Council a few days later stated:

> In light of the results of the 5 and 6 June elections in Czechoslovakia and the joint public declaration of Mr Klaus and Mr Meciar after their talks of 19 and 20 June, the European Council expressed the hope that the ongoing talks between the different political forces will continue in a peaceful and constructive manner and that the important steps in regional and international cooperation already achieved may be further developed without any major difficulty.[63]

Once the decision to divide Czechoslovakia had been taken, the Community strengthened its message. The two successor states were told that unless they established a customs union, a number of serious technical problems could hinder their trade with the EC. The need to reopen negotiations on Europe agreements gave the Community some leverage.[64] On 25 and 26 October 1992, Czech and Slovak leaders signed several agreements including one establishing a customs union.[65]

The division of Czechoslovakia, as of 1 January 1993, went relatively smoothly and the question of recognizing the successor states, the Czech Republic and Slovakia, did not even arise.[66] The Czech

Republic pressed for the two new countries to be treated on the same terms. Slovakia was basically included in the unofficial 'first tier' – those associates most likely to become EU members first. Both new countries signed Europe agreements at the same time (October 1993), even though reform in Slovakia was much less advanced and Slovak-Hungarian relations were still strained.[67] While this contributed to making the divorce a 'velvet' one, the EU's relations with Slovakia soon became more contentious, as noted in Section 7.2.1.

Several member states have been particularly active in encouraging regional cooperation. In 1989, Italy launched what is now called the Central European Initiative (CEI), which also includes Austria and 14 states from eastern and southeastern Europe, the former Yugoslavia and the former Soviet Union.[68] Germany and Denmark have promoted the Council of Baltic Sea States (CBSS), which includes new member states Finland and Sweden, as well as the EU (represented by the Commission). Greece belongs to the Black Sea Cooperation Council.

Links are being strengthened between the EU and the CBSS and the CEI. The Florence European Council (June 1996) requested a Commission report on initiatives to intensify cooperation with the CEI; the report centered on the willingness to fund projects developed within the CEI framework (through PHARE and TACIS).[69] The Commission has pushed for a Union approach to the Baltic Sea region; this has again centered on the willingness to encourage and fund regional cooperation projects within the CBSS framework.[70]

The differentiated approach taken towards enlargement somewhat supersedes the EU's efforts to encourage regional cooperation. Each membership application was judged separately; relations will now be intensified with each of the applicant countries to help them prepare for membership. This will reassure them they could all still join (and thus could reduce tensions), yet encouraging regional cooperation among the applicant countries would also help ensure that the accession of some of them does not damage relations with those left outside.

7.3.2   The WEU's Relations with Eastern Europe

The East European countries have been concerned that Russia may try to reestablish a sphere of influence in Eastern Europe. The Community/Union has shared their concerns to a certain extent; an assertive Russian foreign policy could destabilize the region, disrupt the transformation, exacerbate existing inter-state tensions, and, of course, strain relations with the West. The Europe agreements and structured relationship have been extended partly in response to these concerns. Whether any of these countries is actually threatened militarily by Russia is doubtful, but the East Europeans still feel insecure. Their preferred solution is membership in NATO and the WEU. But this may not be the best way to engender security in Europe, as it could antagonize Russia and recreate a divided Europe.

The WEU's relations with East European countries developed gradually. In June 1991, the WEU foreign and defence ministers agreed to organize ad hoc ministerial meetings with Bulgaria, Czechoslovakia, Hungary, Poland and Romania. Several countries, including apparently the UK, did not want to institutionalize the dialogue because it could undermine NATO's role in this area.[71] And the NATO summit on 7 and 8 November 1991 agreed to establish a North Atlantic Cooperation Council (NACC) with the East European countries and the Soviet Union.[72]

In the fall of 1991, the relationship of the WEU to the future EU and to NATO was still uncertain. A compromise between 'Atlanticists' and 'Europeanists' was then embodied in the Maastricht Treaty. The WEU was to be built up as the defence component of the European Union; it would also be developed as the European pillar of the Atlantic Alliance.[73] WEU Secretary-General Willem Van Eekelen noted that it was then quite logical that those East European countries seeking close ties with the Community would also want close ties with the WEU.[74]

After a WEU Council meeting in Petersberg near Bonn on 19 June 1992, the WEU ministers met with the foreign and defence ministers of Czechoslovakia, Poland, Hungary, Bulgaria and Romania (all soon to be EC associates), as well as Estonia, Latvia and Lithuania.[75] They agreed to establish a Forum of Consultation to discuss European security and stability. The foreign and defence ministers would meet at least once a year, while the WEU Permanent Council (composed of ambassadors) and East European ambassadors would hold twice-yearly consultations, and senior officials from the East European countries and an ad hoc WEU troika could meet regularly.[76] The Forum would create mechanisms for consultation in crises and consider joint training exercises, especially for peacekeeping operations. Van Eekelen characterized the Forum as an instrument of preventive diplomacy.[77]

The WEU initiative at this stage was competing with NACC. Van Eekelen argued that the WEU's Forum was smaller (NACC included all of the former Soviet republics) and therefore could host more structured, in-depth discussions on European security issues.[78] NATO was reportedly not happy that the WEU had created such a forum parallel to NACC.[79]

The WEU's East European partners, however, were not entirely pleased with the level of cooperation in the Forum, or in NACC. Nor were they satisfied with the follow-up to NACC, the Partnership for Peace programme, which was launched by the NATO summit in January 1994 and provided for much closer military cooperation with all the NACC countries and other CSCE members.[80] The East European countries wanted to be distinguished from Russia, which they considered their principle security threat.[81]

At the third annual meeting of the German, French and Polish foreign ministers (the Weimar triangle) on 12 November 1993, Klaus Kinkel and Alain Juppé declared that the WEU should offer associate member status to the EU's associates and that they would propose this to the WEU Council.[82] At the 22 November Council meeting, France and Germany proposed the creation of an 'enhanced status' for the EU's associates and prospective associates.[83] This would not entail a security guarantee, but would involve the associates in the WEU's structures.

Some members were concerned that the status was being offered to non-EU members and, more importantly, to non-NATO members, with all of the implications that could have for the WEU and NATO security guarantees. But the WEU ministers agreed to study the proposal further.[84] Some of the more 'Atlanticist' member states considered the plan to be a rival to NATO's Partnership for Peace. Juppé, however, pointed to the parallelism between EU and WEU links to the East European countries.[85]

On 9 May 1994, the WEU admitted the six EU associates and the three Baltic republics as 'associate partners', without a security guarantee. The WEU Council of Ministers declared that the initiative would help prepare the associate partners for their integration and eventual accession to the EU. It was 'fully complementary' with NATO's Partnership for Peace programme and the Stability Pact.[86] The associate partners can attend every second weekly meeting of the Permanent Council, send liaison officers to planning groups and take part in joint operations to maintain or restore peace and provide humanitarian assistance.

Russia was not pleased with the WEU decision. A foreign ministry spokesman warned that it could cause further division in Europe and that the WEU should have taken Russia into account.[87] Russian concern centered on associate partner status for the Baltic republics; later it voiced concerns that by concluding Europe agreements, the three Baltic republics would be on a fast track to WEU security guarantees.[88]

Their limited participation in the CFSP (through the enhanced dialogue) and WEU provides the associates with some framework for security and defence integration. The associate partnership with the WEU is essentially symbolic, however, as the WEU is still undeveloped as a military organization and it is still unclear whether the EU will formulate a common defence policy. But it also signals the 'beginning of the end' of the EU's civilian power image and means that enlargement could be seen as moving an armed border further eastwards.

This of course raises the sensitive problems of relations with Russia (and other 'outsiders') and with those EU associates that have not yet joined the EU: there is a danger of re-creating a divided Europe.[89] It is not clear that full membership in a military alliance (NATO and/or the WEU) will engender security in Eastern Europe, particularly given the diverse nature of security threats in Europe.

Because NATO has agreed to enlarge to the Czech Republic, Hungary and Poland, they will be eligible for full WEU membership. Other East European countries, once they join the EU, could become observers (the status for EU members that are not members of NATO), but they may not be satisfied with this. There will still be differing memberships in the three organizations, which could block or slow decisionmaking in the security field. It could also prevent an eventual EU-WEU merger (envisaged in the Amsterdam Treaty), since it would give non-NATO members a security guarantee 'through the back door'.

7.3.3   Mediation in the Gabcikovo Dam Dispute

The Community's leadership role in Eastern Europe, and its attempts to negotiate a resolution to the Yugoslav conflict in 1991 and 1992, meant that parties to other disputes might naturally turn to it for good offices. In 1992, Hungary and Czechoslovakia asked the Commission to mediate a dispute over a hydroelectric project on the Danube. The dispute was potentially serious because tensions between Hungary and

Slovakia were already rising as Slovakian nationalism aggravated relations with the Hungarian minority in Slovakia.[90] The Community's involvement demonstrates the extent to which it was considered a political and diplomatic actor in Eastern Europe; the Commission's rather remarkable role in mediating the dispute shows how far its involvement in foreign policy was accepted by the member states.

In 1977, Hungary and Czechoslovakia agreed to build a series of dams on the Danube.[91] The Hungarian democratic opposition, however, coalesced around opposition to the project. In 1989, the Hungarian government halted work on the Nagymáros dam located in its territory (only ten per cent of the work had been completed). The Czechoslovak government protested and demanded financial compensation (having already completed 90 per cent of the project).[92] It also proceeded with the construction of a new diversion dam wholly inside Slovakian territory, which would channel water from the Danube to the Gabcikovo dam and power station, also in Slovakia. In May 1992, Hungary announced it was abrogating the 1977 agreement, and would turn to the EC or the International Court of Justice (ICJ) if Czechoslovakia continued work on the project.[93] Hungary cited environmental concerns as reasons for halting the project; Czechoslovakia pointed out that it provided an alternative source of electricity to coal-fired and nuclear power plants. In an increasingly tense atmosphere the project then became a symbol of Slovakia's new nationhood and sovereignty.[94]

The dispute had earlier come before the Commission. Back in January 1991, Hungary and Czechoslovakia asked the Commission to provide a technical opinion on the environmental impact of the dam project.[95] But in May 1992, Commissioner Andriessen's proposals to set up an independent committee of technical experts to try to resolve the dispute were rejected. The two sides would not commit themselves to accept the committee's final recommendation.[96]

By the autumn of 1992, Germany in particular was increasingly concerned by developments. Foreign Minister Klaus Kinkel raised the issue at a special European Council summit in Birmingham on 19 October 1992. He suggested that a three-party commission be formed to try to resolve the dispute. At a meeting with the Czech foreign minister in Bonn four days later, Kinkel – on behalf of the EC – stressed that a unilateral diversion of the Danube would violate conditions for negotiations with the Community and that the Community would judge both successor states to Czechoslovakia as unreliable partners.[97]

During the same period, the Commission became involved. On 19 October, a Slovakian delegation visited Environmental Commissioner Karl Van Miert, to ask the EC to mediate the dispute. Van Miert responded that the Commission would provide good offices, on the condition that the talks were technical, not political. By emphasizing less emotional technical issues, the Commission attempted to depoliticize the dispute.[98] Commission officials would also participate in a tripartite committee, along with Czechoslovak and Hungarian experts, which would examine the economic and ecological consequences of the project.[99] The member states were quite willing to let the Commission take the lead on this rather tricky issue; the Commission was a neutral party and could thus potentially be an effective mediator.

The Commission delegation was led by Pablo Benavidès Salas, head of the Eastern Europe unit in DG I (later DG IA). Benavidès was allowed much freedom to mediate between the parties; the member states did not interfere with the Commission's work, although Benavidès met frequently with the informal 'advisers' group', composed of officials from the Permanent Representations.

Beginning 21 October, the Commission hosted talks with Czechoslovak and Hungarian negotiators.[100] The talks broke down the next day, however and Hungary said it would invoke CSCE emergency procedures. On 24 October the Slovak state construction company blocked the river, prompting an angry reaction from Hungary, which also questioned the future of cooperation within the Visegrad group. Two days later, Kinkel warned against rash decisions, appearing to condemn the Slovak move. He suggested that the Community's willingness to provide economic aid would be negatively affected.[101]

The dispute reportedly overshadowed all other issues at the summit between Delors, Major and the Visegrad group in London on 28 October. Commission, Hungarian and Slovakian representatives negotiated behind the scenes, apparently successfully. Hungary and Czechoslovakia signed a provisional agreement: work on the dam would stop; Czechoslovakia would ensure that 95 per cent of the normal flow of water would flow in the Danube and would not operate the Gabcikovo dam turbines.[102] A working group of experts nominated by the Commission and the two countries would examine navigation, water management and environmental issues. If no agreement could be reached, the dispute would be submitted to binding international arbitration or the ICJ.[103] One reason why the London agreement was reached is that the Community pointed out much more strongly that its relations with the parties would be endangered if the dispute escalated.[104] Czechoslovakia, however, was still diverting water, leaving the Danube along the Hungarian-Slovak border almost empty. On 6 November, the working group told Czechoslovakia to halt work on the dam by 21 November (which it did).[105] The dispute was disturbing relations within the Visegrad group. A Polish minister announced that the signing of the Visegrad free trade agreement, scheduled for 30 November, was postponed because of the Czechoslovak split and the tensions over the dam.[106]

On 27 November, Benavidès hosted a meeting in Brussels with Czechoslovak and Hungarian high officials to discuss the working group's report. Both sides agreed to apply the London summit agreement and to submit the dispute to the ICJ. They also agreed to continue discussing a Commission proposal to resolve the dispute. The Danube by-channel would be navigable throughout the year and supply the Gabcikovo power station, which would be brought into service only for trial purposes.[107]

In early January 1993, Hungary accused Slovakia – now an independent country – of operating the Gabcikovo dam turbines and redirecting only 25 per cent, rather than 95 per cent, of the Danube's waters back to the river.[108] On 5 February, Hungarian-Slovak talks on water management failed. A meeting with the Commission was postponed until 16 February. Both sides seemed to harden their positions.[109] The meeting in Brussels on 16–17 February 1993 between the Slovakian and Hungarian secretaries of state for foreign affairs and Commissioner van den Broek left the dispute unresolved. The two sides did not agree to take the case to the ICJ: Slovakia argued that the question of state succession had to be resolved first.[110]

Quite a lot of pressure was then put on the parties. On 24 and 25 February, Slovak Prime Minister Meciar met with Delors, Brittan and van den Broek in Brussels; the dam dispute was discussed at those meetings.[111] Benavidès went to Slovakia and Hungary in early March, but could not secure agreement on the submission of the dispute to the ICJ or on a scheme for the temporary management of the Danube's waters.[112] The EP, on 12 March, called for the dispute to be referred to the ICJ and for a rapid solution to the water management problem.[113] Between 15 and 19 March, van den Broek met with the Hungarian president and prime minister and the Slovak president and prime minister.[114]

Finally, after another EC-sponsored meeting on 7 April 1993, chaired by van den Broek, the Hungarian and Slovak state secretaries for foreign affairs agreed to submit the dispute to the ICJ, although they did not agree on a water management system.[115] In July 1993, Hungary and Slovakia referred the dispute to the ICJ. This defused much of the tension, and both countries agreed to continue working on a water management scheme, with the Commission's good offices.[116] The success in convincing the two countries to refer the dispute to the ICJ is now considered a precedent. Relations between the two countries are by no means warm, however, and a final resolution of the dam dispute may be difficult to reach.

Gabriel Munuera argues that 'the basic underlying factor imposing a certain measure of restraint on the parties has been their shared interest in joining the European Union . . . . [N]either Bratislava nor Budapest could afford to jeopardize its privileged position by failing to resolve minority issues and the dispute over the Gabcikovo-Nagymáros project.'[117] The Community could thus exert a considerable amount of leverage on the parties, as it did at the October 1992 London summit.

Munuera, however, charges that more could have been done earlier, had the Community realized the potential dangers of escalation.[118] The Community became involved only at the insistence of the parties to the dispute, and at the instigation of Germany (whose concern arose relatively late as well). This illustrates the need for a CFSP planning and early warning unit (as provided by the Amsterdam Treaty), to provide some warning that disputes are getting out of hand.

7.3.4 The Pact on Stability

With the Yugoslav crisis serving as a stark reminder of the enormous problems left after the fall of communism, the then French prime minister, Edouard Balladur, came up with a proposal to try to prevent such crises from occurring in other East European countries. On 15 April 1993, Balladur proposed a treaty to guarantee stability and peace in Europe, which he would present to the other member states.[119] At a Franco-German summit on 2 June, Kohl backed Balladur's plan, although Germany was concerned that it was intended to keep the East Europeans out of the EU.[120] The proposal was made shortly before the Copenhagen summit, when the European Council agreed on enlargement to Eastern Europe; it may well have been an attempt to put off enlargement, but it also addressed legitimate concerns about conflicts in future member states and would reiterate principles and objectives (regional cooperation, protection of minority rights) already expressed by the Community. Furthermore, it would provide another opportunity for France to lead the Community's *Ostpolitik*, as it became clear that Germany and the UK were going to 'win' the debate on enlargement.

On 9 June, France outlined the plan, on which Balladur and Mitterrand were collaborating closely. The Pact on Stability in Europe would be an exercise in preventive diplomacy; it would be more effective than the CSCE because a smaller group of countries could come up with firmer security commitments and incentives. Sought-after EU membership would only be offered to those states that settled problems which could threaten European security, by concluding good neighbourly agreements. France suggested that the agreements might entail small frontier changes, which would be endorsed by the conference.[121]

For Balladur, the initiative would place the Community at the centre of a new political and security arrangement in Europe, and give the EU something to do under the CFSP.[122] But there were initially many criticisms. The possibility of territorial revisions caused particular concern. Poland, the Czech Republic, Romania and Bulgaria cited the potential for re-opening border and minority disputes as one reason for their doubts about the idea. Some within the Community saw the initiative as primarily serving French domestic political interests.[123] It was a French bid to undermine the CSCE and thus US involvement in Europe.[124] Many East Europeans felt that the EC member states needed to deal with their own unresolved minority and border problems.[125] Hungary, however, backed the plan, because of the large numbers of ethnic Hungarians living in neighbouring states.[126]

The French proposal for a Pact on Stability in Europe was presented to the Copenhagen summit, 21–2 June 1993. The Pact would give the East European countries a forum in which to settle potential sources of conflict. The Community should 'contemplate new long-term accessions only on the express condition that those countries first settle, in the framework of the preparatory conference, the problems liable to threaten European stability.'[127]

Despite the reservations, the Copenhagen European Council asked the Council to study the proposal and report back to it in December.[128] There was growing awareness that the Pact would be useful for pressuring Hungary, Slovakia and Romania (in particular) to reach agreements on minority rights.

At its July meeting, the Council set up a high-level working party to prepare the report on the Pact.[129] In October, the foreign ministers approved the working party's timetable for action and suggested procedures.[130] The special European Council on 29 October 1993, called to welcome the Maastricht Treaty's entry into force, declared that the Pact would be one of the first CFSP joint actions.[131]

On 6 December, the General Affairs Council briefly discussed the Pact. Some member states wanted all the CSCE countries to participate; others, including France, favoured a more restricted list. A consensus was developing, however, to restrict participation to the EU's (then) six associates and the three Baltic republics (not yet associates).[132] Slovenia, embroiled in a dispute with Italy over (paradoxically) minority rights, was to be excluded.[133] Albania, where the problem of minorities was potentially very dangerous (as well as a source of disputes with Greece), also would not participate, presumably because it was much further behind in reforms and in its relations with the EU.[134] This of course meant that the Pact remained uncontroversial, so that all the member states could go along with it, more or less enthusiastically.

The Council presented its proposal for the Pact to the Brussels European Council in December. The objective was

> to contribute to stability by preventing tension and potential conflicts in Europe; it is not concerned with countries in open conflict; it is intended to promote good neighbourly relations and to encourage countries to consolidate their borders and to resolve the problems of national minorities that arise...[135]

The foreign ministers suggested that the project focus on those East European countries that are prospective members 'vis-à-vis which the Union had greater opportunities to exert its influence more effectively': the six associates and the three Baltic republics.[136] The inaugural conference would set up multilateral round tables in addition to the bilateral discussions. The EU's primary role would be to encourage the parties to conclude good neighbour agreements covering the problems of national minorities and borders, and to set up regional cooperation arrangements. A final conference would ratify all the agreements concluded, and forward the Pact to the CSCE, which would act as its guardian. In contrast to France's initial proposals, the Council's report did not mention the possibility of revising borders, nor state that participation in the Pact was a condition for EU membership. The European Council approved the report and called for the inaugural conference to be held in Paris in April 1994. It instructed the Council to implement the initiative as a joint action.[137] On 20 December, the Council approved a joint action under which the EU would convene the inaugural conference.[138] France, in collaboration with Council President Greece, would organize the conference, as host country.[139] The CFSP unit and France then did most of the work on the Pact.[140]

The inaugural conference convened on 26–7 May 1994, in Paris. Nine countries were 'directly concerned' (the three Baltic republics and the six associates), but other CSCE members and international organizations were observers. The participants declared:

> Our aim is to encourage countries which have not yet concluded cooperation and good neighbourliness agreements and arrangements, extending also to issues concerning minorities and borders, to do so...[141]

The conference agreed to set up two regional round tables, for the Baltic region (including the Baltic republics and Poland) and for all the other East European countries (including Poland), chaired by the EU.[142] The round tables were to identify projects to further good neighbourly relations in areas such as regional transborder cooperation, questions relating to minorities, cultural and economic cooperation and the environment.[143] Neighbouring or other countries, as well as international organizations, could join the nine countries 'directly concerned' at their round tables. Slovenia was asked to join the East European round table; Belarus, Moldova, Turkey and Ukraine also participated.[144] The EU convinced an initially hesitant Russia to participate in the Baltic round table.[145]

The EU presidency, and sometimes also the troika, visited several capitals to promote the Pact and encourage cooperation and bilateral negotiations.[146] Quite clearly, attention was focused on the thorny issues of the Hungarian minorities in Slovakia and Romania, and the Russian minorities in the Baltic republics. The troika visited the Baltic republics in July 1994 and Romania, Hungary, and Slovakia in the autumn, to prod them into reaching agreements.[147]

The EU increasingly emphasized regional cooperation, in addition to the bilateral negotiations. In its June 1994 decision to continue the joint action, the Council requested the Commission to take appropriate economic measures to help reach the Pact's objectives. An annex to the Pact contains a list of specific 'good-neighbourly' projects supported by the EU, such as language training and regional economic cooperation. The list includes measures already financed by PHARE (for 200 million ECUs) and projects still being studied (60 million ECUs worth).[148]

The Pact, consisting of a declaration and the agreements included by the participants, was then adopted by the members of the OSCE (formerly the CSCE)[149] on 20–1 March 1995. The final conference was held in Paris (France held the Council presidency).[150] It was fairly low-key, at least in the media, perhaps a reflection of the Pact's modest achievements.

The Pact declaration stated:

> We undertake to combine our efforts to ensure stability in Europe. A stable Europe is one in which peoples democratically express their will, in which human rights, including those of persons belonging to national minorities, are respected, in which equal and sovereign States cooperate across frontiers and develop among themselves good-neighbourly relations.[151]

Over 100 agreements (between the nine directly concerned countries, and between them and other participants) were attached to the Pact. Most of them were concluded before the inaugural conference, including several significant ones, such as the 1991 agreement on minorities between Hungary and Ukraine, the 1992 treaty confirming the Polish-German border, the 1992 friendship treaty between the Czech Republic and Slovakia, and the Polish-Lithuanian treaty concluded a month before the inaugural conference opened (26 April 1994).

A Hungarian-Slovak treaty was agreed on 19 March 1995, a day before the final conference convened. It includes a Council of Europe recommendation providing for minorities to have an autonomous administration where they constitute a majority and the principle of the inviolability of borders.[152] Hungary ratified the agreement over the summer, but Slovakia did not do so until March 1996.[153] Relations, however, have not improved greatly, as Hungary is concerned about Slovakia's failure to pass a law on the use of minority languages.[154]

The EU unsuccessfully pressed Romania and Hungary to agree on a friendship treaty, with minority rights provisions, during the Pact. Romania feared that including minority rights provisions would give ethnic Hungarians too much autonomy, and fuel demands for self-determination.[155] On 16 September 1996, however, they did sign a treaty that includes the Council of Europe recommendation on minorities but rules out territorial autonomy for the Hungarian minority in Romania. The Pact does not include good neighbourly agreements between Russia and Estonia or Latvia.

The OSCE is to supervise the Pact's implementation. In case of disagreements over the implementation of the agreements included in the Pact, the participants can resort to OSCE procedures for conflict prevention and the peaceful settlement of disputes.

It is not certain that a large conference was necessary to meet the EU's objectives. The EU could have instead encouraged states to cooperate within the framework of the CSCE, for example. In this sense, the Pact seems to have served more to give the CFSP something to do (led by France), potentially successful, in contrast to its perceived failures in the former Yugoslavia. The relative lack of agreements concluded during the Pact could indicate either that the Pact's objective was not fully met, or that it was not really necessary – as most of the participants had already concluded good neighbourly agreements.

This, however, does not diminish the significance of publicly vowing to respect certain principles and acknowledging that regional cooperation and good neighbourliness are legitimate concerns for all European states. It has also increased the pressure on specific associates (Hungary, Romania, and Slovakia in particular) to reach agreements with their neighbours. The Pact has been widely cited as one of the CFSP's rare successes.

The Pact's success depends on the effectiveness of the conditionality of EU enlargement. The participants agreed to the plan because they considered it a prerequisite for EU membership. As France's European affairs minister, Alain Lamassoure, declared: 'No country with unsettled border or minority conflicts will be allowed to join.'[156] And Agenda 2000 clearly states: 'Enlargement should not mean importing border conflicts . . . . The Commission considers that, before accession, applicants should make every effort to resolve any outstanding border dispute among themselves or involving third countries.'[157]

CONCLUSION

The Community, then Union, has become much more active in conflict prevention, by trying to reduce the sources of insecurity in Eastern Europe, mediate agreements and encourage regional cooperation. Whether conflicts will actually be prevented remains to be seen, and whether the Union could be considered primarily responsible for this is not certain. The absence of conflict may not necessarily mean that conflict prevention measures were successful; the parties may not have intended to 'escalate' (though disputes could get out of hand for unforeseen circumstances). The EU has found it difficult to convince the associates to cooperate, and there are evident problems in encouraging Slovakia to democratize. Enlargement could exacerbate those problems. However, the Union's conflict prevention activities do seem to have contributed to a more stable and secure environment in Eastern Europe.

The EU's initiatives clearly reflect its own experiences, emphasizing as they do regional cooperation and dialogue in particular. Its attempts to prevent conflict have arisen less because of specific demands from outsiders to act and more because the EU acknowledged that it would have to assume more responsibility for conflict prevention. It is well equipped to address the internal and external sources of conflicts and to encourage democratization and economic development (and much less equipped to deal with violent conflicts). The conditionality of EU membership in particular provides the EU with considerable influence in Eastern Europe. Recognizing this, the member states have worked through the Community/Union to try to prevent conflicts and spread security in Eastern Europe, as the EU can bring much greater leverage to bear than national action could.

8 Explaining the Making of a Foreign Policy Towards Eastern Europe

Since the late 1980s, the Community/Union has formulated and implemented a common, consistent policy towards Eastern Europe. The member states and EC institutions agreed that the principal objective is to support the economic and political transformation in Eastern Europe and thus ensure security. To reach this objective, they agreed on several important decisions (most importantly on enlargement), held to them and mobilized a variety of different national and collective resources.

The Community/Union's policy was very much about security. During the Cold War, the interconnection between security and economic relations with Eastern Europe had already been made clear – partly because the US insisted that there was a negative connection, but also because there was a strong belief (especially in West Germany) that trade and increased contacts would foster political and economic liberalization in Eastern Europe, and therefore enhance Western Europe's security (see Chapter 2). But because trade relations with Eastern Europe were politically significant, the member states sought to retain control over them (no matter how small the volume of trade actually was). Matters of military security were dealt with in NATO. The uneasy connection between economics and security is precisely what limited the Community's relations with Eastern Europe during the Cold War.

When communism collapsed, the interconnection became even more pronounced, and translated into 'functional spillover' between external economic relations and foreign policy, which was reflected in extensive EC-EPC/CFSP collaboration. As David Buchan noted: 'Security and economic issues had become hopelessly intertwined due to the fact that the Community's former enemies in Eastern Europe were now clamouring for aid and trade from Brussels.'[1]

To ensure security in Europe, there was a pressing need to ensure that the transformation in Eastern Europe succeeded. The failure of political and economic reforms could give rise to a variety of security threats. 'Security' in the post-Cold War world acquired a much broader connotation than military security: threats to security could arise from several sources, including ethnic disputes, violations of human rights and economic deprivation.[2] To bolster democratization and economic reform and prevent conflicts, the Community/Union wielded its civilian instruments (including trade, aid, and eventual membership), often on a conditional basis. The view that strengthening ties with the East European countries would foster reform and spread security still influenced policymaking, but jostled (sometimes uneasily) with the new emphasis on conditionality.

The Union *has* helped to spread security and stability in Eastern Europe. Its assistance programmes *have* helped the East European countries carry out economic and political reforms. It has been an important source of external pressure for economic and political reforms and for good neighbourly behaviour, although it is certainly not the only one. It is a focal point for the East European countries, whose foreign policy priorities are still topped by that of EU membership. NATO membership is, of course, also a major priority, but the East European countries maintain that NATO membership is insufficient to guarantee their security: only EU membership would ensure the economic prosperity and democratic consolidation needed for their long-term security and stability.[3]

There is a risk, however, that enlargement will be destabilizing for the EU, for the acceding countries and for the countries excluded from the EU in the short or long term. But at this point, not enlarging would be more destabilizing than enlarging, given the expectations that have been raised. And there are steps that can be taken to minimize the risk of destabilization: the Union should undertake fundamental reforms, the new member states must be well-prepared for membership and links could be strengthened with the excluded countries. Whether such steps are taken will help determine whether the EU continues to have a positive impact on security and stability in Europe.

Many observers have argued that the Union has not done enough in Eastern Europe: it should have set up a 'Marshall Plan' for Eastern Europe;[4] it should allow in more sensitive East European goods; and, most of all, it should have agreed much earlier to enlarge to the East European countries, given them a definitive date for accession (sooner than the current estimate of 2002 for the first stage) and taken the necessary steps to reform the Union in preparation for enlargement.

There was no widespread agreement to grant large amounts of bilateral *or* multilateral aid to Eastern Europe – partly because of qualms about the cost but partly because the effectiveness of aid was by no means assured when the East European economies were still largely state controlled.[5] Excluding Germany, none of the member states has given more aid than the EU has (see Table 4.1). PHARE's budget has increased substantially since its establishment and the programme has been reformed to address criticisms made of it, although more can still be done to improve it. Private investment was also expected to generate economic growth – but would ultimately only be attracted to Eastern Europe if the necessary reforms were undertaken (for which assistance was targeted).

Trade in the sensitive sectors *was* a particularly difficult issue. The intra-EC wrangling over concessions, particularly during the negotiations on the Europe agreements, gave the impression that the member states were fiddling while Rome burned. Yet what is striking is how often the member states gave in to pressures to compromise, from the trade and cooperation agreements and lifting of quantitative restrictions, to the Europe agreements and the Copenhagen European Council decision to accelerate trade liberalization. Most trade between Eastern Europe and the EU is now liberalized.

The EU's enlargement decisions were not made soon enough for many observers nor, certainly, for the East European states.[6] But an early, definite promise of rapid entry for Slovakia, for instance (or even Bulgaria and Romania, before the most recent changes there), would look decidedly foolish from the perspective of the late 1990s. There is little reason to believe that reforms would have proceeded more rapidly (or at all) in those countries had they been integrated sooner into the Community (indeed the troubles experienced by eastern Germany should serve as a warning against rapid integration). The conditional promise of eventual EU enlargement has been one of the most significant external sources of pressure for reform and good neighbourly behaviour; this leverage would dissipate if all the East European countries were guaranteed entry by a certain date. There must also be internal support for reform.

Considering the vast repercussions that eastern enlargement will have for the Union, for the East European countries themselves and for Europe as a whole, it is not surprising that it took time to reach a consensus within the Community in favour of enlargement. Indeed, it is rather astonishing that the Copenhagen decision was taken less than four years after the Berlin Wall fell, given that the reform process in

Eastern Europe is by no means complete and that integration into the EU will be very complex. And considering the implications of enlargement, a slower, more gradual process would be preferable to a rapid, haphazard one. The East European countries want to join the Union because it apparently provides for prosperity, democracy and security. An enlarged Union incapable of meeting those expectations is hardly a desirable outcome, yet could be the end result if the process is not well handled.

The EU may not have fully satisfied its external 'demandeurs' or its critics, but what has been agreed is noteworthy in and of itself. The policy that has been formulated and implemented by the member states and EC institutions is undoubtedly the most wide-ranging EU foreign policy made so far and has set several important precedents.

In the rest of this chapter, the reasons why the Community/Union agreed on a common foreign policy towards Eastern Europe will be explored in more depth. The next four sections will reconsider the questions posed in Chapter 1 and draw out the theoretical implications of the responses to them. Who were the key actors in policymaking? How did they reach decisions? Was the policy strategic or incremental? What was the role of endogenous factors and exogenous pressures?

8.1 WHO WERE THE MAIN ACTORS?

The member states have obviously been the primary actors in the making of a policy towards Eastern Europe; it could hardly be otherwise. But what is significant is that so many member states played an important role; the policy was not a German or Franco-German line legitimized by the EU. Leadership was exercised by a number of different member states, at different times, illustrating the extent to which the member states shared the view that the EU should formulate and implement a common foreign policy towards Eastern Europe. In particular, Belgium (in 1988–9), France, Germany, the UK and Italy (together and separately) were quite active in pushing common initiatives.

Germany undoubtedly was a key actor in the policymaking process: its geographical position alone dictates that it must be concerned with stability and security in Eastern Europe. It gives the most aid (see Table 4.1) and is the biggest trader with Eastern Europe (see Table 8.1). German support for common initiatives (such as the structured relationship and Pact for Stability) and for enlargement was crucial – but Germany did not always lead the policymaking process, nor were its views always adopted by the collectivity. The UK was also an early proponent of enlargement (if it was not linked to deepening). Germany would have preferred that the EU enlarge to three countries in the first stage, yet the Commission (or a majority of it) and other member states (notably Italy and the Scandinavian states) successfully pushed to widen the first intake.[7] Part of the reason why other actors were so active in the policymaking process is

Table 8.1   Trading Partners, 1993
(% EC trade with Bulgaria, Czech Republic, Hungary,
Poland, Romania, and Slovakia)

Share of total EC imports from Eastern Europe	
Germany	58
Italy	13
France	8
UK	6
Netherlands	6
Share of total EC imports from Eastern Europe (suppliers)	
Poland	38
Czech Republic	24
Hungary	20
Romania	8
Slovakia	6
Bulgaria	5
Share of total EC exports to Eastern Europe	
Germany	53
Italy	14
France	8
Netherlands	7
UK	7
Main receivers of EC exports to Eastern Europe	
Poland	38
Czech Republic	24
Hungary	19
Romania	9
Bulgaria	5
Slovakia	5

Source: Eurostat, *Rapid Reports*, no. 11, 1994.

that they sought to balance Germany's potential dominance in the region; Germany too sought 'cover' from the Community/Union, and that entailed making compromises.

The presidency was especially important in brokering agreements and launching initiatives. Both France and Ireland called special European Council meetings specifically to discuss the events in Eastern Europe, in November 1989 and April 1990. The Dutch presidency helped broker the first three Europe agreements. The British presidency launched a high-profile political dialogue with the Visegrad group in the fall of 1992. Denmark played a large part in pushing through the Copenhagen European Council decisions. The German presidency in the fall of 1994 pressed for the implementation of the structured relationship.

Looking within the governments of the member states, foreign ministers (and their officials) in particular have been heavily involved, on almost all aspects of the policy (a 'cartel of elites', in consociationalist terms). Even prior to Maastricht, 'the Council' acted simultaneously as the General Affairs Council and the gathering of foreign ministers within EPC. Decisions on trade and aid were taken by the foreign ministers in the context of the overall foreign policy towards Eastern Europe. However, the heads of state or government, in the European Council (a body which was set up to ensure consistency across the different policymaking frameworks), also played a prominent role. They took or endorsed the big decisions on enlargement, for example. Changes in government or of ministers did not lead to dramatic shifts in policy: for example, although French President Chirac has become a backer of enlargement, his predecessor Mitterrand took the initial leap in favour of it.[8]

The member states were not the only key actors. To a unique extent, the Commission has also been involved in the making of a policy towards Eastern Europe. There are two remarkable aspects of its role. The first is that the Commission was so active in a region where it had previously been marginalized and in foreign policymaking in general. The second is that its mediation role was crucial. On several occasions, the Commission 'upgraded the common interest', mediating solutions that were more than the lowest common denominator (as in, for example, the Copenhagen European Council decisions to improve the trade provisions of the Europe agreements). The Commission's role in this case seems to fit with neofunctionalist hypotheses.

Functional spillover allowed the Commission to elbow its way into areas that might earlier have fallen within the domain of EPC. With respect to policy towards Eastern Europe, it

> seemed to loom large in the counsels of Political Cooperation and to occupy a position which would have raised eyebrows at the time the Single European Act was passed. It would have been deemed rank heresy a decade before that.[9]

When communism faltered in Eastern Europe, the Commission was already becoming a more dynamic force and seized the opportunity to influence the making of a civilian foreign policy. The expansion of the Community's role in Eastern Europe necessarily entailed an increased role for the Commission. With the G-24 and PHARE programmes, it became an important actor in its own right. The Commission has also been a primary source of economic and political initiatives, from economic assistance to ideas for a European Political Area to 'Agenda 2000'.

The East European states clearly perceived the Commission's political importance (helping to reinforce its position). Virtually every month, an East European president, prime minister, or foreign minister has visited the Commission to discuss economic and political relations with the Community/Union; Commissioners have also frequently visited Eastern Europe to hold talks with leaders. The Commission's role in mediating the Gabcikovo dam dispute reflected the perception of its importance.

The Commission's activity contributed to its new position in CFSP policymaking under the Maastricht Treaty, although the Treaty provisions do not reflect the extent to which the Commission was involved in making the policy towards Eastern Europe. The Commission's dynamism, however, may have provoked a backlash. The member states now seem more determined to control the Commission's position in CFSP, for example. Commission President Jacques Santer does not have the personality, network, or disposition that enabled Delors to push successfully for a greater role, but in implementing Agenda 2000 and the new pre-accession strategy, the Commission will continue to play a leading part in the policy.

As to the Commission's mediation role, it was instrumental in improving the trade concessions in the Europe agreements. Afterwards, it supported East European demands for further concessions in its reports to the Lisbon, Edinburgh and Copenhagen European Councils. By December 1992, the Commission was pushing a reluctant

European Council to accept the prospect of eventual membership for the associates. In 'Agenda 2000', the Commission argued for policy reforms and suggested that membership negotiations begin with five associates, instead of the three Visegrad frontrunners or all ten countries.

The Commission's proposals went much further than what the most reluctant member states wanted, tipping the median point of any possible agreement higher than it would have been otherwise. In convincing the reluctant member states to reconsider their positions (rather than insist on the lowest common denominator), the Commission thus 'upgraded the common interest'.

It is somewhat surprising that the Commission (at the very least an understaffed and somewhat disorganized body) was able to play such an active role in policymaking. Without doubt, the way Delors ran the Commission helped (that is, from the top down as opposed to fostering collegiate decisionmaking), as did his reliance on a network of friends and allies in strategic places (including Kohl and Mitterrand).[10] Even the brief (January 1993–January 1995) division of responsibility for relations with Eastern Europe between two directorate-generals did not weaken the Commission's role: it was a very active period, with the proposals to the Copenhagen European Council and the setting up of the pre-accession strategy.

The other Community body involved in policymaking is the European Parliament. But while the EP did ensure that some issues were addressed, its role was fairly limited in this case, reflecting its limited powers in external relations. It voiced concerns for human rights (for example, in Romania) and held up agreements as a result. It also pressed for more funds for PHARE and launched a few initiatives (scientific cooperation, border cooperation, the democracy programme) within that framework. But the EP was more a follower than an initiator in policymaking.

8.2   HOW WERE DECISIONS REACHED?

All of the member states agreed on the primary objective of ensuring the success of the reforms and thus engendering prosperity and security in Eastern Europe. Agreement on how to achieve this objective, however, was at times difficult to reach. What is important is that these differences were overcome. Agreements reached at one stage were later 'upgraded' even further.

The member states *did* try to shape the common policy to reflect their own concerns. Germany's desire to 'erase' its border with Poland (with the help of PHARE aid) stems partly from a desire to ease communications and ties with ethnic Germans living there. Its emphasis on minority rights stems from its own concerns with the rights of ethnic Germans in other East European countries.[11] France's attempts to maintain its traditional links (and therefore influence) with Romania could partly explain why it pushed for closer EC/EU-Romanian ties. Italy's concerns for the rights of ethnic Italians in Slovenia and Greece's concerns for the rights of ethnic Greeks in Albania (initially) impeded the development of those countries' relations with the EU.

Germany has been particularly keen on integrating the Czech Republic, Hungary and Poland (above all) into the EU – for reasons of security and simple economics, and perhaps to atone for the past. Sweden has expressed opposition to letting the Visegrad countries join before the Baltic republics, an example of the 'centrifugal' influence of geographical and historical ties.[12] France, and other member states, were initially not keen on enlargement at all, apparently concerned for the implications it would have for the intra-Community balance of power.

The member states have also tried to limit the extent of the common policy: export credit policy remained resolutely a matter for intergovernmental cooperation; good neighbour and cooperation agreements were still concluded on a bilateral basis; and some member states complained about the Community's role in granting balance of payments loans and tried to reduce the Commission's autonomy in allocating PHARE resources. They have competed over PHARE contracts and the sponsoring of prestigious aid projects.

The member states protected specific economic interest groups, by blocking or delaying trade concessions. There was sympathy from other member states for many of these concerns: Portuguese objections to free trade in textiles were considered legitimate enough for an agreement to be reached to grant extra EC aid to textile producers there. Spain's concerns about steel imports from Bulgaria and Romania were not easily dismissed by free trade advocates because of the crisis in the Community steel industry. Where objections were not considered legitimate, there was much pressure on the member state to back down, as in the example of France and meat imports under the Europe agreements.

The efforts to limit or direct the policy, however, pale when compared to the extent of the common policy agreed by the member states and the compromises made to reach those agreements. That there should be a common policy towards Eastern Europe was not at issue; this was accepted, if not actively advocated. A side-payment was occasionally necessary to reach agreements, as in, for example, the aid to Portuguese textile workers. Sometimes package deals of a sort were put together to satisfy member state concerns: the southern member states won a higher-profile EU role in the Mediterranean, to balance the EU's policy towards Eastern Europe; France's Stability Pact plan may have been welcomed so that it would accept the prospect of enlargement more easily. These deals entail greater EU involvement and more resources, which is difficult to fit into approaches based on the self-interest of the member states.

The problem-solving style of decisionmaking still seems to capture the process of making policy towards Eastern Europe better than does the bargaining style, highlighted by intergovernmentalist (and consociationalist) approaches. The policy is not a series of decisions made on the basis of the lowest common denominator of the various national positions. On virtually every decision, the member states made concessions: trade barriers were lowered and then lowered again, several times; initiatives sponsored by one or more member states were supported by the others (even if they had not been received enthusiastically); PHARE funding was increased; the prospect of enlargement was accepted; and the structured relationship was established.

Policymaking occurred in a situation of empathetic interdependence: the member states were inclined to work for collective solutions of larger overall value to the 'problem' of encouraging reform in Eastern Europe, even at the expense of direct gains to themselves. Furthermore, the member states made compromises during the process of interaction at the EC/EU level. This supports the constructivist view that state preferences can change during that process. Why the member states agreed to make compromises on the common policy will be examined further in Section 8.4.

8.3   WAS THE POLICY STRATEGIC OR INCREMENTAL?

To what extent has the EU 'controlled' the policy towards Eastern Europe? Did the East European countries set the agenda? Has policymaking been largely characterized by incrementalism, or has it had a more strategic orientation?

Clearly the East European countries have been persistent deman- deurs. Time and again they made ever greater demands on the Community/Union, for better market access, aid, political dialogue and above all, a firm commitment to membership and a timetable for enlargement. The collective responses seemed to fuel higher expecta- tions. The East Europeans objected to certain options, such as a con- federation or partial membership, thus limiting any potential response from the Community/Union.

Although the East European states are 'weak' states, their demands had surprising resonance. Partly this was because the reforming governments had to be able to show their electorates that the EU was listening to them (a key consideration behind the Andreatta-Hurd initiative, for example). The urgent need to 'do something' for Eastern Europe – in a completely new geopolitical environment – also meant that the East European demands had a better chance of being heard. The perceived imperative of helping Eastern Europe gave the East European countries leverage.

The decision on enlargement taken at the June 1993 Copenhagen European Council followed months of pressure from the East Europeans for a declaration on membership, during which the Community had insisted relations would develop within the frame- work of the Europe agreements. There were fears that *not* responding positively to the membership demands could destabilize the region. Perhaps the decision on membership was thus taken too soon: the Community should have reflected a great deal more about the wisdom of enlargement, rather than allow itself to be 'pushed' into a decision. Once taken, there was no going back on it, particularly given the continuing pressure from the East European countries to move quickly to membership negotiations.

A concrete strategy for an enlarged EU did not appear until 'Agenda 2000', and has been criticized by the member states. Indeed, the continuing lack of agreement on how the Union should be reformed so that it can enlarge successfully to Eastern Europe lends much support to the view that the Union lacks a long-term vision for enlargement. In addition, a strategy for an enlarged EU (and its rela- tions with its neighbours) is in some ways impossible without defining where the EU's borders will eventually end. Defining these, however, means giving up a great deal of leverage over those membership aspirants that would be excluded from the EU.

Seen this way, the Community/Union seems to have taken a series of incremental, reactive steps: its initial actions did not entirely satisfy East European demands, so it was forced to take further steps to try to fulfill them (which required upgrading previous agreements within the Community/Union). Unable to meet the ultimate demand for accession in the short term, the EU tried several intermediate solutions, none of which fully pleased the East Europeans. External pressures were the main source of a Community/Union policy. The policymaking process was characterized by 'disjointed incrementalism'.[13]

Yet the Community/Union did not simply respond defensively and incrementally to the East European demands for market access, aid, dialogue and membership. From the trade and cooperation agreements through to the Pact for Stability, it has fashioned a distinct policy, which can be seen as more purposive (or proactive) than reactive. The self-styled logic seems to apply, if only in part: the Community/Union pursued its own interests, often on its own initiative.

With the end of the Cold War, the Community/Union stepped into a leadership role in Europe, and tried to shape the new European 'architecture' in line with its own interests and objectives. It promoted democracy, the protection of human rights and the market economy; this would create the conditions for long-term stability and security in Eastern Europe and thus in Western Europe as well. The instruments which the Community/Union used to achieve its objectives changed, from trade and aid to conflict prevention measures, with changing circumstances in Eastern Europe. The use of different instruments did not arise solely in response to East European demands: the Community/Union more often devised the new instruments itself and imposed its own views. The instruments are interconnected: PHARE helps the associates meet the Copenhagen conditions; the Stability Pact was addressed to possible future member states; the pre-accession strategy builds on the Europe agreements.

The idea of concentric circles (reflecting German, Commission and French ideas) was a novel response to internal exigencies (deepening in the wake of German unification) and external demands for closer ties. The Europe agreements, a new type of association agreement, were to be the framework for the development of bilateral relations with the associates. The structured relationship refashioned relations as the EU considered necessary, while the associates were less than pleased with its multilateralism. Although the enhanced dialogue on CFSP matters was partially a response to East European demands for gradual integration, the associates have rarely come up with ideas to exploit the possibilities it offers: proposals for joint CFSP declarations and participation in CFSP joint actions have come from the EU.

The policy itself reflects a sense of identity and interest that transcends member state boundaries. The emphasis placed on regional cooperation, democratization and minority rights (as manifested most clearly in the Pact for Stability) reflects EU concerns and a particular EU vision, based on its own experience, of how to prevent conflicts and ensure security in the region. The membership conditions can be seen as a sort of inventory of shared characteristics that form the basis for a collective identity. The East European countries wanted to 'rejoin Europe'; the EU's response defined what a European identity entails.

Conditionality certainly was not applied in response to East European demands. In the Community's earlier dealings with Eastern Europe, most member states held the view that trade and closer contacts would be the way to encourage peaceful change. Yet as some East European states launched reforms, the Community began to apply conditionality, to use its civilian instruments to try to create the basis for security and stability in Europe. The conditionality of membership in particular has given the EU considerable influence for encouraging reforms and preventing conflicts in Eastern Europe.

The evolving norm of conditionality, however, competes with the older view that integration is a better way to try to ensure stability and security in Eastern Europe. Both views reflect collective interests and experiences, but the issue arose often in the discussions on relations with the East European countries and continues to arise with respect to enlargement in stages.

There was much support from *within* the Community/Union for enlargement. It was widely seen as an 'historical necessity'. The enlargement issue figured high on Community discussions as early as the autumn of 1989. Germany long argued that expanding to the east would stabilize the region and consolidate the democratic and economic transformation there.[14] The UK heartily agreed (though also because enlargement might have the double advantage of slowing down integration). Supporters of enlargement could point to the strength of the outside demands to persuade doubters, but support for expansion did not arise solely because of those demands. By 1993, the situation in Eastern Europe had evolved so dramatically that the time seemed right to offer the prospect of membership, on a conditional basis. Timing here is crucial in another sense: only once Maastricht

Treaty ratification was assured and the issue of EFTAn membership settled did the member states agree to offer membership. The issue of the extent to which the policy has been strategic and controlled or incremental and reactive is an open one. The East Europeans were clearly quite insistent in their demands and the Community/Union had to come up with a response, either to stall or to act positively. But the way in which the Community/Union responded to the demands and sought to shape its relations with the region reflects its own interests, norms and goals, not all of which were always consensual.

8.4 THE ROLE OF EXOGENOUS AND ENDOGENOUS FACTORS

Exogenous Factors

The East European demands for Community/Union action were undoubtedly *the* most important external pressures for a common policy. The member states could not escape from the fact that the Community/Union was the focus of East European foreign policies; this necessarily overshadowed their bilateral relations with the countries of the region. They would at least have to work together to respond to East European demands; they had limited freedom to go it alone, even if they had so wanted. Numerous issues – enlargement in particular – could *only* have arisen within the Community/Union context and could only be handled in that context. The East European expectations that the Community/Union was a unified actor with resources to distribute were one of the key factors pushing the member states to behave that way. (And as the externalization hypothesis states, these external demands led to further institutionalization: the Community expanded its competences; the Commission's role in CFSP increased; procedures to ensure consistency were formalized; and the prospect of enlargement prompted the reforms, albeit limited, of the Amsterdam Treaty.)

More generally, the external environment favoured an active common policy. The ending of the imposed division of Europe was an extraordinary event; relations with the other 'half' were necessarily of a different order than the Community's relations with other countries. While more people died elsewhere as a result of the Cold War (in proxy wars, for example), its most dangerous manifestation was in

Europe: this was the fault line on which the world's survival was poised. During the Cold War, the Community/EPC had tried to overcome that division, or at least reduce the threat it posed. Once the Cold War ended, this goal was realizable; the Community, then Union, tried to ensure that Europe would not return to such a predicament.

In addition, the East European countries are European; the issue of identity was key here. The East Europeans had been cut off from post-World War II processes of economic and political interaction that they might otherwise have participated in and they demanded to be reincorporated into 'Europe'. The East European countries were seen as victims of Soviet domination; in post-Cold War Europe, the task became one of reintegrating the victims into Europe. This made it difficult to resist EU enlargement, rather as it was impossible to block German unification.

The end of the Cold War also meant that the Community *could* act in a region where Cold-War politics had previously restricted its competences. In the new environment, civilian power could have much more influence, as overwhelming military security concerns diminished. Paradoxically, the recent focus on NATO enlargement may enhance the need for the EU to act as a stabilizer in Eastern Europe: it has the right tools for a wider-encompassing 'politics of inclusion'.[15]

Communism also fell during a particularly dynamic time in the Community's history. In the late 1980s, the Community was manifesting a new assertiveness and confidence. Increasingly, its member states accepted (or expected) that it should and could assume a leading role in some aspects of international affairs, at a time when the change in the international environment seemed to have facilitated such a role for a civilian power. It was, therefore, particularly attractive to the East Europeans.[16] A less confident Community might have passed up the opportunity to lead efforts to support reform in Eastern Europe, regardless of any demands on it to do so. Nonetheless, it took time for the member states to agree to work together and only with signs of major change in Poland and Hungary. There was a profound synergy between internal dynamism and the external environment.

To a varying extent, two other third parties played a role in 'pushing' the Community/Union to conduct a common foreign policy towards Eastern Europe, the Soviet Union/Russia and the US. During the Cold War, the Community tried (gingerly) to reduce the Soviet

Union's dominance in Eastern Europe, refusing to conclude an agreement with the CMEA and rewarding the more independently inclined states, Romania and Yugoslavia (Chapter 2). In the immediate aftermath of the Cold War, the Soviet Union did not occupy such a prominent place in the Community's policy towards Eastern Europe; the attempted coup in August 1991, however, changed that. Europe agreements were concluded with Romania and Bulgaria, to bring them closer to the Community. There have been concerns (perhaps exaggerated) that strictly applying conditionality could drive the East European countries into a Russian-led grouping. As Russian foreign policy seemed to take on a more nationalistic tone, the East European countries feared it would try to re-establish its old 'sphere of influence'. While the membership decisions, structured relationship and WEU associate partnership status were not devised specifically in opposition to the new form of Russian 'threat', it was a consideration, along with, however, several other factors.

The influence of another outsider, the US, is even less clear. It greeted the EEC-CMEA declaration of June 1988 with concern: the East European commitment to reforms was, in American eyes, still uncertain. It stalled on West European proposals to loosen COCOM restrictions even in early 1990. Yet the US supported the Commission's role as G-24 aid coordinator and the Community's leading role in general. In December 1989, Secretary of State James Baker declared: 'The promotion of political and economic reforms in the East is a natural vocation for the European Community.'[17] The US periodically criticized the extent to which the EC/EU opened its markets to East European goods. It has pressured the EU to embrace those states left out of the first round of NATO enlargement. But all in all, US encouragement or pressure has not forced the Community/ Union to act. Regardless of the US position, it would have been the focal point for the East Europeans and had its own reasons to be active in the region.

Endogenous Factors

'Endogenous' here refers to intra-EU factors, both at the domestic level (within states) and at the level of the member states acting within the EU. Domestic-level factors were not a significant source of pressure favouring the making of a common foreign policy. Public opinion in general did not figure much in national positions on the policy towards Eastern Europe, although EU-wide polls have shown

some support (but not enthusiasm) for enlargement to the Visegrad countries (see Table 8.2).
Domestic interest groups neither hindered nor encouraged foreign policymaking. Many aspects of the policy (for example, PHARE involvement in infrastructure investment and macro-financial support) were intended to encourage economic operators to invest in Eastern Europe, in line with liberal economic beliefs about the benefits of trade and foreign investment. There is certainly interest in trading

Table 8.2   EU Public Opinion on Enlargement to Eastern Europe, 1996
Question: For each of the following countries, are you in favour or not of it becoming part of the European Union in the future?

	EU15 + −	B + −	Dk + −	D + −	Gr + −	E + −	F + −	Irl + −
Bulgaria	37 42	27 52	30 57	28 54	53 34	51 18	25 58	35 51
Czech Rep.	44 36	32 48	46 43	43 41	55 31	51 18	29 54	35 32
Estonia	37 40	25 53	57 34	35 46	46 38	47 20	21 61	30 34
Hungary	51 30	38 43	49 41	56 30	59 29	53 17	36 48	43 27
Latvia	38 39	27 51	58 33	37 44	44 39	44 19	22 59	32 33
Lithuania	37 40	26 52	57 34	35 46	45 39	48 19	22 59	31 34
Poland	49 33	38 44	56 35	37 48	58 31	55 16	42 44	50 23
Romania	38 42	28 52	32 56	22 61	57 32	53 18	30 55	38 30
Slovakia	38 41	27 52	38 51	36 47	49 35	48 19	22 60	27 37
Slovenia	34 43	26 52	32 56	27 52	48 35	48 19	19 61	27 37

	I + −	L + −	NL + −	A + −	P + −	Fin + −	S + −	UK + −
Bulgaria	48 33	20 59	54 33	20 57	35 38	44 38	48 24	37 37
Czech Rep.	53 29	33 48	65 23	40 41	35 38	55 28	59 16	42 32
Estonia	43 35	26 52	60 27	23 51	28 43	69 19	65 14	34 37
Hungary	59 24	36 44	71 19	53 29	40 34	67 19	63 14	46 29
Latvia	43 34	28 50	62 25	25 49	28 43	63 23	64 14	35 36
Lithuania	43 35	27 51	58 29	23 51	28 43	63 24	64 15	34 37
Poland	61 24	37 43	69 22	29 49	41 34	61 25	63 15	49 27
Romania	54 28	24 57	54 35	18 60	35 38	44 39	48 25	39 35
Slovakia	47 33	23 56	58 29	33 46	29 43	45 37	50 24	33 39
Slovenia	46 34	19 59	52 33	38 43	28 44	40 41	45 27	31 40

Key: + in favour; − not in favour; B Belgium; Dk Denmark; D Germany; Gr Greece; E Spain; F France; Irl Ireland; I Italy; L Luxembourg; NL Netherlands; A Austria; P Portugal; Fin Finland; S Sweden; UK United Kingdom
Source: *Eurobarometer* no. 45, 1996.

with and investing in Eastern Europe, but the voices in favour of liberalized trade with the region seemed fainter than those opposed.

The objections of domestic interest groups to freer trade with Eastern Europe were continuously overruled, with the important exception of trade in the sensitive sectors (but even there, concessions were made). This is because trade policy was part of a wider foreign policy: greater issues were at stake and required compromises from the member states. The political importance of liberalizing trade with Eastern Europe outweighed the risk of enraging domestic interest groups. That the foreign ministers and heads of state or government were making key decisions is crucial: keenly aware of the political significance of economic relations with the associates, they effectively overruled other government ministers who might have sympathized more with the concerns of interest groups.

At the level of the member states interacting within the EC/EU, the 'politics of scale' was undoubtedly at work. All of the member states recognized that the 'problem' of increasing prosperity and security in Eastern Europe would be better solved jointly. National action alone could not cope with the enormity of the task. The member states would have a great deal more influence and be much more effective, if they acted jointly rather than separately. The most appropriate instruments to use to encourage reform and spread stability in the region were Community or EPC/CFSP instruments (trade, association, political dialogue, membership) or would best be wielded at the Union level (aid, conflict prevention).

The smaller member states (the Benelux especially) consistently advocated formulating a common policy towards Eastern Europe. In part, this reflects a concern that otherwise a directorate of the large member states would dominate relations with the region, as was most evident in the EBRD negotiations. The smaller member states clearly lack the resources to encourage reform. A common Community/Union policy meant that they would be much more involved in relations with Eastern Europe – and share the benefits of economic relations – than might otherwise have been possible.

The large member states, however, have also created a common policy towards Eastern Europe. A purely national policy would have been ineffective anyway. Germany, France and Italy have to a certain extent acted on their own in Eastern Europe, but always as a supplement or complement to a common Community policy. Germany has been anxious to 'multilateralize' policy towards Eastern Europe.[18] Confronted with a united Germany, potentially dominant in Eastern

Europe, France has backed an active Community/Union policy, which it would try to lead.[19] Italy has traditionally supported multilateral cooperation and has strongly supported a common policy towards Eastern Europe, also to counter potential German dominance in the region. The UK, whose trade with and aid to Eastern Europe is relatively small (see Tables 4.1 and 8.1), has worked almost solely with the Community/Union framework to formulate and implement civilian policy towards the region.

Furthermore, there was agreement that the Community/Union *should* assume a leading role in relations with Eastern Europe. The Strasbourg European Council in December 1989 declared that the Community 'remains the cornerstone of a new European architecture'.[20] The member states seemed keenly aware that this was a turning point in history and that the Community should play a role in the transformation of the international system in Europe. It had to support the reform process in Eastern Europe and help reshape Europe's institutional architecture.[21] This indicates a sense of collective identity, that facilitated the making of the common policy.

Both endogenous and exogenous factors thus contributed positively to the making of a common foreign policy and in this case, were mutually reinforcing.

8.5 THEORETICAL IMPLICATIONS

Intergovernmental approaches cannot fully explain the continual compromising, or the sense of collective interest and identity, that have characterized the making of a policy towards Eastern Europe. Rationalist theories cannot take into account the possibility that interaction at the Community/Union level could transform interests and identities, which thereby diminishes the force of those theories in the EU context. Concepts used by some neoliberal institutionalists, such as empathetic interdependence, do have some relevance here – but are best seen from a more 'interpretive' standpoint. Theories about the domestic determinants of cooperation do not help, as neither domestic interest groups nor public opinion played a major role in determining the member states' positions.

A combination of constructivism and neofunctionalism may thus be more useful for explaining the making of a common policy towards Eastern Europe. Neofunctionalist insights into spillover, the Commission's role, and the supranational (problem-solving) style of decisionmaking help explain why and how the policy was agreed. The constructivist emphasis on how the process of interaction can transform interests and identities helps illuminate the development of the problem-solving style of decisionmaking and helps explain why the self-styled logic can partly apply in this case. But the exogenous factors were also important, clearly favouring the making of a common foreign policy.

This does not, however, mean that neofunctionalism and constructivism are useful for explaining every case of EU foreign policymaking. The policy towards Eastern Europe is unique, as is the nature of foreign policymaking within the EU – highly dependent as it is on the particular issues at hand. Eastern Europe after 1989 – being right next to the Community and now part of the same geopolitical space – had an immediacy that facilitated the formulation of a common policy and supporting reform there had an urgency that demanded an adequate collective response. The EU is considered, by insiders and outsiders, to have a particular responsibility for Eastern Europe. Eastern Europe had to be integrated into democratic, prosperous and secure Europe; not only was the Community/Union considered the most appropriate institution for that task, but, especially in East European eyes, it epitomized 'Europe' (and hence the enlargement issue dominated the policy agenda).

8.6   WHAT FUTURE FOR EU FOREIGN POLICYMAKING?

Even though the international system now allows more room for civilian powers (perhaps backed by coalitions of the willing with peace-keeping capabilities) and the EU is expected to formulate more foreign policy decisions, it does not follow that the EU will do so. There are many issues on which the member states cannot agree, or do not share common interests; the 'logic of diversity' still prevails. There are also many situations in which the EU simply does not possess the right instruments, even for its own near abroad. It has proven quite unsuited to dealing with violent conflicts, for example. Even where the EU does possess the right policy instruments, it may not have as much influence; privileged ties with the former Soviet republics and several Mediterranean countries may not be enough for the EU to have an impact, because it will not hold out the prospect of enlargement to them – a very powerful instrument in the case of Eastern Europe. A capability-expectations gap[22] clearly exists in many areas.

But a point that might be drawn from this case is that the EU member states can develop and recognize their common interests and formulate a common policy to further those interests. They can hammer out an agreement on the specifics of that policy, compromising their original positions in the process. The logic of diversity may still prevail in some cases; CFSP may still produce only symbolic positions. But the member states have nonetheless been engaged in a process in which their interests and identities are changing and from which common foreign policies can emerge.

The effects of enlargement on this process, however, remain to be seen. It may well be that the 'logic of integration'[23] will stall, having produced the very policy that now renders uncertain its future vitality.

An increase in the number of member states will have far-reaching effects on the EU. It will take time to integrate the new member states into policy networks, which will affect policymaking especially in the Community pillar. Enlargement will inevitably influence any development of 'community' feeling and solidarity within the EU. The socialization of new member states will take time, although it will be easier with an enlargement in stages (as the group will grow larger more gradually). An increase in the EU's membership could alter the decisionmaking style from the (at least occasional) use of a problem-solving approach, which relies on a sense of common values, to the much more prevalent use of bargaining or confrontation.

How difficult it will be to forge a consensus within the Union on foreign policy remains to be seen. The enhanced political dialogue seems to be fairly successful and the East European countries have aligned themselves with many CFSP statements and common positions. But consensus-building is bound to take more time in a larger, more diverse group. Member states might be tempted to 'go it alone' to a greater extent than now.

In the case of making policy towards Eastern Europe, the formal rules and procedures were less important than the general willingness on the part of the member states to formulate and implement a common foreign policy. This willingness arose partly out of the socialization and identity-shaping processes that were spawned by the formal institutional set-up. With a larger group of states, the formal rules may become more important if decisions are to be made at all. Institutional reform will be necessary to avoid paralysis.

These uncertainties about the future shape of an EU should not cloud what has been achieved thus far. The EU has agreed on an extraordinarily far-reaching foreign policy towards Eastern Europe.

That policy has been driven by a fundamental belief that integration and interdependence among democratic states with market economies will ultimately lead to a more stable and secure Europe. As a result, in the first decade of the 21st century, perhaps ten East European countries will accede to the EU, radically changing Europe's institutional and geopolitical landscape.

Notes

1 CONCEPTUALIZING EU FOREIGN POLICYMAKING

1. The Treaty was approved in December 1991 at the Maastricht European Council, signed in February 1992 and entered into force, after a turbulent ratification phase, on 1 November 1993.
2. The Community's relations with the former East Germany, also previously a CMEA member, will be covered up until German unification.
3. Brian White, 'Analysing Foreign Policy: Problems and Approaches', in Michael Clarke and Brian White, eds, *Understanding Foreign Policy: The Foreign Policy Systems Approach* (Aldershot: Edward Elgar, 1989), p. 1.
4. See the definition in Michael Smith, 'The European Union, Foreign Economic Policy and the Changing World Arena', *Journal of European Public Policy*, vol. 1, no. 2, Autumn 1994, p. 287.
5. On the diminishing usefulness of military power, see in particular Joseph Nye, 'Soft Power', *Foreign Policy*, no. 80, Fall 1990.
6. Smith, 'The European Union', p. 287.
7. David Allen, 'Conclusions: The European Rescue of National Foreign Policy?', in Christopher Hill, ed., *The Actors in Europe's Foreign Policy* (London: Routledge, 1996), p. 303.
8. Smith, 'European Union', pp. 287–8.
9. See Christopher Hill, 'The Capability-Expectations Gap, or Conceptualizing Europe's International Role', *Journal of Common Market Studies*, vol. 31, no. 3, September 1993, pp. 315–18.
10. As Gunnar Sjöstedt defines international actorness, in *The External Role of the European Community* (Westmead: Saxon House, 1977), p. 15.
11. Another such case is the common policy towards Central America. See Hazel Smith, *European Union Foreign Policy and Central America* (London: Macmillan, 1995).
12. White, 'Analysing Foreign Policy', pp. 6–7.
13. Eberhard Rhein, 'The Community's External Reach', in Reinhardt Rummel, ed., *Toward Political Union: Planning a Common Foreign and Security Policy* (Boulder: Westview, 1992), p. 36.
14. Justice and home affairs matters (discussed in the third pillar of the Maastricht Treaty) could also have foreign policy implications, but 'output' from the third pillar is still rather limited.
15. According to the 1987 Single European Act, Maastricht Treaty and Amsterdam Treaty (agreed in June 1997, but at the time of writing, not yet ratified).
16. On consistency, see Simon Nuttall, *European Political Co-operation* (Oxford: Clarendon Press, 1992), pp. 319–20; Horst-Günter Krenzler and Henning C. Schneider, 'The Question of Consistency', in Elfriede

Regelsberger, Philippe de Schoutheete de Tervarent and Wolfgang Wessels, eds, *Foreign Policy of the European Union: From EPC to CFSP and Beyond* (Boulder: Lynne Rienner, 1997); and Nanette Neuwahl, 'Foreign and Security Policy and the Implementation of the Requirement of "Consistency" under the Treaty on European Union', in David O'Keeffe and Patrick Twomey, eds, *Legal Issues of the Maastricht Treaty* (London: Chancery Law Publishing, 1994).

17. See the similar definitions of joint foreign policies and joint foreign policy actions in Roy Ginsberg, *Foreign Policy Actions of the European Community: The Politics of Scale* (Boulder: Lynne Rienner, 1989), pp. 2–3.

18. The three European Communities are the European Coal and Steel Community (or ECSC, established in 1952), the European Atomic Energy Community (or Euratom, established in 1958) and the most important, the European Economic Community (or EEC, established in 1958). In some usages of the term, 'European Community' has implied all three Communities.

19. Sometimes 'European Community' was used to indicate the Community and the member states, acting within the bounds of the EEC and EPC. 'European Community and its member states' also increasingly indicated the collectivity (often in EPC declarations). Neither of these definitions will be used here.

20. It is divided into various directorates general (DGs), and headed by 20 Commissioners (two each from the large member states; one each from the others).

21. The foreign ministers are thus key decisionmakers on both trade and foreign policy. On the Council, see Fiona Hayes-Renshaw and Helen Wallace, *The Council of Ministers* (London: Macmillan, 1997).

22. The ECSC and Euratom have similar powers, but only Euratom can conclude association agreements with third parties. D. Lasok and J. W. Bridge, *Law and Institutions of the European Communities* (London: Butterworths, 1991), pp. 60–1.

23. During negotiations, the Commission consults with a special committee (the 'article 113 committee') of government officials. See Rohini Acharya, *Making Trade Policy in the EU*, Discussion Paper 61 (London: Royal Institute of International Affairs, 1996).

24. The European Court of Justice in the 1970 ERTA case ruled that the EC could conclude agreements with outsiders in any area where it exercised power internally; later, it ruled that the EC could do so whenever it was necessary to attain one of the EC's specific objectives. Paul Taylor, *The Limits of European Integration* (New York: Columbia University Press, 1983), pp. 123–4.

25. Iain MacLeod, Ian Hendry, and Stephen Hyett, *The External Relations of the European Communities: A Manual of Law and Practice* (Oxford: Clarendon Press, 1996), Chapter 18.

26. One example is the trade and cooperation agreement signed with the Palestinian Authority in February 1997.

27. Two previous attempts to establish a framework for making European foreign policy had failed: the European Defence and Political

Communities in the early 1950s, and the Fouchet Plans in the 1960s. See Nuttall, *European Political Co-operation*, Chapter 2, for an account of EPC's origins.

28. See 'First Report of the Foreign Ministers to the Heads of State and Government of the Member States of the European Community of 27 October 1970 (Luxembourg Report)', in *European Political Co-operation* (Bonn: Press and Information Office of the Federal Government, 1982), p. 31.

29. Renaud Dehousse and Joseph H. H. Weiler, 'EPC and the Single Act: From Soft Law to Hard Law?', in Martin Holland, ed., *The Future of European Political Cooperation: Essays on Theory and Practice* (London: Macmillan, 1991), p. 124.

30. Michael E. Smith, *The 'Europeanization' of European Political Co-operation: Trust, Transgovernmental Relations, and the Power of Informal Norms*, Center for German and European Studies Working Paper 2.44 (Berkeley: University of California, 1996), p. 42.

31. The name derives from the first meeting place, Schloss Gymnich, in Germany.

32. Nuttall, *European Political Co-operation*, p. 15.

33. 'European Correspondents' prepared the Political Committee's meetings.

34. Political Committee opinions appear on Coreper's agenda, and 'CFSP counsellors' have been attached to each member state's permanent representation. See Krenzler and Schneider, 'Question of Consistency', pp. 137–8.

35. This was a compromise on a proposal for a 'Mr or Ms CFSP', who would play an important role in formulating foreign policy and representing the EU.

36. The Secretariat was to reduce the increasing burden of assuming the presidency. It helped draft replies to questions from members of the EP about EPC (just about the EP's only involvement in EPC).

37. Nuttall, *European Political Co-operation*, pp. 314–15.

38. The difference between common positions and joint actions has been obscure. The Amsterdam Treaty states that joint actions address specific situations where operational action by the EU is considered necessary, and common positions define the EU's approach to a particular matter.

39. This procedure was codified in Maastricht Treaty article 228a: economic relations can be interrupted following a common position or joint action adopted to that effect in CFSP.

40. See Simon Nuttall, 'Interaction between European Political Co-operation and the European Community', *Yearbook of European Law*, no. 7, 1987.

41. The October 1994 CFSP common position on Rwanda is one example of this. OJ L283, 29 October 1994.

42. The WEU is also to be developed as the European pillar of NATO. This satisfied those who wanted to develop the WEU as *the* European defence organization, and those who argued for NATO's continuing predominance. See Anand Menon, Anthony Forster and William

Wallace, 'A Common European Defence?', *Survival*, vol. 34, no. 3, Autumn 1992.

43. See, for example, Hans van den Broek, 'Why Europe Needs a Common Foreign and Security Policy', *European Foreign Affairs Review*, vol. 1, no. 1, July 1996.

44. Martin Holland, 'Introduction: EPC Theory and Empiricism', in Holland, ed., *Future*, p. 5.

45. On foreign policy models, see Michael Clarke, 'Foreign Policy Analysis: A Theoretical Guide', in Stelios Stavridis and Christopher Hill, eds., *Domestic Sources of Foreign Policy: West European Reactions to the Falklands Conflict* (Oxford: Berg, 1996).

46. On the literature, see Jeremy Richardson, 'Interests, Ideas and Garbage Cans of Primeval Soup', in Jeremy Richardson, ed., *European Union: Power and Policy-Making* (London: Routledge, 1996), and Thomas Risse-Kappen, 'Exploring the Nature of the Beast: International Relations Theory and Comparative Policy Analysis Meet the European Union', *Journal of Common Market Studies*, vol. 34, no. 1, March 1996.

47. According to the mainstream definition, cooperation occurs 'when actors adjust their behavior to the actual or anticipated preferences of others, through a process of policy coordination'. Robert Keohane, *After Hegemony: Cooperation and Discord in the World Political Economy* (Princeton: Princeton University Press, 1984), p. 51. Integration goes further, bringing states more closely together. See Paul Taylor, 'A Conceptual Typology of International Organization', in A. J. R. Groom and Paul Taylor, eds, *Frameworks for International Co-operation* (London: Pinter, 1990).

48. For a useful review of various concepts and approaches used to conceptualize EU foreign policy, see Roy Ginsberg, 'Concepts of European Foreign Policy Revisited: Narrowing the Theoretical Capability-Expectations Gap', paper presented at the European Community Studies Association conference, Seattle, May 1997 (cited with author's permission).

49. The seminal neorealist work is Kenneth Waltz, *Theory of International Politics* (Reading, MA: Addison-Wesley, 1979). See also Joseph Grieco, *Cooperation Among Nations: Europe, America, and Non-Tariff Barriers to Trade* (Ithaca: Cornell University Press, 1990), and John J. Mearsheimer, 'Back to the Future: Instability in Europe after the Cold War', *International Security*, vol. 15, no. 1, Summer 1990.

50. Alfred Pijpers argues that the member states agreed only to modest foreign policy cooperation because they did not want to create a 'third force' challenging the Cold War balance of power. 'European Political Cooperation and the Realist Paradigm', in Holland, ed., *Future*. Peter van Ham considers that neorealism is 'powerful in explaining the origins and initial development of the European Community and it has proved helpful in analysing the EC's economic and political relations with the "Other Europe".' *The EC, Eastern Europe and European Unity: Discord, Collaboration and Integration Since 1947* (London: Pinter, 1993), pp. 205–6.

51. See Robert Keohane, 'Neoliberal Institutionalism: A Perspective on World Politics', in Robert Keohane, *International Institutions and State Power* (Boulder: Westview Press, 1989).

52. As Mancur Olson noted: unless the number of individuals in a group is quite small, or unless there is coercion or some separate incentive to make individuals act in their common interest, rational, self-interested individuals will not act to achieve their common or group interests. In *The Logic of Collective Action: Public Goods and the Theory of Groups* (Cambridge, MA: Harvard University Press, 1971), p. 2.

53. See Robert Keohane and Stanley Hoffmann, 'Institutional Change in Europe in the 1980s', and Andrew Moravscik, 'Negotiating the Single European Act', both in Robert Keohane and Stanley Hoffmann, eds, *The New European Community: Decisionmaking and Institutional Change* (Boulder: Westview Press, 1991); and Andrew Moravscik, 'Preferences and Power in the European Community: A Liberal Intergovernmentalist Approach', *Journal of Common Market Studies*, vol. 31, no. 4, December 1993.

54. Ginsberg, *Foreign Policy Actions*, p. 3.

55. Stanley Hoffmann, 'Obstinate or Obsolete? The Fate of the Nation-State and the Case of Western Europe', *Daedalus*, Summer 1966, especially pp. 881–2.

56. See Paul Taylor, *The European Union in the 1990s* (Oxford: Oxford University Press, 1996), pp. 77–97, and 'The European Community and the State: Assumptions, Theories and Propositions', *Review of International Studies*, vol. 17, no. 2, April 1991.

57. Joseph Weiler and Wolfgang Wessels, 'EPC and the Challenge of Theory', in Alfred Pijpers, Elfriede Regelsberger and Wolfgang Wessels, eds, *European Political Cooperation in the 1980s: A Common Foreign Policy for Western Europe?* (Dordrecht: Martinus Nijhoff, 1988), pp. 243–58.

58. Keohane, *After Hegemony*, pp. 122–3.

59. Ibid., p. 125.

60. Smith, *'Europeanization'*, p. 10.

61. This is one of three 'decision styles', distinguished by Fritz Scharpf. The other two are 'bargaining', or the appeal to the participants' self-interest and resort to incentives and 'confrontation', or appeal to the interests of the dominant actor or coalition and resort to coercion as the ultimate sanction. In 'The Joint-Decision Trap: Lessons from German Federalism and European Integration', *Public Administration*, vol. 66, no. 3, Autumn 1988, pp. 258–9.

62. Andrew Hurrell, 'International Society and the Study of Regimes: A Reflective Approach', in Volker Rittberger, ed., *Regime Theory and International Relations* (Oxford: Clarendon Press, 1995), p. 67.

63. See Helen Milner, 'International Theories of Cooperation among Nations: Strengths and Weaknesses', *World Politics*, vol. 44, no. 3, April 1992.

64. Moravscik, 'Preferences and Power'.

65. Robert D. Putnam, 'Diplomacy and Domestic Politics: The Logic of Two-Level Games', *International Organization*, vol. 42, no. 3, Summer

1988. Simon Bulmer has argued that such an approach should be used to analyze EPC, in 'Analysing European Political Cooperation: The Case for Two-Tier Analysis', in Holland, ed., *Future*.
66. Ginsberg, *Foreign Policy Actions*, p. 18.
67. Smith, *'Europeanization'*, p. 10.
68. Alexander Wendt, 'Collective Identity Formation and the International State', *American Political Science Review*, vol. 88, no. 2, June 1994, p. 384.
69. Joseph Nye, 'Neorealism and Neoliberalism', *World Politics*, vol. 40, no. 2, January 1988, p. 246.
70. Wayne Sandholtz, 'Choosing Union: Monetary Politics and Maastricht', *International Organization*, vol. 47, no. 1, Winter 1993, p. 3.
71. Alexander Wendt, 'Anarchy is What States Make of It: The Social Construction of Power Politics', *International Organization*, vol. 46, no. 2, Spring 1992, p. 393. See also: Ronald L. Jepperson, Alexander Wendt and Peter J. Katzenstein, 'Norms, Identity, and Culture in National Security', and Paul Kowert and Jeffrey Legro, 'Norms, Identity, and Their Limits: A Theoretical Reprise', both in Peter J. Katzenstein, ed., *The Culture of National Security: Norms and Identity in World Politics* (New York: Columbia University Press, 1996).
72. Wendt, 'Anarchy', p. 399.
73. Wendt, 'Collective Identity Formation', p. 386.
74. Ibid., p. 391.
75. Wendt, 'Anarchy', p. 417.
76. Ole Wæver, 'Identity, Integration and Security: Solving the Sovereignty Puzzle in E.U. Studies', *Journal of International Affairs*, vol. 48, no. 2, Winter 1995, pp. 419–20, 429.
77. Wendt, 'Anarchy', p. 423.
78. See Karl Deutsch et al., *Political Community and the North Atlantic Area: International Organization in the Light of Historical Experience* (Princeton: Princeton University Press, 1957), and Taylor, *Limits*, Chapter 1.
79. Martin Holland, *European Community Integration* (London: Pinter, 1993), p. 130.
80. Ernst Haas, *The Uniting of Europe: Political, Economic and Social Forces 1950–1957* (London: Stevens and Sons, 1958), pp. 311–13.
81. Philippe Schmitter, 'Three Neo-Functional Hypotheses About International Integration', *International Organization*, vol. 23, no. 1, Winter 1969, p. 162. The most 'creative talent' is surely that of Jean Monnet, the 'father' of European integration. François Duchêne, *Jean Monnet: The First Statesman of Interdependence* (New York: W. W. Norton and Co., 1994).
82. For example, Keohane and Hoffmann, 'Institutional Change', p. 28, Hoffmann, 'Obstinate or Obsolete?', and Pijpers, 'European Political Cooperation'.
83. Thomas Risse-Kappen points out, however, that neofunctionalism lacked a theory of social action to explain the transition from the utility-maximizing self-interest of the actors involved in European integration (its fundamental assumption) to integration based on

collective understandings about a common interest. 'Exploring the Nature of the Beast', p. 56.

84. Haas, *Uniting of Europe*, p. 16.
85. Ibid., pp. 13–19.
86. Ibid., pp. 490–527. Jacques Delors has called this the 'Community method'. See Charles Grant, *Delors: Inside the House that Jacques Built* (London: Nicholas Brealey, 1994), p. 224.
87. Leon Lindberg, *The Political Dynamics of European Economic Integration* (Stanford: Stanford University Press, 1963), pp. 74–6.
88. Lindberg, *Political Dynamics*, p. 285.
89. Philippe de Schoutheete, *La Coopération Politique Européenne* (Brussels: Editions Labor, 1980), p. 118.
90. Dehousse and Weiler, 'EPC and the Single Act', p. 132.
91. Smith, '*Europeanization*', p. 36.
92. Ibid., p. 10.
93. Ginsberg, *Foreign Policy Actions*, p. 10.
94. Ibid., p. 36.
95. Christopher Hill and William Wallace, 'Introduction: Actors and Actions', in Hill, ed., *The Actors*, p. 9.
96. Panayiotis Ifestos, *European Political Cooperation: Towards a Framework of Supranational Diplomacy?* (Aldershot: Avebury, 1987), pp. 136–7.
97. Ernst Haas, 'Turbulent Fields and the Theory of Regional Integration', *International Organization*, vol. 30, no. 2, Spring 1976.
98. Schmitter, 'Three Neo-Functional Hypotheses', p. 165.
99. See Ernst Haas and Edward Thomas Rowe, 'Regional Organizations in the United Nations: Is There Externalization?', *International Studies Quarterly*, vol. 17, no. 1, March 1973, p. 6.
100. Christopher Hill warned that there has been a gap between the Community's actual capabilities and the expectations of its ability to act, in 'Capability-Expectations Gap'.

2 THE COMMUNITY'S RELATIONS WITH EASTERN EUROPE THROUGH 1988

1. See John Pinder, *The European Community and Eastern Europe* (London: Pinter, 1991), Chapter 2, for the early history of the relations between the Communities and the Soviet bloc.
2. While the *Ostpolitik* began when Willy Brandt became Chancellor in 1969, West Germany set up trade missions in East European countries already from 1963. Timothy Garton Ash, *In Europe's Name: Germany and the Divided Continent* (London: Vintage, 1993), p. 36.
3. Charles Ransom, *The European Community and Eastern Europe* (London: Butterworths, 1973), pp. 15–16 and pp. 38–9.
4. Peter Marsh, 'The Development of Relations between the EEC and the CMEA', in Avi Shlaim and G. N. Yannopoulos, eds, *The EEC*

and Eastern Europe (Cambridge: Cambridge University Press, 1978), p. 45.

5. Ransom, *The European Community*, pp. 39–46.
6. Regulation no. 109/70 in OJ L19, 26 January 1970.
7. Decision no. 69/494 in OJ L326, 29 December 1969.
8. Decision no. 74/34 in OJ L30, 4 February 1974. See also European Parliament, Working Document 425/1974, 'Report on the European Community's Relations with the East European State-Trading Countries and COMECON' (the Klepsch Report), 9 January 1975, p. 11.
9. Commission of the European Communities, *Bulletin of the European Communities* (hereinafter *EC Bulletin*) no. 5, 1974, pt. 2330. Trade policy was limited by GATT rules anyway. Czechoslovakia was a founding member of GATT; Poland (1967), Romania (1971) and Hungary (1973) joined later, under special protocols. To reciprocate MFN benefits, state-trading countries agreed to increase their imports by a certain percentage each year.
10. Marsh, 'The Development of Relations', pp. 49–52.
11. *EC Bulletin* no. 11, 1974, pt. 1301.
12. Decision 75/210 in OJ L99, 21 April 1975.
13. Under GATT rules, restrictions could be imposed against imports from state-trading countries, but were to be progressively reduced – a vague enough undertaking to justify their continued use. Susan Senior Nello, *The New Europe: Changing Economic Relations between East and West* (New York: Harvester Wheatsheaf, 1991), pp. 29–33.
14. The East European states borrowed heavily from the West in the late 1960s and early 1970s; servicing the debt became a serious problem by the late 1970s.
15. Ransom, *The European Community*, pp. 39–40.
16. Ibid., p. 40.
17. Edmund Wellenstein, 'The Relations of the European Communities with Eastern Europe' in David O'Keeffe and Henry G. Schermers, eds, *Essays in European Law and Integration* (Deventer, the Netherlands: Kluwer, 1982), p. 204.
18. Senior Nello, *The New Europe*, pp. 42–6.
19. West Germany, for example, concluded economic cooperation agreements with the Soviet Union, Poland, Hungary, Czechoslovakia and Bulgaria in the early 1970s (part of *Ostpolitik*). The use of cooperation agreements later declined as Eastern Europe's economic situation and the international political climate deteriorated in the early 1980s. Jurgen Notzold, 'Political Preconditions of East-West Economic Relations', *Aussenpolitik*, vol. 36, no. 1, 1985, p. 43.
20. See Susan Senior Nello, *EC-East European Economic Relations: Cooperation Agreements at the Government and Firm Levels*, EUI Working Paper no. 85/183 (Florence: European University Institute, 1985), pp. 1–11.
21. Decision 74/393 in OJ L208, 30 July 1974.
22. Wellenstein, 'The Relations', p. 206.
23. Carl A. Ehrhardt, 'The EC in the Network of its Bilateral Agreements', *Aussenpolitik*, vol. 31, no. 4, 1980, p. 373.

24. Trade with the CMEA was only four per cent of the EC's total foreign trade. Peter Marsh, 'The European Community and East-West Economic Relations', *Journal of Common Market Studies*, vol. 23, no. 1, September 1984, p. 2. East Germany remained antagonistic to the EC, although it could afford to do so because its goods entered West Germany free of tariffs, under the provisions of the EEC Treaty's protocol relating to intra-German trade.

25. Quoted in Frans A. M. Alting von Geusau, *Beyond the European Community* (Leyden: A. W. Sijthoff, 1969), p. 149.

26. These involved undertakings by the five states to limit the quantity of goods exported to the EC, or not to sell products below a certain price. John Maslen, 'The European Community's Relations with the State-Trading Countries, 1981–1983', *Yearbook of European Law*, no. 3, 1983, pp. 330–1.

27. Such agreements were periodically renewed. Maslen, 'The European Community's Relations, 1981–1983', p. 331.

28. Peter Marsh, 'E.E.C. Foreign Economic Policy and the Political Management of East-West Economic Relations', *Millennium*, vol. 9, no. 1, Spring 1980, p. 46.

29. Marsh, 'E.E.C.', p. 42.

30. Robert M. Cutler, 'Harmonizing EEC-CMEA Relations: Never the Twain Shall Meet?', *International Affairs*, vol. 63, no. 2, Spring 1987, p. 264.

31. Ransom, *The European Community*, p. 28.

32. The GSP offers developing countries tariff reductions for their industrial products and some agricultural products.

33. Both agreements are in OJ L352, 29 December 1980.

34. John Maslen, 'A Turning Point: Past and Future of the European Community's Relations with Eastern Europe', *Rivista di Studi Politici Internazionali*, no. 4, 1988, p. 560.

35. In 1970, a three-year trade agreement went into effect between the Community and Yugoslavia. In 1971, Yugoslavia was granted the GSP. Another trade agreement was signed in 1973, and a trade and cooperation agreement was concluded in 1980. See Patrick F. R. Artisien and Stephen Holt, 'Yugoslavia and the E.E.C. in the 1970s', *Journal of Common Market Studies*, vol. 28, no. 4, June 1980.

36. John Pinder, 'Economic Integration and East-West Trade: Conflict of Interests or Comedy of Errors?', *Journal of Common Market Studies*, vol. 16, no. 1, September 1997, p. 4. In 1971, the CMEA approved a 'complex program of socialist economic integration' to facilitate enterprise links and encourage joint planning. It did not increase the CMEA's powers over external trade and commercial policies; some CMEA members, especially Romania, opposed such a move and the CMEA operated on the basis of unanimity. Arie Bloed, *The External Relations of the Council for Mutual Economic Assistance* (Dordrecht: Martinus Nijhoff, 1988), pp. 9–10 and 73–4, and Chapter 8.

37. Maslen, 'The European Community's Relations, 1981–1983', p. 325.

38. The Klepsch Report, pp. 21–2.

39. Pinder, 'Economic Integration', pp. 4–5.
40. It was drafted by the UK, which participated in EPC before it formally acceded to the Community in 1973. Nuttall, *European Political Co-operation*, p. 61.
41. Marsh, 'The Development of Relations', pp. 54–5. In 1974, the CMEA's statute was revised to allow it to stipulate trade agreements with third parties, but these would not bind the CMEA members unless they each so agreed. Bloed, *External Relations*, p. 92 and pp. 110–13.
42. The Klepsch Report, pp. 21–2. The member states had accepted only in May 1974 that the EC would handle trade agreements with East European countries.
43. European Parliament, 'Report drawn up on behalf of the Committee on External Economic Relations on Relations between the European Community and the Council for Mutual Economic Assistance (CMEA) and the Eastern European member states of the CMEA' (the Seeler Report), PE Doc A2-187/86, 19 December 1986, p. 17.
44. Susan Senior Nello notes that the Community's stance could have led the Soviet Union to increase the CMEA's supranational powers, and therefore its own, the opposite effect intended. Susan Senior Nello, *Recent Developments in Relations between the EC and Eastern Europe*, EUI Working Paper no. 89/381 (Florence: European University Institute, 1989), pp. 5–6.
45. Margaret Thatcher maintains that her visit to Hungary in early February 1984 'was the first foray in what became a distinctive British diplomacy towards the captive nations of eastern Europe. The first step was to open greater economic and commercial links with the existing regimes, making them less dependent upon the closed COMECON system.' Margaret Thatcher, *The Downing Street Years* (London: HarperCollins, 1993), p. 457. But well before then, the UK had agreed to the Community stance on the CMEA, whose objective was the same.
46. Pinder, 'Economic Integration', pp. 8–13.
47. Marsh, 'The Development of Relations', pp. 54–5.
48. John Maslen, 'The European Community's Relations with the State-Trading Countries of Europe, 1984–1986', *Yearbook of European Law*, no. 6, 1986, pp. 336–7.
49. European Parliament, 'Report drawn up on behalf of the Committee of External Economic Relations on relations between the European community and the East European state-trading countries and the CMEA (COMECON)' (the Irmer Report), Working Document 1-531/82, 28 July 1982, p. 40.
50. Maslen, 'The European Community's Relations, 1981–1983', p. 337.
51. Maslen, 'The European Community's Relations, 1984–1986', p. 338.
52. As quoted, ibid., p. 338.
53. Ibid., p. 340. Normalization being defined as a situation where each party is willing to deal on an official basis with the other. The East European countries would accredit diplomatic missions to the Communities.
54. *EC Bulletin* no. 6, 1985, pts. 2.3.37–38 and pt. 1.2.9, and no. 7/8, 1985, pt. 2.3.38.

55. The Seeler Report, p. 15. The declaration would be concluded with the 'EEC', then the formal name of the Community.
56. Senior Nello, *Recent Developments*, p. 9.
57. Maslen, 'The European Community's Relations, 1984–1986', pp. 339–42.
58. Wojciech Morawiecki, 'Actors and Interests in the Process of Negotiations Between the CMEA and the EEC', *Legal Issues of European Integration*, vol. 15, no. 2, 1989, pp. 26–7.
59. *Agence Europe* no. 4784, 18 May 1988. The Soviet compromise was probably encouraged by the West German announcement the week before that credits worth DM3.5 billion would be made available to the Soviet Union by a West German-led bank consortium. Quentin Peel, 'Comecon and EC Close to Recognition', *The Financial Times*, 17 May 1988.
60. *Agence Europe* no. 4786, 20 May 1988 and David Buchan, 'Trade Blocs to Recognise Each Other', *The Financial Times*, 25 May 1988.
61. Joint Declaration on the Establishment of Official Relations between the European Economic Community and the Council for Mutual Economic Assistance, in OJ L157, 24 June 1988.
62. Barbara Lippert, 'EC-CMEA Relations: Normalisation and Beyond', in Geoffrey Edwards and Elfriede Regelsberger, eds, *The European Community and Inter-regional Cooperation* (London: Pinter, 1990), p. 124.
63. Maslen, 'A Turning Point', p. 564.
64. Ibid., p. 565. Romania did not establish diplomatic ties with the Communities until March 1990 (see Section 3.2.2). The informal 'advisers' group', composed of Commission and member state officials, handled the decisions regarding the opening of East European embassies in Brussels.
65. In 1967, NATO had approved the Harmel Report, which emphasized the importance of pursuing detente and strengthening defence.
66. William Wallace, 'Political Cooperation: Integration through Intergovernmentalism', in Helen Wallace, William Wallace and Carole Webb, eds, *Policy-Making in the European Community* (Chichester: John Wiley and Sons, 1983), pp. 375–6.
67. Nuttall, *European Political Co-operation*, p. 60.
68. Alfred Pijpers, 'European Political Cooperation and the CSCE Process', *Legal Issues of European Integration*, vol. 10, no. 1, 1984, p. 143.
69. Pijpers, 'European Political Cooperation', p. 138.
70. In the 1970 FRG-USSR bilateral treaty, West Germany agreed to respect existing borders; the Soviet Union wanted wider confirmation of the status quo.
71. Michael Clarke, 'Britain and European Political Cooperation in the CSCE', in Kenneth Dyson, ed., *European Detente: Case Studies of the Politics of East-West Relations* (London: Frances Pinter, 1986), p. 241. The Commission thus participated in the preparations via the *EPC* machinery, a way of limiting its input.
72. Nuttall, *European Political Co-operation*, p. 58.

73. *EC Bulletin* no. 7/8, 1975, pt. 1201.
74. Carl Ehrhardt, 'EEC and CMEA Tediously Nearing Each Other', *Aussenpolitik*, vol. 28, no. 2, 1977, p. 170.
75. Karl E. Birnbaum and Ingo Peters, 'The CSCE: A Reassessment of its Role in the 1980s', *Review of International Studies*, vol. 16, no. 4, October 1990, p. 310.
76. 'Final Act of the Conference on Security and Co-operation in Europe, Helsinki, 1 August 1975', reprinted in Arie Bloed, ed., *From Helsinki to Vienna: Basic Documents of the Helsinki Process* (Dordrecht: Martinus Nijhoff, 1990).
77. Clarke, 'Britain', p. 243.
78. Pijpers, 'European Political Cooperation', pp. 143–6.
79. See Thatcher, *Downing Street Years*, p. 457, and Dominique Moïsi, 'French Policy Toward Central and Eastern Europe', in William Griffith, ed., *Central and Eastern Europe: The Opening Curtain?* (Boulder: Westview, 1989), pp. 359–62.
80. Nuttall, *European Political Co-operation*, p. 118.
81. Jan Zielonka, 'Introduction: Eastern Europe in Transition', in Gary K. Bertsch, Heinrich Vogel, and Jan Zielonka, eds, *After the Revolutions: East-West Trade and Technology Transfer in the 1990s* (Boulder: Westview, 1991), pp. 2–4.
82. Stephen Woolcock, *Western Policies on East-West Trade* (London: Routledge and Kegan Paul, 1982), p. 8. COCOM, an informal, non-treaty organization, consisted of all the NATO member countries except Iceland, plus Japan. The Community was not even an observer. Members agreed not to sell products on three sets of lists to the communist bloc. The lists – for munitions, atomic energy, and industrial-commercial goods – were reviewed every few years. See Gary K. Bertsch, *East-West Strategic Trade, COCOM and the Atlantic Alliance* (Paris: The Atlantic Institute for International Affairs, 1983).
83. Beverly Crawford, 'The Roots of European Self-Assertion in East-West Trade', in Beverly Crawford and Peter W. Schulze, eds, *The New Europe Asserts Itself: A Changing Role in International Relations* (Berkeley: University of California, 1990), p. 256.
84. For the West German view, see Hans-Dietrich Genscher, 'Toward an Overall Western Strategy for Peace, Freedom and Progress', *Foreign Affairs*, vol. 61, no. 1, Fall 1982.
85. Stephen George, using a world systems approach, argues that the member states could agree on a stance on East-West trade because the capitalist, wealthy West European countries in the 'core' had to maintain their markets in Eastern Europe and guarantee their supplies of raw materials, even if it meant clashing with the US. In 'European Political Cooperation: A World Systems Perspective', in Holland, ed., *Future*, pp. 63–4. But there *were* other concerns: economic relations were considered important to pry open the regimes and hopefully engender liberalization.
86. And the different national interpretations of the Soviet move added to the appearance of an uncoordinated, confused response. Wallace, 'Political Cooperation', p. 393. In the 1981 London Report, the member

states agreed to allow any three member states to call an emergency meeting within 48 hours.

87. Maslen, 'The European Community's Relations, 1981–1983', p. 338.
88. To try to help stabilize Poland's economy, the EC responded favourably, but in a poorly coordinated way, to requests for food aid. Nuttall, *European Political Co-operation*, p. 199.
89. Miles Kahler, 'The United States and Western Europe: The Diplomatic Consequences of Mr. Reagan', in Kenneth Oye, Robert Lieber and Donald Rothchild, eds, *Eagle Defiant: United States Foreign Policy in the 1980s* (Boston: Little, Brown and Company, 1983), p. 279.
90. The Declarations are in *European Political Co-operation (EPC)* (Bonn: Press and Information Office of the Federal Government of Germany, 1982), p. 245 and pp. 251–2.
91. Kahler, 'The United States', p. 293.
92. Marsh, 'The European Community', p. 8.
93. Belgium has long pushed for consistency between the EC and EPC/CFSP. Christian Franck, 'Belgium: The Importance of Foreign Policy to European Political Union', in Hill, ed., *Actors*, pp. 151–3.
94. The declaration is in *European Political Co-operation (EPC)*, p. 297.
95. Their declaration is in *European Political Co-operation (EPC)*, pp. 302–4. No agreement could be reached to convene the foreign ministers during the Christmas holidays. Greece subsequently withdrew its agreement to most of the 4 January declaration and objected to any hint that sanctions would be imposed on the Soviet Union. Nuttall, *European Political Co-operation*, pp. 201–2.
96. Maslen, 'The European Community's Relations, 1981–1983', p. 339.
97. Regulation 596/82 in OJ L72, 16 March 1982.
98. The regulation was renewed once in December 1982. Denmark's parliament voted against the renewal because it was a recourse to article 113 for political purposes; the government suspended its application in Denmark (and the Commission then initiated proceedings against Denmark for breaching the CCP). To counter these objections, subsequent EC regulations implementing sanctions refer to 'discussions in the context of EPC'. This implies that EPC deliberations are sufficient grounds for an EC decision. Nuttall, *European Political Co-operation*, pp. 262–3.
99. Nuttall, *European Political Co-operation*, pp. 203–4.
100. Conclusions of the Presidency, European Council, *EC Bulletin* no. 3, 1982, pt. 1.3.6.
101. Kahler, 'The United States', p. 297.
102. See Declaration of the foreign ministers on 21 and 22 June 1982 in *EC Bulletin* no. 6, 1982, pt. 2.2.44, and the Conclusions of the European Council in Brussels, 28–9 June 1982, in *EC Bulletin* no. 6, 1982, pt. 1.5.2. The EP also expressed its concern.
103. As Thatcher points out, the US decision in April 1981 to resume grain sales to the Soviet Union also irritated Europe; the US was unwilling to take measures that would hurt its economy, yet expected the Europeans to make sacrifices. Thatcher, *Downing Street Years*, p. 256.

104. Julie E. Katzman, 'The Euro-Siberian Gas Pipeline Row: A Study in Community Development', *Millennium*, vol. 17, no. 1, Spring 1988, pp. 28–37.
105. North Atlantic Assembly, *East-West Economic Relations* (Brussels: North Atlantic Assembly, 1984), p. 22, and Maslen, 'The European Community's Relations, 1981–1983', p. 342.
106. Katzman, 'Euro-Siberian', p. 27.
107. See North Atlantic Assembly, *East-West*, pp. 27–30 and Michael Mastanduno, 'The Management of Alliance Export Control Policy: American Leadership and the Politics of COCOM', in Gary K. Bertsch, ed., *Controlling East-West Trade and Technology Transfer: Power, Politics and Policies* (Durham: Duke University Press, 1988), p. 268.
108. Maslen, 'The European Community's Relations, 1981–1983', p. 343.
109. Robert J. McCartney, 'W. Europe Considers Formal Trade Ties with Soviet Bloc', *The Washington Post*, 5 August 1987.
110. Katzman, 'Euro-Siberian', p. 39.

3 DEVELOPING A COMMON FOREIGN POLICY TOWARDS EASTERN EUROPE, 1988–9

1. As reflected in the titles of books, such as: Reinhardt Rummel, ed., *The Evolution of an International Actor: Western Europe's New Assertiveness* (Boulder: Westview, 1990) and Crawford and Schulze, eds, *The New Europe Asserts Itself*.
2. Conditionality entails the linking, by a state or international organization, of perceived benefits to another state (such as aid or trade concessions), to the fulfilment of economic and/or political conditions.
3. In so doing, the Community resembled Christopher Hill's 'power bloc model' of European foreign policy, according to which the Community/EPC uses its economic strength for political purposes, more so than the 'civilian model', in which it relies on persuasion and negotiation. Christopher Hill, 'European Foreign Policy: Power Bloc, Civilian Model – or Flop?', in Rummel, ed., *Evolution of an International Actor*.
4. Norms are 'shared (thus social) understandings of standards for behavior.' Audie Klotz, *Norms in International Relations: The Struggle against Apartheid* (Ithaca: Cornell University Press, 1995), p. 14.
5. To a limited extent, human rights concerns had influenced the Community/EPC's foreign relations during the Cold War (particularly in relations with South Africa). EC aid and membership for Greece, Spain, and Portugal were linked to democratization. The first time a Community agreement mentioned human rights was in the 1989 revision of the Lomé convention. But conditionality developed furthest in relations with Eastern Europe from the late 1980s.
6. On the changing nature of international politics, see Nye, 'Soft Power'.
7. See Franck, 'Belgium: The Importance', pp. 152–3 and Christian Franck, 'Belgium: Committed Multilateralism', in Christopher Hill, ed.,

National Foreign Policies and European Political Cooperation (London: George Allen and Unwin, 1983), pp. 86–7.

8. See, for example, *Agence Europe* no. 4948, 4 February 1989.
9. David Usborne, 'EC must act together on East Europe, says Delors', *The Independent*, 17 November 1988. Gorbachev's Soviet Union was apparently a more attractive investment opportunity than elsewhere in Eastern Europe. Government-backed loans to East European states were not much of an issue; East European states were also either not reforming or burdened by debt.
10. *Agence Europe* no. 4827, 18–19 July 1988.
11. Andriana Ierodiaconou, 'Foreign Ministers Split Over Response to East Bloc Reform', *The Financial Times*, 17 October 1988.
12. Usborne, 'EC Must Act Together on East Europe'. The Community was concluding trade and cooperation agreements with the fastest reformers (Hungary and Poland, at that stage); this was conditionality applied in practice, but the norm had not yet been articulated.
13. *Agence Europe* no. 4903, 30 November 1988.
14. Nuttall, *European Political Co-operation*, p. 275. The statement was finalized in joint meetings of the Political Directors and the Permanent Representatives, an example of EPC-EC collaboration.
15. Document no. 88/490, 3 December 1988, *EPC Documentation Bulletin*, vol. 4, no. 2, 1988.
16. The Commission's document urged the Community to respond positively to the economic reforms in Eastern Europe. It would thereby have an instrument to pressure the East European states to respect CSCE commitments. The member states should outline a global position on relations with Eastern Europe, and agree to harmonize export aid policy and use the consultation procedure for national cooperation agreements. *Agence Europe* no. 4957, 17 February 1989.
17. Jacques Delors, 'Statement on the Broad Lines of Commission Policy' in *EC Bulletin Supplement 1/89*, p. 12.
18. *Agence Europe* no. 4948, 4 February 1989.
19. *Agence Europe* no. 4960, 22 February 1989.
20. Timothy Garton Ash, *The Magic Lantern: The Revolution of '89 Witnessed in Warsaw, Budapest, Berlin and Prague* (New York: Random House, 1990), p. 14.
21. *Agence Europe* no. 4997, 17–18 April 1989.
22. *Agence Europe* no. 5002, 24–5 April 1989 and *EC Bulletin* no. 4, 1989, pt. 2.2.11. As for Community coordination of export credit policy, the Council only reiterated the importance of transparency regarding export credits to East European countries; no further action was taken.
23. David Buchan, 'EC Moves to Coordinate Policy on Eastern Europe', *The Financial Times*, 25 April 1989.
24. *Agence Europe* no. 5044, 26–7 June 1989.
25. Document no. 89/178 in *EPC Documentation Bulletin*, vol. 5, no. 1, 1989. An indication of the Commission's growing role in EPC was the more frequent usage of 'the Community and its member states' in declarations on Eastern Europe.

26. 'Political Declaration concerning East-West relations, released at the Paris meeting of industrialized countries, held on 14 to 16 July 1989', Document no. 89/184, *EPC Documentation Bulletin*, vol. 5, no. 2, 1989. The Commission's management of this aid programme is discussed in Chapter 4.

27. As Jeanne Kirk Laux maintains in *Reform, Reintegration and Regional Security: The Role of Western Assistance in Overcoming Insecurity in Central and Eastern Europe*, Working Paper no. 37 (Ottawa: Canadian Institute for International Peace and Security, 1991), p. 5.

28. Peter Ludlow, 'The Politics and Policies of the European Community in 1989', in Centre for European Policy Studies, *The Annual Review of European Community Affairs 1990* (London: Brassey's, 1990), p. xlvii.

29. Simon Nuttall, 'The Commission: The Struggle for Legitimacy', in Hill, ed., *The Actors*, p. 142.

30. Nuttall, *European Political Co-operation*, pp. 280–1.

31. *Agence Europe* no. 5141, 29 November 1989.

32. Nuttall, *European Political Co-operation*, p. 277. After Maastricht, the working groups were merged.

33. *EC Bulletin* no. 9, 1989, pts. 2.2.10–11.

34. *EC Bulletin* no. 11, 1989, pt. 2.2.19. Such impromptu presidency-Commission joint visits were the product of cooperation between the French presidency and the Commission. This probably reflected France's desire that the Community (and France) play a highly visible role in Eastern Europe and balance Germany's potential dominance there; collaboration with the Commission was also a way of keeping it in check.

35. Barbara Lippert, Rosalind Stevens-Ströhmann, et al., *German Unification and EC Integration: German and British Perspectives* (London: Pinter, 1993), pp. 12–13.

36. *EC Bulletin* no. 11, 1989, pt. 2.2.15.

37. 'Statement Concerning the Events in Central and Eastern Europe', 22 November 1989, Document no. 89/301, *EPC Documentation Bulletin*, vol. 5, no. 2, 1989.

38. The European Council also approved a statement on German unification.

39. Nuttall, *European Political Co-operation*, p. 278.

40. *EC Bulletin* no. 12, 1989, pt. 1.1.14.

41. 'Statement Concerning Central and Eastern Europe', Document no. 89/314, *EPC Documentation Bulletin*, vol. 5, no. 2, 1989.

42. *Agence Europe* no. 5112, 16–17 October 1989.

43. 'Communication from the Commission to the Council: Implications of Recent Changes in Central and Eastern Europe for the Community's Relations with the Countries Concerned', SEC (90) 111 final, 23 January 1990, p. 3.

44. Commission of the European Communities, External Relations Information no. 1/89, 'The European Community's Relations with Comecon and its East European Members', January 1989, p. 4.

45. David Usborne, 'Howe Moves to Head Off EC Split', *The Independent*, 25 October 1988.

46. 'Statement on the Period of the German Presidency – Abstracts', 16 June 1988, Document no. 88/168, *EPC Documentation Bulletin*, vol. 4, no. 1, 1988.
47. Relations with the GDR will be discussed in Section 5.1.
48. The agreement with the USSR entered into force on 1 April 1990 (OJ L68, 15 March 1990). Trade and cooperation agreements were later concluded with other East European countries (some newly-independent) as they implemented reforms: an agreement with Albania entered into force on 1 December 1992 (OJ L343, 25 November 1992); agreements with Latvia and Lithuania entered into force on 1 February 1993, and with Estonia on 1 March 1993 (all three are in OJ L403, 31 December 1992); and an agreement with Slovenia entered into force on 1 September 1993 (OJ L189, 29 July 1993).
49. Senior Nello, *Recent Developments*, p. 16.
50. In December 1988, Commissioner Willy De Clercq maintained that to increase its exports to the EC, Hungary needed to improve the quality of its goods, not demand the removal of QRs. *Agence Europe* no. 4914, 14 December 1988.
51. Many countries feared that they would be excluded from the Community altogether because restrictions existing in only a few member states would be extended to the entire EC, creating a 'Fortress Europe'.
52. For Bulgaria and Romania, restrictions on a few highly sensitive products would remain after 1995. All of the agreements contain a safe-guard clause allowing the parties to take protective measures against imports.
53. The agreements with Czechoslovakia and Romania are also concluded with Euratom, because the areas of cooperation include nuclear energy and safety. Because the economic cooperation measures exceed Rome Treaty provisions, the agreements were based on articles 113 and 235, and were approved by the EP.
54. See Maslen, 'A Turning Point', pp. 571–2.
55. Senior Nello, *Recent Developments*, pp. 30–1.
56. Péter Balázs, 'Trade Relations between Hungary and the European Community', in Marc Maresceau, ed., *The Political and Legal Framework of Trade Relations between the European Community and Eastern Europe* (Dordrecht: Martinus Nijhoff, 1989), p. 65.
57. *EC Bulletin* no. 4, 1987, pt. 2.2.28.
58. David Buchan, 'Hopes Rise for Trade Deal with Hungary', *The Financial Times*, 23 March 1988.
59. *Agence Europe* no. 4765, 16 April 1988 and Senior Nello, *Recent Developments*, p. 28.
60. David Buchan, 'Outlook for EC-Hungary Accord Brightens', *The Financial Times*, 14 June 1988.
61. Maslen, 'A Turning Point', p. 562.
62. *Agence Europe* no. 4915, 15 December 1988.
63. *Agence Europe* no. 4960, 22 February 1989.
64. *EC Bulletin* no. 4, 1989, pt. 2.3.1; *Agence Europe* no. 4991, 8 April 1989.

65. *EC Bulletin* no. 4, 1989, pt. 2.2.15.
66. *Agence Europe* no. 5019, 22–3 May 1989.
67. David Buchan, 'EC Cool on Loans for Poland to Encourage Reform', *The Financial Times*, 23 May 1989. In 1989, Poland's total external debt was US$43.029 billion; it was classified as a severely indebted middle-income country. World Bank, *World Debt Tables 1991–1992: External Debt of Developing Countries Volumes 1 and 2* (Washington, DC: The World Bank, 1991).
68. *Agence Europe* no. 5017, 19 May 1989. The G-7 announced they would support the rescheduling of Poland's debt in the Paris Club, provided Poland met IMF conditions.
69. *Agence Europe* no. 5065, 27 July 1989.
70. David Buchan, 'Poles and EC Agree Economic Cooperation and Trade Pact', *The Financial Times*, 26 July 1989.
71. Senior Nello, *Recent Developments*, p. 31.
72. *Agence Europe* no. 4829, 21 July 1988, and no. 4853, 16 September 1988.
73. In August, for example, the police used force to break up demonstrations on the 20th anniversary of the Warsaw Pact invasion.
74. OJ L88, 31 March 1989.
75. Senior Nello, *Recent Developments*, p. 31.
76. *Agence Europe* no. 5157, 20 December 1989.
77. *Agence Europe* no. 5172, 15–16 January 1990.
78. *EC Bulletin* no. 3, 1990, pt. 1.2.15.
79. *Agence Europe* no. 5206, 3 March 1990. Dienstbier was reacting to the EC debate on association (see Chapter 5).
80. *Agence Europe* no. 4736, 4 March 1988.
81. *EC Bulletin* no. 2, 1989, pt. 2.2.25.
82. *Agence Europe* no. 5028, 3 June 1989.
83. *Agence Europe* no. 5047, 30 June 1989.
84. *Agence Europe* no. 5123, 1 November 1989.
85. See *Thirty-seventh Review of the Council's Work, 1 January–31 December 1989* and *Agence Europe* no. 5166, 6 January 1990.
86. *Agence Europe* no. 5204, 1 March 1990.
87. *Thirty-fifth Review of the Council's Work, 1 January–31 December 1987*, p. 106.
88. *Twenty-second General Report on the Activities of the European Communities 1988*, p. 412.
89. As outlined in a reply to two questions by MEPs, in Document no. 89/112, *EPC Documentation Bulletin*, vol. 5, no. 1, 1989.
90. Document no. 89/102, *EPC Documentation Bulletin*, vol. 5, no. 1, 1989.
91. Maslen, 'A Turning Point', p. 566.
92. *Agence Europe* no. 4937, 20 January 1989.
93. *Agence Europe* no. 4977, 16 March 1989.
94. *EC Bulletin* no. 4, 1989, pt. 2.2.16.
95. 'Statement concerning Romania', Document no. 89/343, *EPC Documentation Bulletin*, vol. 5, no. 2, 1989.
96. *Agence Europe* no. 5159, 22 December 1989; *EC Bulletin* no. 12, 1989, pt. 2.2.33.

97. *Agence Europe* no. 5167, 8–9 January 1990. Immediately after the violent fall of the Ceausescu regime in December 1989, the Commission and the French presidency sent a delegation to Romania to assess the country's recovery needs. *Agence Europe* no. 5162, 29 December 1989.
98. *Agence Europe* no. 5172, 15–16 January 1990.
99. *Agence Europe* no. 5209, 8 March 1990.
100. *Agence Europe* no. 5218, 21 March 1990.
101. *Agence Europe* no. 5272, 11–12 June 1990.
102. *Agence Europe* no. 5276, 16 June 1990.
103. 'Statement by the Twelve on Romania', EPC Press Release P. 44/90, 18 June 1990.
104. *EC Bulletin* no. 6, 1990, pt. 1.4.5.
105. *Agence Europe* no. 5297, 16–17 July 1990, and no. 5298, 18 July 1990.
106. *EC Bulletin* no. 10, 1990, pt. 1.4.9.
107. *EC Bulletin* no. 1/2, 1991, pt. 1.3.19.
108. Commission of the European Communities, 'Action Plan for Coordinated Aid to Poland and Hungary', COM (89) 470 final, 27 September 1989, and *EC Bulletin* no. 10, 1989, pts. 1.1.1–2.
109. As Italy had the most quantitative restrictions on goods from Eastern Europe of all the member states, this was a significant gesture. See Senior Nello, *The New Europe*, p. 33. Some member states were apparently not enthused about extending the GSP, as it was supposed to be for developing countries. *Agence Europe* no. 5103, 4 October 1989.
110. Regulation no. 3381/89, in OJ L326, 11 November 1989, later replaced by Regulation 2727/90.
111. *EC Bulletin* no. 10, 1989, pt. 1.1.5.
112. Regulation no. 3691/89, in OJ L362, 12 December 1989, later replaced by Regulation no. 2727/90. The restrictions were not lifted by Spain or Portugal, still in their accession transition period.
113. Regulation 2727/90, in OJ L262, 26 September 1990.
114. In February 1990, six member states – including France, Spain, and Italy – blocked a Commission proposal to eliminate levies on sheep and goat meat imports. *Agence Europe* no. 5193, 14 February 1990.
115. 'The Economic Interpenetration between the European Union and Eastern Europe', in European Commission, *European Economy*, no. 6, 1994, p. 161.
116. Commission of the European Communities, 'European Community Relations with the Countries of Central and Eastern Europe', Background Brief BB17, June 1993.
117. *Agence Europe* no. 5135, 20–1 November 1989.
118. Crawford, 'The Roots', p. 276.
119. *Agence Europe* no. 5270, 8 June 1990.
120. *Agence Europe* no. 5742, 3 June 1992, and 'Cold War Group's Successor Set for October Launch', *Reuter*, 30 March 1994. COCOM was to be replaced by a forum to control high-technology exports that would include the former Soviet bloc countries. In July 1996, 31 countries agreed the 'Wassenaar Arrangement' to curb arms exports.

4   AID

1. See Jacques Pelkmans and Anna Murphy, 'Catapulted into Leadership: The Community's Trade and Aid Policies Vis-à-Vis Eastern Europe', *Journal of European Integration*, vol. 14, nos. 2–3, 1991.

2. Accounts differ regarding who actually proposed the idea. Some observers argue that Kohl, taking up Delors' suggestions, did. Claus-Dieter Ehlermann, 'Aid for Poland and Hungary, First Assessment', *European Affairs*, no. 4, 1989, p. 23. Others say Bush did. Giles Merritt, *Eastern Europe and the USSR: The Challenge of Freedom* (London: Kogan Page, 1991), p. 21, and Grant, *Delors*, pp. 165–6. George Ross maintains that Canadian Prime Minister Brian Mulroney formally proposed it. In *Jacques Delors and European Integration* (Cambridge: Polity Press, 1995), fn. 104, pp. 263–4.

3. The Commission could act quickly because Delors mobilized his personal network, rather than the director generals. Grant, *Delors*, p. 105. G-24 coordination is carried out by detached national officials (from EC and non-EC states) and by personnel shifted from DG VIII (Development). The unit remains short-staffed.

4. The Council's conclusions did not mention the G-7: those member states not in the G-7 were apparently touchy about 'submitting' themselves to the G-7's will. *Agence Europe* no. 5060, 19 July 1989.

5. That is, the twelve EC member states, the six members of the European Free Trade Association, or EFTA (Austria, Finland, Iceland, Norway, Sweden and Switzerland), the US, Japan, Canada, Australia, New Zealand and Turkey. *Agence Europe* no. 5063, 24–5 July 1989.

6. *Agence Europe* no. 5069, 2 August 1989, and no. 5070, 3 August 1989.

7. 'G-24 Takes Stock of Assistance to Central and Eastern Europe', Commission of the European Communities Press Release IP (93) 341, 5 May 1993.

8. 'First Annual Report from the Commission to the Council and the European Parliament on the Implementation of Economic Aid to the Countries of East and Central Europe as of 31 December 1990', SEC (91) 1354 final, 24 July 1991, (hereinafter 'PHARE Annual Report 1990'), pp. 14–16.

9. See 'Second Annual Report from the Commission to the Council and the European Parliament on the Implementation of Community Assistance to the Countries of East and Central Europe (PHARE) in 1991', COM (93) 172 final, 10 May 1993 (hereinafter 'PHARE Annual Report 1991'), p. 16, and UN Economic Commission for Europe, *Economic Survey of Europe in 1991–1992*, Chapter 5.

10. Initially, there was some semantic confusion and the G-24 programme was referred to as Operation PHARE. But the two are separate programmes and PHARE refers exclusively to the EC's programme, as is made crystal clear in Commission, *PHARE, Assistance for Economic Restructuring in the Countries of Central and Eastern Europe: An Operational Guide* (Luxembourg: OOPEC, 1992), p. 6.

11. In 1992, the Community and the EBRD signed the 'Bangkok Agreement', providing for closer cooperation. 'Fourth Annual Report

from the Commission to the Council and the European Parliament on the Implementation of Community Assistance to the Countries of East and Central Europe (PHARE) in 1993' (hereinafter PHARE Annual Report 1993), in COM (95) 13 final, 20 February 1995, p. 51 and 71. In June 1995, the Commission and EBRD signed an agreement on financing joint ventures in Eastern Europe. *Agence Europe* no. 6508, 24 June 1995.

12. Nuttall, *European Political Co-operation*, p. 279.
13. Interview with commission official in Brussels, March 1996.
14. Commission of the European Communities, 'Action Plan: Coordinated Assistance from the Group of 24 to Bulgaria, Czechoslovakia, the German Democratic Republic, Romania and Yugoslavia', SEC (90) 843 final, 2 May 1990. One indication of the difficulties the over-stretched Commission could encounter: Andriessen was late for a talk with the Bulgarian foreign minister because planners had not taken account of time zone differences. David Buchan, 'Flying Dutchman Plans Aid for East Europe', *The Financial Times*, 16 January 1990.
15. 'The Development of the Community's Relations with the Countries of Central and Eastern Europe', SEC (90) 196 final, 1 February 1990.
16. Council of the European Communities, General Secretariat, Press Release 4300/90 (Presse 9), 5 February 1990.
17. 'Presidency Conclusions: Special Meeting of the European Council, Dublin, 28 April 1990', in Annex, *Agence Europe* no. 5245, 30 April–1 May 1990.
18. *Agence Europe* no. 5278, 20 June 1990.
19. *Agence Europe* no. 5279, 21 June 1990.
20. EC Office of Press and Public Affairs, Washington, DC, 'Declaration of Ministers of the "Group of 24" Engaged in Economic Assistance to Central and East European Countries', *European Community News* no. 29/90, 5 July 1990.
21. *EC Bulletin* no. 1/2, 1991, pt. 1.3.9. In September 1991, the G-24 decided to extend aid to Albania, Estonia, Latvia and Lithuania. Aid to Yugoslavia was suspended on 8 November 1991. It was then extended to Slovenia in October 1992 and to the Former Yugoslav Republic of Macedonia (FYROM) in July 1993.
22. The acronym is officially French but can be translated into English (Poland/Hungary: Assistance for Restructuring Economies).
23. European Commission, 'PHARE: A Performance Review 1990–1993', April 1994, p. i.
24. This objective is repeated at the beginning of each 'PHARE: Infocontract', published several times a year by DG I.
25. Regulation no. 3906/89, in OJ L375, 23 December 1989. A second regulation, no. 2698/90 (OJ L257, 21 September 1990), amends the first, and does not refer to a specific budget or time scale (as the earlier one did). The legal basis is article 235, as it goes beyond the EC's competences.
26. Under Regulation 2698/90. In July 1993, Czechoslovakia was removed from the list of beneficiaries and the Czech republic and Slovakia added. Aid to Yugoslavia was suspended in November 1991; in August

1992, it was extended to Slovenia. In December 1991, PHARE was extended to Albania, Estonia, Latvia and Lithuania. PHARE was extended to FYROM and Bosnia-Herzegovina (but only for projects in direct support of the peace process) by the end of 1995.

27.	'PHARE Annual Report 1991', p. 4.
28.	'Communication from the Commission to the Council: Follow up to Commission Communication on "The Europe Agreements and Beyond: A Strategy to Prepare the Countries of Central and Eastern Europe for Accession"', COM (94) 361 final, 27 July 1994, Annex IV.
29.	'Essence of Essen', *The Economist*, 3 December 1994.
30.	Presidency Conclusions, European Council Meeting on 9 and 10 December 1994 in Essen, SN 300/94, Annex IV, part XI.
31.	Presidency Conclusions, European Council – Cannes, 26–7 June 1995, SN 211/95, Part B, p. 39. 4.685 billion ECUs was allocated for cooperation with the Mediterranean non-member countries in 1995–9.
32.	Spain in particular has supported measures that weaken PHARE, as PHARE is seen as a drain on resources that should be directed to the Mediterranean or Latin America. Interviews with commission officials, June 1994.
33.	See 'PHARE Annual Report 1991', p. 10; 'Third Annual Report from the Commission to the Council and the European Parliament on the Implementation of Community Assistance to the Countries of East and Central Europe (PHARE) in 1992' (hereinafter 'PHARE Annual Report 1992') in COM (95) 13 final, 20 February 1995, p. 12; 'PHARE Annual Report 1993', p. 54.
34.	European Commission, 'The PHARE Programme Annual Report 1995' (hereinafter 'PHARE Annual Report 1995'), COM (96) 360 final, 23 July 1996, p. 10.
35.	Staff grew from 24 in January 1990 to 125 at the end of 1993. 'PHARE Annual Report 1990', pp. 17–18; 'PHARE Annual Report 1993', p. 60. *The Economist* points out that the Commission's personnel policy is inflexible, so that staff are not easily transferred where needed. 'EC Aid to the East: Good Intentions, Poor Performance', 10 April 1993.
36.	European Commission, 'What is PHARE?', May 1994, p. 15. Since 1990, Commission delegations have opened throughout Eastern Europe. There were over 100 people posted in the delegations in 1992. See David Buchan, *Europe: The Strange Superpower* (Aldershot: Dartmouth, 1993), pp. 55–65.
37.	Member states lobbied the Commission for consultant contracts; the southern member states complained that consultants from northern Europe were winning the bulk of contracts. With the increasing decentralization of PHARE management, this is less of an issue.
38.	As a recent evaluation of PHARE noted. See 'European Parliament Receives an Independent Evaluation of PHARE and TACIS', European Commission Press Release IP/97/748, Brussels, 11 August 1997.
39.	European Commission, 'PHARE 1994 Annual Report'(hereinafter 'PHARE Annual Report 1994'), COM (95) 366 final, 20 July 1995 p. 27.

40. The member states' representatives come from the permanent representations in Brussels and national expert offices. If the committee rejects a measure, the Commission can turn to the Council for a decision. On only one occasion did the committee reject a Commission proposal, on a programme for Albania. 'PHARE Annual Report 1992', p. 8.
41. Funds committed but not spent could be disbursed in the following year. 'PHARE Annual Report 1990', pp. 4–5.
42. SEC (90) 111 final, p. 8.
43. *EC Bulletin* no. 11, 1992, pt. 1.4.6.
44. 'PHARE Annual Report 1993', p. 48.
45. 'PHARE Annual Report 1995', pp. 10–11.
46. The criticisms have come from the recipients, observers, MEPs, and the Court of Auditors. 'European Parliament Hearing on PHARE and TACIS Programmes', *European Report* no. 1863, 2 June 1993, and Lionel Barber, 'Brussels Misjudgments Have Cost Millions, Watchdog Says', *The Financial Times*, 27 November 1992.
47. Andrew Hill, 'Brittan Admits Flaws in Aid', *The Financial Times*, 10 June 1993.
48. See European Commission, 'PHARE General Guidelines 1993–1997', 5 July 1993, and 'PHARE Annual Report 1993', p. 56. The 1993 Court of Auditors report charged that PHARE procedures were too heavy, the recipient countries were not involved enough and programmes started very slowly. The Commission reacted quite angrily to the report, noting that much had been done to counter those charges. 'Commission Answers Allegations over Eastern Europe/CIS Aid', European Commission Press Release Memo/94/69, 16 November 1994. A 1997 evaluation of PHARE criticized its 'preoccupation with financial and procedural control to the detriment of substantive programme design and performance'. European Commission Press Release IP/97/748.
49. 'PHARE Annual Report 1995', pp. 44–6.
50. Tempus (along with a vocational training foundation) was launched by the extraordinary European Council summit in Paris in November 1989. It encourages cooperation between EC and East European universities, and provides grants for staff exchanges.
51. 'PHARE Annual Report 1993', p. 47, and 'PHARE: A Performance Review 1990–1993', pp. 2–4.
52. *Agence Europe* no. 5978, 12 May 1993.
53. 'Copenhagen Summit Set to Endorse Substantial Package on East', *European Report* no. 1866, 12 June 1993.
54. Conclusions of the Presidency, European Council in Copenhagen, 21–2 June 1993, SN 180/93, Annex II, paragraph iii.
55. COM (94) 361 final, p. 16.
56. *Agence Europe* no. 6346, 28 October 1994.
57. Presidency Conclusions, SN 300/94, Annex IV, part XI.
58. *EU Bulletin* no. 3, 1997, pt. 1.4.53.
59. COM (89) 470 final, p. 4.

60. *EIB Information* no. 62, December 1989, p. 3. Spain objected to EIB loans to Eastern Europe because Latin America was not eligible for them. See, for example, *Agence Europe* no. 5418, 26 January 1991. After a Council agreement, the EIB Board of Governors authorized the first loan package to Asian and Latin American countries in February 1993.

61. In December 1993, the Council decided that the EIB could lend up to 3 billion ECUs for 1994–6 to ten East European countries. *EC Bulletin* no. 12, December 1993, pt. 1.7.46. Since July 1993, the EIB can lend to Slovenia. See *info Phare* no. 8, July 1995, p. 11. For 1997–9, the EIB can lend 3.52 billion ECUs to the 11 countries. European Investment Bank, 'EIB Financing in Central and Eastern Europe', February 1997.

62. *Agence Europe* no. 5256, 17 May 1990.

63. *EC Bulletin* no. 11, 1991, pt. 1.3.12. The first loan was not granted until September 1994, because of a lack of appropriate projects. It helped to modernize a steel works in Poland. *Agence Europe* no. 6309, 7 September 1994.

64. *Agence Europe* no. 6197, 24 March 1994. One of the first proposed loans, to help complete the Mochovce nuclear power station in Slovakia, generated enormous controversy and had to be shelved. *Agence Europe*, 6 April 1995.

65. European Commission, 'Report on the Implementation of Macro-Financial Assistance to Third Countries in 1994', *European Economy*, no. 2, 1995, p. 305. The EC has since extended such assistance to Israel, Algeria, Moldova, Ukraine and Belarus. One of the G-24's first actions, in December 1989, was the establishment of a US$1 billion stabilization fund for the Polish currency. Five member states contributed over half of the amount, but the Community itself did not participate. *Agence Europe* no. 5153, 14 December 1989.

66. The IMF and World Bank have been lending much more to the East European countries: the EU's share in total macro-financial relief declined from 54 per cent in 1990 to 17 per cent in 1994. 'Report on Macro-Financial Assistance in 1994', pp. 5–7.

67. European Commission, 'Report from the Commission to the Council and the European Parliament on the Implementation of Macro-Financial Assistance to Third Countries in 1995', COM (96) 695 final, 8 January 1997, p. 2. Assistance to Albania is in the form of a grant.

68. Additional G-24 support was forthcoming at a G-24 representatives' meeting the same month. *EU Bulletin* no. 3, 1997, pts. 1.4.56–7.

69. COM (96) 695, pp. 60–1; *EC Bulletin* no. 1/2, 1996, pt. 1.4.81.

70. *Agence Europe* no. 6205, 7 April 1994.

71. *Agence Europe* no. 6273, 14 July 1994 and no. 6348, 31 October–1 November 1994.

72. Commission of the European Communities, *The European Community and its Eastern Neighbours* (Luxembourg: OOPEC, 1990), p. 18.

73. 'Statement concerning the European Council to the European Parliament', 25 October 1989, Document no. 89/245, *EPC Documentation Bulletin*, vol. 5, no. 2, 1989.

74. Among those who also suggested a similar idea are Alfred Herrhausen, the late president of Deutsche Bank, and Giscard d'Estaing. Paul Menkveld, *Origin and Role of the European Bank for Reconstruction and Development* (London: Graham and Trotman, 1991), pp. 25–6, and *Agence Europe* no. 5105, 6 October 1989.

75. Menkveld, *Origin and Role*, p. 32. See also Thatcher, *Downing Street Years*, p. 759.

76. *Agence Europe* no. 5138, 24 November 1989. The EIB lends far more to member states than to non-members: in 1988–1989, the EIB lent 1.3 billion ECUs outside the EC (mainly to the ACP countries) and 21.1 billion ECUs inside. Menkveld, *Origin and Role*, p. 32.

77. 'Statement Concerning the Events in Central and Eastern Europe', Document no. 89/301, *EPC Documentation Bulletin*, vol. 5, no. 2, 1989.

78. *Agence Europe* no. 5143, 1 December 1989.

79. *EC Bulletin* no. 12, 1989, pt. 1.1.14.

80. Several other states joined later, including South Korea, Israel, Egypt and Mexico. Menkveld, *Origin and Role*, pp. 49–50. The EBRD, however, only lends to eligible countries in Eastern Europe and the former Soviet Union.

81. *Agence Europe* no. 5170, 12 January 1990.

82. *Agence Europe* no. 5181, 27 January 1990.

83. *Agence Europe* no. 5257, 18 May 1990, and no. 5258, 19 May 1990. The Commission and EIB representatives abstained from the vote.

84. *Agence Europe* no. 526, 1 June 1990. After Attali's resignation on 25 June 1993, over revelations of financial impropriety, the smaller states nominated former Danish finance minister Henning Christophersen. 'After Attali', *The Economist*, 3 July 1993. France, however, successfully pushed for the job to remain in French hands, and Jacques de Larosière, head of the central bank, was elected president. 'Now the Deluge', *The Economist*, 24 July 1993.

85. *Agence Europe* no. 5186, 3 February 1990.

86. The US had 10 per cent, Japan 8.5 per cent and the Soviet Union six per cent. The EIB's participation was controversial: in March 1990, the US, Japan and EFTAn members opposed full membership for the EIB (but not for the Commission), since it was not a state. *Agence Europe* no. 5212, 12–13 March 1990. United Germany retained the same share as West Germany. With the breakup of the Czechoslovak, Yugoslav and Soviet federations, the EBRD's membership grew to include all the resulting republics (except Serbia and Montenegro). In April 1996, EBRD finance ministers agreed to double the bank's capital to 20 billion ECUs.

87. COM (94) 361 final, p. 17.

88. Menkveld, *Origin and Role*, p. 52 and Peter Uvin, '"Do As I Say, Not As I Do": The Limits of Political Conditionality', in Georg Sorensen, ed., *Political Conditionality* (London: Frank Cass, 1993), p. 67.

89. 'Political Aspects of the Mandate of the European Bank for Reconstruction and Development', EBRD publication (no date). No country has yet been suspended from the EBRD for violating these principles.

5   ASSOCIATION

1. Lippert and Stevens-Ströhmann, *German Unification*, p. 125.
2. See *Agence Europe* no. 4814, 30 June 1988.
3. *Agence Europe* no. 5134, 18 November 1989 and *EC Bulletin* no. 12, 1989, pt. 2.2.32.
4. *Agence Europe* no. 5213, 14 March 1990.
5. Regulation 3800/91 (OJ L357, 28 December 1991) takes the GDR off the list of PHARE beneficiaries. The eastern Länder became eligible for structural funds: an extra 3 billion ECUs was set aside for them between 1991 and 1993.
6. 'Address by Mr Jacques Delors at the College of Europe in Bruges', *EC Bulletin* no. 10, 1989, pt. 3.2.1.
7. At Delors' last European Council, in December 1994, Kohl praised him for being 'the man who said yes to German unity without hesitation.' Andrew Marshall, 'EU Closer to Letting in Central Europeans', *The Independent*, 12 December 1994. On the Kohl-Delors friendship, see Grant, *Delors*, pp. 139–42.
8. *Agence Europe* no. 5131, 15 November 1989.
9. Thatcher in fact sought to slow down German unification through 1990 (particularly since it was soon coupled with deeper European integration), but could not convince the US or France to support her. Thatcher, *Downing Street Years*, pp. 792–9, 813–15.
10. And Franco-German relations were rocky until January 1990, when Kohl took a stand on the Polish border issue (the Oder-Neisse line) and called for close Franco-German cooperation to push for deeper European integration. Lippert and Stevens-Ströhmann, *German Unification*, pp. 16–17.
11. Ian Davidson, Robert Mauthner and David Buchan, 'EC Heads Pledge Economic Help for Eastern Europe', *The Financial Times*, 20 November 1989.
12. 'A Ten-Point Program for Overcoming the Division of Germany and Europe', reprinted in Harold James and Marla Stone, eds, *When the Wall Came Down: Reactions to German Unification* (London: Routledge, 1992), pp. 33–41.
13. David Spence, *Enlargement Without Accession: The EC's Response to German Unification*, RIIA Discussion Paper no. 36 (London: Royal Institute of International Affairs, 1991), p. 8, and 'Deeper, still, and deeper', *The Economist*, 16 December 1989.
14. 'Statement Concerning Central and Eastern Europe', Document no. 89/314, *EPC Documentation Bulletin*, vol. 5, no. 2, 1989.
15. Address to the EP by Delors, in *EC Bulletin Supplement* 1/90.
16. Even Genscher argued that if the GDR asked to join the Community, then the EC should examine the request before *1993*. *Agence Europe* no. 5177, 22–3 January 1990.
17. Lippert and Stevens-Ströhmann, *German Unification*, pp. 24–5.
18. *Agence Europe* no. 5214, 15 March 1990 and no. 5221, 24 March 1990. In February 1990, the Commission had formed several special working

groups to study the implications of German unification and make arrangements for the GDR's 'accession'.

19. Spence, *Enlargement*, p. 9. The EP would thus have to relinquish its power of assent on membership applications; instead, the cooperation procedure was used to approve the transitional measures. Benno Teschke, 'The Incorporation of the Five New Länder into the European Community: Political, Legal and Economic Aspects', *European Access*, no. 2, April 1992, p. 8.

20. Françoise de La Serre and Christian Lequesne, 'France and the European Union', in Alan Cafruny and Glenda Rosenthal, eds, *The State of the European Community Vol. 2: The Maastricht Debates and Beyond* (London: Lynne Rienner, 1993), p. 146.

21. 'The Community and German Unification' in 'The European Community and Germany Unification', *EC Bulletin Supplement* 4/90.

22. On that date, the GDR adopted the CCP. GDR products could circulate within the EC if they complied with EC rules. The EIB, ECSC and Euratom could extend loans to the GDR. Commission of the European Communities, London Office, 'Background Report: The European Community and German Unification', 2 October 1990; *Agence Europe* no. 5287, 2–3 July 1990, and no. 5288, 4 July 1990. The former CMEA countries were allowed to export at zero tariff into the new eastern Länder, provided the goods were already covered by purchasing commitments. But trade between the former GDR and the East European countries collapsed following unification, partly because of the general economic collapse in the former GDR. Lippert and Stevens-Ströhmann, *German Unification*, p. 109.

23. The summit also discussed a possible IGC on political union, making manifest the link between deepening integration and German unification. 'Statement Concerning the Dublin European Council Meeting of 28 and 29 April 1990', Document no. 90/195, *EPC Documentation Bulletin*, vol. 6, 1990.

24. Lippert and Stevens-Ströhmann, *German Unification*, p. 25.

25. The Treaty on the Final Settlement with respect to Germany was signed in Moscow on 12 September 1990 by both Germanies, the Soviet Union, the US, France and the UK. It came into force on 15 March 1991.

26. Teschke, 'Incorporation', pp. 8–9. Germany had agreed that the balance among the member states in the institutions would remain the same. The EP, however, felt that in the name of democracy, the 16 million additional citizens had to be represented in the EP. In July 1990, it decided that the population of the soon-to-be former GDR would be represented by 18 non-voting observers. Lippert and Stevens-Ströhmann, *German Unification*, pp. 33–6. No final decision on EP representation could be reached until the December 1992 European Council. In the June 1994 EP elections, the UK, France and Italy each elected 87 MEPs, Germany 99.

27. Timothy Garton Ash, 'Poor but Clubbable', *The Independent*, 19 January 1990.

28. Spence, *Enlargement*, p. 1.

29. William Wallace, 'From Twelve to Twenty-Four? The Challenges to the EC Posed by the Revolutions in Eastern Europe', in Colin Crouch and David Marquand, eds, *Towards Greater Europe? A Continent Without an Iron Curtain* (Oxford: Blackwell, 1992), p. 40.

30. David Usborne, 'EC Takes Steps to a New Europe', *The Independent*, 8 May 1990. He had just signed a trade and cooperation agreement with the Community.

31. John Palmer, 'Hungarians Join The Growing Queue for EC Membership', *The Guardian*, 18 July 1990.

32. See Tibor Palankai, *The European Community and Central European Integration: The Hungarian Case*, Occasional Paper Series no. 21 (New York: Institute for East-West Security Studies, 1991), pp. 19–20.

33. Jiri Dienstbier, 'Central Europe's Security', *Foreign Policy*, no. 83, Summer 1991, p. 127.

34. Teschke, 'Incorporation', p. 10.

35. Presentation of the Commission's 1990 programme, in *EC Bulletin Supplement 1/90*, pp. 6–8. Delors referred to six East European countries, so he presumably included the GDR in this calculation.

36. In 1990, over half of the budget was spent on CAP and about 20 per cent on structural funds. The allocation for CAP has since decreased to under half of the budget. See European Commission, *The Community Budget: The Facts in Figures* (Luxembourg: OOPEC), published annually.

37. Negotiations began in June 1990; the EEA treaty was signed in May 1992. After the Swiss rejected it in a referendum in December 1992, the treaty had to be revised.

38. Austria applied in July 1989, Sweden in July 1991, Finland in March 1992, Switzerland in May 1992 and Norway in November 1992. The Swiss application was later frozen.

39. France in particular insisted on deeper integration in response to German unification. Spence, *Enlargement*, pp. 1–8.

40. 'Les Voeux de M. François Mitterrand', *Le Monde*, 2 January 1990. 'Atlanticists' in Eastern and Western Europe suspected that this was an attempt to exclude the US from the European security architecture. Jan Zielonka, *Security in Central Europe*, Adelphi Paper no. 272 (London: Brassey's, 1992), p. 45.

41. See Ole Wæver, 'Three Competing Europes: German, French, Russian', *International Affairs*, vol. 66, no. 3, July 1990, p. 484.

42. Anna Michalski and Helen Wallace, *The European Community: The Challenge of Enlargement* (London: Royal Institute of International Affairs, 1992), pp. 11–12. In an August 1990 speech in Aspen, Colorado, Prime Minister Thatcher declared that the East Europeans 'have not thrown off central command and control in their own countries only to find them reincarnated in the European Community.' The text of the speech is reprinted in *The Daily Telegraph*, 6 August 1990.

43. In April 1990, Kohl and Mitterrand jointly wrote to the other Community leaders to support the convening of an IGC on political union. Interestingly, Genscher may have initially opposed deepening,

because it would delay widening to East European countries; heavily criticized, he was forced to change his stance. John Eisenhammer, 'Weakened for the Strasbourg Scrum', *The Independent*, 8 November 1989.

44. The East European countries did worry that the Maastricht Treaty would delay their entry into the Community because it would take longer for them to prepare for membership. See Jolanta Adamiec, *East-Central Europe and the European Community: The Polish Perspective*, RIIA Discussion Paper no. 47 (London: Royal Institute of International Affairs, 1993), pp. 8–11.

45. George Graham, 'EC Ministers Agree on Urgent Visits to East Europe', *The Financial Times*, 16 October 1989 and *Agence Europe* no. 5112, 16–17 October 1989.

46. David Usborne, 'Delors Frames EC "Ostpolitik"', *The Independent*, 16 November 1989.

47. The Warsaw Pact existed until spring 1991, although it was defunct before then.

48. *EC Bulletin* no. 12, 1989, pt. 1.1.14.

49. David Allen, 'West European Responses to Change in the Soviet Union and Eastern Europe', in Reinhardt Rummel, ed., *Toward Political Union: Planning a Common Foreign and Security Policy in the European Community* (Boulder: Westview, 1992), p. 122.

50. Barry Buzan, et al., *The European Security Order Recast: Scenarios for the Post-Cold War Era* (London: Pinter, 1990), p. 209.

51. See de La Serre and Lequesne, 'France', p. 156; and Istvàn Körmendy, 'The Hungarian View: An EC Associate's Perspective from Central Europe', in Rummel, ed., *Toward Political Union*, p. 243.

52. This proved embarrassing when Turkey applied to join in 1987, and thus made many within the Community wary about even promising eventual membership. See Michalski and Wallace, *The European Community*, pp. 120–4.

53. Allen, 'West European Responses', pp. 122–3.

54. See John Redmond, 'The Wider Europe: Extending the Membership of the EC', in Cafruny and Rosenthal, eds, *The State of the European Community*, p. 221, and J. M. C. Rollo and Helen Wallace, 'New Patterns of Partnership', in Gianni Bonvicini, et al., *The Community and the Emerging European Democracies: A Joint Policy Report* (London: Royal Institute of International Affairs, 1991), p. 64.

55. Françoise de La Serre, 'The EC and Central and Eastern Europe', in Leon Hurwitz and Christian Lequesne, eds, *The State of the European Community: Politics, Institutions, and Debates in the Transition Years 1989–1990* (Harlow: Longman, 1991), p. 311.

56. 'Statement on the Programme of Activities of the Irish Presidency', Document no. 90/001, *EPC Documentation Bulletin*, vol. 6, 1990. The Irish presidency was keen on ensuring consistency: it organized two meetings on Eastern Europe in which the foreign ministers participated in their Council and EPC capacities and were joined by the Permanent Representatives and Political Directors. They took place on 20 January and 21 April 1990. Nuttall, *European Political Co-operation*, p. 278. The

Irish presidency also began the practice of merging the agendas of EPC and EC Council meetings.

57. 'Communication from the Commission to the Council: Implications of Recent Changes in Central and Eastern Europe for the Community's Relations with the Countries Concerned', SEC (90) 111 final, 23 January 1990, p. 5.

58. Commission of the European Communities, 'The Development of the Community's Relations with the Countries of Central and Eastern Europe', SEC (90) 196 final, 1 February 1990, p. 6.

59. 'Statement Concerning the Dublin European Council Meeting of 28 and 29 April 1990', Document no. 90/195, *EPC Documentation Bulletin*, vol. 6, 1990. On the Commission's proposal, see *Agence Europe* no. 5239, 21 April 1990.

60. Special Meeting of the European Council, Dublin, 28 April 1990, Presidency Conclusions, *EC Bulletin* no. 4, 1990, pt. I.8.

61. Commission of the European Communities, 'Association Agreements with the Countries of Central and Eastern Europe: A General Outline', COM (90) 398 final, 27 August 1990, p. 1. The term 'Europe agreements' apparently arose from a dinner conversation between Delors and the Polish prime minister in early February 1990; Delors said the EC wanted to put the 'European flag' in each country. Interview with Commission official in Brussels, March 1996.

62. Meetings were held once each presidency in the capital of the Community's president, between the political director of each country concerned and the political directors of the presidency and the Commission. Nuttall, *European Political Co-operation*, pp. 292–3.

63. COM (90) 398 final, pp. 1–2. These are the five conditions set for G-24 assistance, but future associates had to prove they were making progress in meeting them.

64. *Agence Europe* no. 5396, 20 December 1990. The negotiations were carried out with each country separately. The Commission had discussed whether one Europe agreement or three separate ones should be negotiated, but the three East European countries refused a single agreement.

65. Interview with Commission official, March 1996. Before the SEA (which specified the need for consistency), the Commission's involvement in negotiating arrangements for political dialogue would have been limited, to say the least. See Taylor, *Limits*, pp. 121–32.

66. David Buchan, 'East Europe Hopes of EC Integration Being Dashed', *The Financial Times*, 26 March 1991.

67. In early April, Polish President Lech Walesa requested that the preamble refer to Poland's future accession to the EC. *EC Bulletin* no. 4, 1991, pt. 1.3.3.

68. David Buchan, 'Brussels Opens Its Doors to Trade With Eastern Europe', *The Financial Times*, 19 April 1991, and *Agence Europe* no. 5473, 17 April 1991.

69. Martin Delgado, 'EC's Deaf Ear to Polish Trade Plea', *The European*, 17 May 1991.

70. *Agence Europe* no. 5534, 13 July 1991.

71. *Agence Europe* no. 5545, 31 July 1991.
72. *EC Bulletin* no. 7/8 1991, pt. 1.4.19. At this stage, the Yugoslav war, which broke out in June 1991, does not seem to have motivated the Community to strengthen relations with the East European countries. But as the war spread to Bosnia in 1992, concerns for minority rights and 'good neighbourliness' increasingly influenced the Community's policy (see Chapter 7).
73. *EC Bulletin* no. 9, 1991, pts. 1.3.13 and 1.3.16. In August the three prospective associates had asked to be included in political cooperation. David Buchan and David Gardner, 'A New Wave of Eastern Approaches: Eastern Europe is Knocking on the EC's Door', *The Financial Times*, 6 September 1991.
74. *Agence Europe* no. 5555, 29 August 1991.
75. *Agence Europe* no. 5562, 7 September 1991 and no. 5563, 9–10 September 1991.
76. Belgian, German, Greek and Dutch farmers had also demonstrated. Alexandra Frean, 'Europe's Farmers Rebel', *The European*, 4 October 1991.
77. In July, they suggested that the EC should instead encourage the resumption of agricultural trade between the Soviet Union and the East European countries. *Agence Europe* no. 5544, 29–30 July 1991.
78. *Agence Europe* no. 5563, 9–10 September 1991. The quantity was an extra 1400 tons of meat in a market where yearly turnover is 7,000,000 tons. Josef C. Brada, 'The European Community and Czechoslovakia, Hungary, and Poland', RFE/RL Research Institute, *Report on Eastern Europe*, vol. 2, no. 49, 6 December 1991, p. 28.
79. Brada, 'The EC and Czechoslovakia', p. 28. Just before the meeting, Delors had attacked the reluctance to offer further concessions: 'It's no good making fine speeches with a sob in your voice on Sunday, and then on Monday morning opposing the trade concessions enabling those countries (in Eastern Europe) to sell their goods and improve their living standards.' Buchan and Gardner, 'A New Wave of Eastern Approaches'.
80. *Agence Europe* no. 5565, 12 September 1991. The September meeting was held between the usual negotiators, but the Polish side stated that it was not a formal negotiating session. *Agence Europe* no. 5570, 19 September 1991.
81. A safeguard clause would also allow the EC to stop meat imports if they seriously disrupted the market and EC health provisions would be rigorously applied. Lucy Walker, 'EC Opens Trade Doors to the East', *The European*, 4 October 1991 and *Agence Europe* no. 5578, 30 September–1 October 1991.
82. *Agence Europe* no. 5627, 11 December 1991. Germany (generally known as an advocate for free trade) and Spain were also allowed to protect their coal industry for four years.
83. Quoted in Grant, *Delors*, p. 158.
84. The Council could not conclude agreements providing for political dialogue with third countries in its own capacity or on behalf of the member states. MacLeod, Hendry and Hyett, *External Relations*,

pp. 371–2. Under the 1997 Amsterdam Treaty, the Council can authorize the presidency to negotiate international agreements which fall within the CFSP framework; the Council would then conclude them unanimously.

85. These agreements needed only the Council's approval and a favourable EP opinion.
86. *EC Bulletin* no. 9, 1992, pt. 1.3.11.
87. 'MEPs Endorse Hungarian and Polish Association Agreements', *European Report* no. 1796, 19 September 1992.
88. *EC Bulletin* no. 10, 1993, pt. 1.3.14. See Chapter 7 on the breakup of Czechoslovakia.
89. The Commission also proposed to negotiate a trade agreement with Albania and formulate a policy towards the newly recognized Baltic republics. *EC Bulletin* no. 9, 1991, pts. 1.3.13, 1.3.17, and 1.3.18.
90. Though in April 1991, Andriessen had told the Bulgarian prime minister that an agreement could be signed within a few months. *Agence Europe* no. 5482, 29–30 April 1991. Also in April, Romania signed a friendship treaty with the Soviet Union, a sign that applying conditionality could end up chasing the East European states back into the Soviet/Russian sphere of influence. (The treaty was never ratified, given the breakup of the Soviet Union.) Vladimir Socor, 'The Romanian-Soviet Friendship Treaty and its Regional Implications', RFE/RL Research Institute, *Report on Eastern Europe*, vol. 2, no. 18, 3 May 1991.
91. *EC Bulletin* no. 9, 1991, pt. 1.3.17.
92. 'Statement on Romania', EPC Press Release P. 95/91, 3 October 1991.
93. In the Portuguese presidency's answer to 'Question No. H–1233/91 by Ms Banotti on EC/Romania relations', Document no. 92/014 in *EPC Documentation Bulletin*, vol. 8, 1992.
94. Luxembourg European Council, 'Declaration on Human Rights', *EC Bulletin* no. 6, 1991, pt. I.45; and 'Resolution of the Council and of the Member States meeting in the Council on Human Rights, Democracy and Development', *EC Bulletin* no. 11, 1991, pt. 2.3.1. In addition, the Maastricht Treaty specifies that the EU will respect fundamental rights (title I, article F) and that one of the CFSP's objectives is to develop and consolidate democracy and respect for human rights (title V, article J.1, paragraph 3).
95. *Agence Europe* no. 5704, 4 April 1992.
96. *Agence Europe* no. 5706, 8 April 1992 and no. 5714, 22 April 1992.
97. *EC Bulletin* no. 5, 1992, pt. 1.2.12. Without the clause, suspension or denunciation of agreements would have to be justified on other grounds and in accordance with the provisions of the agreements themselves and international law on treaties.
98. *EC Bulletin* no. 5, 1992, pt. 1.2.13. On 29 May 1995, the Council decided that agreements with *all* third countries will contain a clause stating that respect for human rights and democratic principles is an essential element of the agreements, as well as a suspension mechanism enabling the Community to react in the event of violation of essential elements of the agreements. *EU Bulletin* no. 5, 1995, pt. 1.2.3. See European

Commission, 'On the Inclusion of Respect for Democratic Principles and Human Rights in Agreements between the Community and Third Countries', COM (95) 216 final, 23 May 1995.

99. As do the trade and cooperation agreements concluded with Albania (1992), the Baltic states (1993) and Slovenia (1993), and the partnership and cooperation agreements signed with the former Soviet republics since 1994. The clause in the trade and cooperation agreements with Albania and the Baltic states allowed for the immediate suspension of the agreement; the clause in all other agreements allows for measures to be taken only after consultations.

100. *Agence Europe* no. 5728, 13 May 1992. This affected the first three associates too: in November 1992, the Commission imposed safeguard measures on steel tube imports from Czechoslovakia, Hungary and Poland. *Agence Europe* no. 5860, 19 November 1992.

101. *Agence Europe* no. 5831, 8 October 1992.

102. 'Textiles and Agriculture Stunt Association Accord Progress', *European Report* no. 1805, 21 October 1992.

103. *Agence Europe* no. 5859, 18 November 1992 and no. 5885, 23 December 1992. Greek-Bulgarian relations in 1992 were strained, over Bulgaria's recognition of Macedonia in January 1992. Although it had hinted that Bulgaria's relations with the EC could be disrupted, Greece did not block the Europe agreement. Kjell Engelbrekt, 'Greek-Bulgarian Relations: A Disharmonious Friendship', *RFE/RL Research Report*, vol. 2, no. 28, 9 July 1993, p. 30.

104. *EC Bulletin* no. 1/2, 1993, pt. 1.3.9, and no. 3, 1993, pt. 1.3.8. Both agreements contain an extra safeguard clause for steel products, permitting either party to impose QRs for five years.

105. In July 1992, the Commission proposed changing the procedure: it, rather than the Council, would take the final decision, which the Council could overturn by a qualified majority vote. France, Italy and Spain supported the proposal; the northern member states worried that it would increase protectionism. *Agence Europe* no. 5888, 30 December 1992. In February 1994, the Council decided that it would retain the power to take final decisions, but that it would decide by simple majority. *Agence Europe* no. 6166, 9 February 1994.

106. *EC Bulletin* no. 10, 1993, pt. 1.3.13; *Agence Europe* no. 6105, 10 November 1993 and no. 6123, 8 December 1993. Italy has been blamed for holding up the agreement, but several member states did not want to create a precedent for future decisionmaking on antidumping measures and forced the issue in the Bulgarian case. Bulgaria had relatively few 'friends' in the Community.

107. See Marc Maresceau, 'Les Accords Européens: Analyse Générale', *Revue du Marché Commun et de l'Union Européenne*, no. 369, June 1993 and Claude-Pierre Lucron, 'Contenu et Portée des Accords entre la Communauté et la Hongrie, la Pologne et la Tchécoslovaquie', *Revue du Marché Commun*, no. 357, April 1992.

108. The association councils have met yearly since the Europe agreements entered into force and have generally covered progress in integrating the associate into the EU.

109. Political matters are discussed informally in meetings with other associates; many bilateral dialogues are based on troika, rather than full Council, meetings. The dialogues with other regional groupings take place yearly or every 18 months, with all ministers; meetings with the ministerial troika are also held. The transatlantic declaration provides for more regular consultations at all levels. See Jörg Monar, 'Political Dialogue with Third Countries and Regional Political Groupings: The Fifteen as an Attractive Interlocutor', in Regelsberger, de Schoutheete de Tervarent and Wessels, eds, *Foreign Policy of the European Union*.

110. And Bulgaria and Romania have been particularly concerned about the imposition of an EU-wide visa requirement for their nationals in 1995. None of the other East European associates is subject to this requirement.

111. While there has been agreement 'in principle' to open EU programmes to participation by the associates, it has proved difficult to do so. Only in April 1995 did the Council sign protocols permitting participation in Community framework programmes, specific programmes and projects. But disagreements continued through 1997 over financing the associates' participation and whether they could sit on the management committees.

112. See *Agence Europe* no. 5545, 31 July 1991 and Lucron, 'Contenu et Portée', p. 298.

6 INTEGRATION

1. Eurostat, 'Statistics in Focus', no. 3, 1995.
2. Commission of the European Communities, 'Europe and the Challenge of Enlargement', *EC Bulletin Supplement* 3/92.
3. Commission of the European Communities, 'Towards a Closer Association with the Countries of Central and Eastern Europe', SEC (92) 2301 final, 2 December 1992.
4. Paul Ames, 'EC Nations Welcome Closer Links with Eastern Europe, Edgy About Membership', *Associated Press*, 8 December 1992.
5. Conclusions of the Presidency, European Council in Edinburgh 11–12 December, 1992, SN 456/92, Part D.
6. 'Poor Relations', *The Economist*, 1 May 1993.
7. Commission of the European Communities, 'Towards a Closer Association with the Countries of Central and Eastern Europe', SEC (93) 648 final, 18 May 1993.
8. Lionel Barber, 'Commission Opens Doors for Eastern Europe', *The Financial Times*, 6 May 1993. The rivalry stemmed from the fact that from January 1993 to January 1995, both were in charge of different aspects of relations with Eastern Europe, as a result of the division of DG I. See 'Uncivil War in the European Community', *The Economist*, 30 January 1993.
9. Interview in Brussels, March 1996.

10. 'Council Gives Thumbs Up to Quicker Trade Access for East', *European Report* no. 1858, 12 May 1993.
11. Lionel Barber, 'EC and E Europe Progress', *The Financial Times*, 9 June 1993. Greece and Portugal were the least enthusiastic, Portugal because of the textiles concessions. 'EC Welcomes Plan for Closer East Europe Ties', *Reuter*, 10 May 1993 and *Agence Europe* no. 5997, 10 June 1993.
12. European Council Conclusions, SN 180/93, pp. 30–1. The Commission then negotiated additional protocols with the six associates incorporating the concessions; they were concluded on 20 December 1993 (OJ L25, 29 January 1994).
13. Michalski and Wallace, *The European Community*, p. 139.
14. From 1992, Russian 'peacekeepers' had been deployed in several hotspots throughout the former Soviet Union and Russia was exerting strong pressure on recalcitrant republics to join the Commonwealth of Independent States.
15. In 1992–3, the East European states began to demand NATO membership as well.
16. For example, in mid-September 1991, UK Prime Minister Major called on the EC to offer membership for the East European and Baltic states as soon as they were ready. A few days later, Mitterrand argued that the Community should be reinforced before it grew larger. Ian Davidson and Ivo Dawnay, 'Major Urges EC to Admit East European States', *The Financial Times*, 13 September 1991 and Quentin Peel, 'Mitterrand Plea to Strengthen Community', *The Financial Times*, 20 September 1991.
17. The Community would instead conclude 'partnership and cooperation' agreements with them. *EC Bulletin* no. 3, 1992, pts 1.3.5, 1.3.11–12. Agreements have since been signed with almost all of the CIS members.
18. One 1993 study estimated that admitting the Visegrad countries would add 26 billion ECUs to the structural funds budget (almost half of the entire EU budget); 1992–3 estimates on additional CAP spending for the Visegrad countries range from 2.4 to 40.4 billion ECUs. Susan Senior Nello and Karen E. Smith, *The Consequences of Eastern Enlargement of the European Union in Stages*, Robert Schuman Centre Working Paper no. 97/51 (Florence: European University Institute, 1997).
19. Stanley Hoffmann maintains that Mitterrand's opposition to enlargement was caused by an obsession with German power. In 'French Dilemmas and Strategies in the New Europe', in Robert Keohane, Joseph Nye and Stanley Hoffmann, eds, *After the Cold War: International Institutions and State Strategies, 1989–1991* (Cambridge: Harvard University Press, 1993), p. 140.
20. As Richard Baldwin notes in *Towards an Integrated Europe* (London: Centre for Economic Policy Research, 1994), p. 187.
21. In October 1993, he suggested that the Council of Europe become the confederation, with annual summits, regular ministerial meetings, and a permanent secretariat. Marcel Scotto and Claire Tréan, 'M. Mitterrand relance l'idée d'une confédération européenne', *Le Monde*, 10–11 October 1993.
22. 'Mitterrand: Confederazione Tra Est e Cee', *Il Sole 24 Ore*, 13 June 1991. Such cooperation was already on course. Since 1990, several

meetings of European environment ministers have been held. Following on from a 1990 proposal by Dutch Prime Minister Ruud Lubbers, a European Energy Charter Treaty was signed in June 1994 by almost 50 countries, including the US and Russia.

23. Vaclav Havel, 'Don't Make Us Europe's Second-Class Citizens', *The European*, 14 June 1991.

24. 'Report of the Committee on Institutional Affairs on the Structure and Strategy for the European Union with regard to its Enlargement and the Creation of a Europe-Wide Order', Rapporteur: Klaus Hänsch, Document A3-0189/92, 21 May 1992.

25. Holger Schmieding, 'The EFTA Option for Eastern Europe: Comecon and the Community', *The Financial Times*, 2 August 1989. See also Palankai, *The European Community*, pp. 20–2. Richard Baldwin noted that there have been three stages in European integration: the common market, the Single European Act and the Maastricht Treaty. Prospective members were being asked to jump right to the third stage; joining the single market first would be a better alternative. Baldwin, *Towards*, Chapter 9.

26. See Körmendy, 'The Hungarian View', pp. 251–2.

27. Frans Andriessen, 'Towards a Community of Twenty-Four', speech to the 69th Plenary Assembly of Eurochambers, Brussels, 19 April 1991, Rapid Database Speech/91/41.

28. *Agence Europe* no. 5482, 29–30 April 1991.

29. Partial membership 'would cause the Union to unravel as an entity and would only further institutional proliferation with all its negative effects.' Mathias Jopp, *The Strategic Implications of European Integration*, Adelphi Paper no. 290 (London: Brassey's, 1994), p. 70.

30. See Andrew Marshall, 'UK Faces Life on the Outside Looking In', *The Independent*, 26 September 1992; 'Pressing On', *The Economist*, 3 October 1992; and the interview with Mitterrand in *The Financial Times*, 9 December 1992.

31. This issue is not new by any means. See Helen Wallace with Adam Ridley, *Europe: The Challenge of Diversity* (London: Routledge and Kegan Paul, 1985), written at a time when the Community was contemplating institutional reform and moving towards enlargement to Spain and Portugal.

32. Redmond, 'The Wider Europe', p. 221.

33. The Commission takes part in political dialogue. In the case of Eastern Europe, the dialogue inevitably covered EC issues, such as economic relations and enlargement. Likewise, during the Commission's meetings with East European politicians, political issues were discussed: in April 1993, for example, van den Broek discussed the situation in the former Yugoslavia with the Bulgarian and Romanian governments. *EC Bulletin* no. 4, 1993, pts 1.3.12 and 1.3.15. This again highlights the 'blurring' of the EC-EPC dividing line.

34. On 9 April 1990 the leaders of the three countries discussed their 'return to Europe'. In February 1991, they established the Visegrad group, to press for integration into the EC and other organizations.

35. In September 1991, the Commission had proposed initiating a multi-lateral political dialogue with the associates, in response to their desire to be involved in political cooperation. *EC Bulletin* no. 9, 1991, pt. 1.3.13.
36. *EC Bulletin* no. 5, 1992, pt. 1.2.17.
37. 'Europe and the Challenge of Enlargement'.
38. Article O states that any European state may apply for EU membership; article F proclaims that the governments of member states are founded on the principle of democracy and that the Union is to respect fundamental human rights.
39. Michalski and Wallace, *The European Community*, p. 54.
40. 'Conclusions of the Presidency at the European Council in Lisbon, 26 and 27 June 1992', in *EC Bulletin Supplement* 3/92, pp. 23–4.
41. 'Report to the European Council in Lisbon on the likely development of the common foreign and security policy (CFSP) with a view to identifying areas open to joint action vis-à-vis particular countries or groups of countries', Annex I, Conclusions of the Lisbon European Council, *EC Bulletin* no. 6, 1992, p. 20.
42. Enlargement to the EFTAns was also in doubt: the Lisbon European Council decided that enlargement to the EFTAns could not proceed until the Maastricht Treaty was ratified and the Delors-II budget package approved.
43. David Buchan, 'EC To Meet East Europe Leaders', *The Financial Times*, 21 July 1992. France also wanted all the EC leaders to attend the summit meeting, an indication perhaps of resentment of the British initiative in an area where France wanted to lead.
44. Quoted in Michalski and Wallace, *The European Community*, p. 114.
45. *Agence Europe* no. 5827, 2 October 1992.
46. 'Meeting of the Ministers of Foreign Affairs of the European Community and the Visegrad Countries – Joint Statement', Council of the European Communities Press Release 9033/92 (Presse 170), Luxembourg, 5 October 1992, p. 3. The Community promised to help the Visegrad countries with the approximation of their laws to the *acquis communautaire*, and to develop joint infrastructure projects.
47. The Gabcikovo dam dispute between Hungary and Slovakia dominated behind the scenes at the summit; see Section 7.3.3.
48. Andrew Marshall, 'EC to Improve Links with East Europe', *The Independent*, 29 October 1992.
49. 'Joint Declaration of the EC Community and its Member States and the Visegrad Group of Poland, Hungary and Czechoslovakia on Political Dialogue', European Union Press Release, 29 October 1992.
50. SEC (92) 2301 final, p. 3.
51. SEC (92) 2301 final, p. 4.
52. *Agence Europe* no. 5876, 11 December 1992.
53. Conclusions of the Presidency, SN 456/92, Part D: External Relations.
54. Austria, Sweden and Finland joined the EU on 1 January 1995; Norway declined to join after a referendum rejected membership.
55. 'Copenhagen Strikes Disappointing Chord Among East Europeans', *European Report* no. 1851, 17 April 1993.

Notes

56. 'EC/Poland – Suchocka Chastises Community Inaction', *European Report* no. 1864, 5 June 1993.
57. 'Poor Relations', *The Economist*, 1 May 1993.
58. *Agence Europe* no. 5936, 10 March 1993.
59. SEC (93) 648 final, p. 3.
60. SEC (93) 648 final, p. 2.
61. SEC (93) 648 final, p. 2. Commissioner van den Broek had pushed heavily for the creation of a European Political Area. See the interview with him in Lionel Barber and David Gardner, 'A Brief to Build Bridges', *The Financial Times*, 8 March 1993.
62. The package included trade concessions and PHARE reform. 'Copenhagen Summit Set to Endorse Substantial Package on East', *European Report* no. 1866, 12 June 1993.
63. 'Political Dialogue Remains Only Obstacle to Copenhagen Conclusion on East', *European Report* no. 1868, 19 June 1993.
64. Germany has been concerned to convince France that enlargement should occur; strengthening Franco-German cooperation, as in the 'Weimar dialogue', would help achieve that goal. The Weimar dialogue was launched at a meeting of the French, German and Polish foreign ministers in August 1991; since then, the ministers have met yearly. See Hans Stark, 'L'est de l'Europe et l'Allemagne: des rapports complexes', *Politique Étrangère*, no. 4/91, winter 1991, pp. 869–70; and Jean-Christophe Romer and Thomas Schreiber, 'La France et l'Europe Centrale', *Politique Étrangère*, no. 4/95, winter 1995. The French and German foreign ministers have also met with their counterpart in Romania (traditionally close to France).
65. Conclusions of the Presidency, SN 180/93, p. 13.
66. Whether the associates accept the aims of political union is also a subjective decision, as 'political union' remains undefined.
67. Conclusions of the Presidency, SN 180/93, p. 12. The European Council also called for free trade agreements with the three Baltic states, to replace the trade and cooperation agreements. The agreements were signed on 18 July 1994 and entered into force on 1 January 1995. *EC Bulletin* no. 12, 1994, pts. 1.3.37–43.
68. Péter Balázs, *The EU's Collective Regional Approach to its Eastern Enlargement: Consequences and Risks*, CORE Working Paper 1/1997 (Copenhagen: Copenhagen Research Project on European Integration, 1997), pp. 11–21.
69. A Polish request to participate in the IGC was rebuffed: Commission President Jacques Santer said only EU member states can take part. *Agence Europe* no. 6457, 7 April 1995.
70. Douglas Hurd and Klaus Kinkel, 'Welcome to our Eastern Cousins', *The Times*, 26 April 1994.
71. John Major, 'Raise Your Eyes, There is a Land Beyond', *The Economist*, 25 September 1993.
72. *Agence Europe* no. 6265, 2 July 1994.
73. Andrew Marshall, 'EU Drives East Towards a "Greater Europe"', *The Independent*, 29 January 1994.
74. Interview with Sir Leon Brittan in *Le Monde*, 14 April 1994.

75. Andrew Marshall, 'Germany Pushes Cause of Eastern Neighbours', *The Independent*, 19 July 1994.
76. Andrew Marshall, 'Central Europe Lines up to Board the Brussels Bandwagon', *The Independent*, 21 March 1994, and 'Southward Swing', *The Economist*, 14 January 1995. The EFTAn enlargement heightened these concerns. This is partly why Greece was also pushing for enlargement to Cyprus. The June 1994 Corfu European Council agreed that Cyprus and Malta would be included in the next phase of enlargement. The December 1994 Essen European Council also agreed that the EU would launch a 'Euro-Mediterranean partnership'.
77. Tom Buerkle, 'For Spain, the EU is All About Money', *International Herald Tribune*, 10 July 1995.
78. On terminology, see Claus-Dieter Ehlermann, *Increased Differentiation or Stronger Uniformity*, EUI Working Paper RSC no. 95/21 (Florence: European University Institute, 1995), and Helen Wallace and William Wallace, *Flying Together in a Larger and More Diverse European Union*, Working Document 87 (The Hague: Netherlands Scientific Council for Government Policy, 1995).
79. Nino Andreatta, 'Una Politica Estera per l'Italia', *Il Mulino*, no. 5, September–October 1993, p. 888.
80. 'Back to the Drawing-Board', *The Economist*, 10 September 1994.
81. Stephen Kinzer, 'German Plan for Phased Union of Europe Provokes Controversy', *The New York Times*, 4 September 1994.
82. Lionel Barber, 'Opportunity for Fine-Tuning', *The Financial Times*, 10 May 1995.
83. Conclusions of the Presidency, in *EC Bulletin* no. 6, 1994, pt. I.13.
84. Commission documents: 'The Europe Agreements and Beyond: A Strategy to Prepare the Countries of Central and Eastern Europe for Accession', COM (94) 320 final, 13 July 1994, and 'Follow Up to Commission Communication on "The Europe Agreements and Beyond: A Strategy to Prepare the Countries of Central and Eastern Europe for Accession"', COM (94) 361 final, 27 July 1994.
85. One Polish official complained, 'The EC's concessions are rather modest and far short of expectations.' Boris Johnson, 'Eastern Recruits Cool Over EC Status', *The Daily Telegraph*, 2 February 1994.
86. European Commission, 'Trade and Aid in Relations Between the European Union, the Countries of Central and Eastern Europe and the Countries of the Commonwealth of Independent States', MG/PRH/FW/vf, 9 June 1994. Commissioner van den Broek also argued that tariff quotas had not been fully used up by East European exporters. Interview in The Philip Morris Institute for Public Policy Research, *Is the West Doing Enough for Eastern Europe?*, November 1994, p. 45.
87. Günter Burghardt and Fraser Cameron, 'The Next Enlargement of the European Union', *European Foreign Affairs Review*, vol. 2, no. 1, 1997, p. 13. The most problematic areas will be the *acquis* on social and environmental policy, as has been widely noted. Less noted is that the acceding countries will, in all probability, join the EU when some member states have reached stage three of EMU. Part of the *acquis* will

include the obligations of stage two, including fiscal discipline and liberalization of capital movements, which may be difficult for the new member states to meet. See Senior Nello and Smith, *Consequences*. The *acquis* will also include provisions on justice and home affairs, and the East European states are expected to strengthen their external borders and adopt EU immigration policies. Ian Traynor, 'Fortress Europe shuts window to the East', *The Guardian*, 9 February 1998.

88. *Agence Europe* no. 6366, 28–9 November 1994.
89. Presidency Conclusions, SN 300/94, p. 3.
90. On 7 February 1994, the Council and Commission had stated that Europe agreements would be negotiated with the three Baltic states as soon as possible. *EU Bulletin* no. 1/2, 1994, pt. 1.3.40. Negotiations formally opened in December 1994; the agreements were signed on 12 June 1995. The Europe agreement with Slovenia was held up by Italian objections over the rights of ethnic Italians in Slovenia and the property rights of Italians who left Yugoslavia after World War II. Negotiations began in March 1995; the agreement was initialled on 15 June 1995, but not signed until 10 June 1996. Upon entry into force of the agreement, EU citizens who have lived in Slovenia for three years will be able to acquire real estate. Other EU nationals will be able to do so four years later.
91. See Balázs, *The EU's Collective Regional Approach*, pp. 11–14.
92. COM (94) 361 final, 27 July 1994, pp. 6–7. France, Spain and Portugal initially opposed the initiative. Lionel Barber, 'EU to Tackle Blueprint for Enlargement', *The Financial Times*, 28 November 1994. Between 1992 and 1994, the Community initiated only two anti-dumping cases (on steel products), and activated the safeguard clauses twice (on steel and cherries). 'The Economic Interpenetration between the European Union and Eastern Europe', *European Economy*, no. 6, 1994, pp. 163–70.
93. Baldwin notes that the Europe agreements set up a 'hub-and-spoke bilateralism' which marginalizes the 'spoke' (East European) economies. Because trade between the East European countries is not as liberalized as that with the 'hub' (the Community), East-East trade is hindered, and investment thus discouraged. Baldwin, *Towards*, pp. 133–6.
94. This would mean that goods made or assembled in several associated countries would still benefit from preferential trade access. French and Portuguese manufacturers were concerned that such moves would lead to job losses. Lionel Barber, 'EU to Amend Origin Rules', *The Financial Times*, 2 December 1994. The associates were not thrilled with the proposal either.
95. The White Paper was published in May 1995, after consultation with the associates. 'Preparation of the associated countries of Central and Eastern Europe for integration into the internal market of the Union', COM (95) 163 final, 3 May 1995.
96. Burghardt and Cameron, 'Next Enlargement', pp. 18–19.
97. As van den Broek noted in the interview in *Is the West Doing Enough For Eastern Europe?*, p. 43.

98. *Agence Europe* no. 6119, 2 December 1993 and no. 6246, 8 June 1994.
99. They discussed the proposed Pact for Stability (see Chapter 7), relations with Russia, the situation in the former Yugoslavia, and minority rights issues. *EC Bulletin* no. 9, 1993, pt. 1.3.7 and *Agence Europe* no. 6069, 22 September 1993.
100. The initiative follows closely on a Franco-German proposal to offer the associates some form of association with the WEU (see Chapter 7). Andreatta had first mentioned the proposal to German Foreign Minister Klaus Kinkel, but he was more interested in pursuing initiatives with France. Interviews in Rome, July 1995.
101. The political crisis that has rocked Italy since 1992, along with its severe budget problems (whose resolution was made urgent by the EMU criteria), had sharply reduced its ability to carry out an active foreign policy; Andreatta's proposal was thus a way for Italy to exercise greater leadership, relatively cheaply.
102. Text of the letter from the UK and Italian foreign ministers (Coreu).
103. The far right had just done well in Russian parliamentary elections, while there were worries that Ukraine would not dismantle its nuclear arsenal. Stephen Nisbet, 'Britain, Italy Urge Closer EC-East Europe Links', *Reuter*, 20 December 1993.
104. Andrew Marshall, 'East Pushes for Tighter Integration with EU', *The Independent*, 3 March 1994, and 'Delors Returns to Notion of Political Initiative', *European Report* no. 1926, 16 February 1994.
105. *EC Bulletin* no. 3, 1994, pt. 1.3.37 and *Agence Europe* no. 6186, 9 March 1994. The decision was taken within the CFSP context, prepared in Political Committee meetings on 17–18 January and again on 28 February–1 March 1994, but was not a joint action. Links with the third pillar were held up because cooperation within the EU on justice and home affairs was proving to be a sensitive matter.
106. There have been several joint statements (mostly on human rights) and the associates have participated in démarches on human rights and in the implementation of a joint action on the Nuclear Non-Proliferation Treaty review conference. Janis Emmanouilidis, 'The CEEC and CFSP – More Than a First Acquaintance with the Second Pillar?', *CFSP Forum*, nos. 3/4, 1996. As Barbara Lippert has noted, the associates are both the objects of a joint action (the Stability Pact) and possible participants in others. In 'Relations with Central and Eastern European Countries: The Anchor Role of the European Union', in Regelsberger, de Schoutheete de Tervarent and Wessels, eds, *Foreign Policy*, p. 210.
107. On 19 April, the troika of foreign ministers, plus van den Broek, held talks with the foreign ministers of the six associates. *EC Bulletin* no. 4, 1994, pt. 1.3.21. There was supposed to have been a meeting with the full Council the previous month, but the EFTAn membership negotiations were still in progress and the meeting had to be postponed. *Agence Europe* no. 6187, 10 March 1994.
108. COM (94) 320 final, p. 3.
109. COM (94) 361 final, pp. 1–2.
110. *Agence Europe* no. 6312, 10 September 1994 and *EC Bulletin* no. 10, 1994, pt. 1.3.20.

111. *Agence Europe* no. 6346, 28 October 1994. Coreper's prominent role would ensure consistency.
112. 'Council Agrees to Structured Dialogue and White Paper for Spring', *European Report* no. 1981, 5 October 1994.
113. Andrew Marshall, 'German Plan to Reach Out to Central Europe Triggers Row with EU Partners', *The Independent*, 5 October 1994.
114. *Agence Europe* no. 6329, 5 October 1994.
115. 'Essence of Essen', *The Economist*, 3 December 1994; *Agence Europe* no. 6366, 28–9 November 1994.
116. Coreper will prepare the sectoral meetings; ambassadors could jointly prepare foreign ministers meetings. Coreper is to ensure the horizontal coherence of the dialogue. Presidency Conclusions, SN 300/94, Annex IV, pp. 9–10.
117. The invitation was late in reaching the associates, however. Some observers say that reservations from London and Paris caused the uncertainty. Others point out that the southern member states were complaining about the neglect of Mediterranean economic and security issues. *Agence Europe* no. 6364, 25 November 1994 and Tony Barber, 'Norway Shows the Way for EU Doubters', *The Independent*, 30 November 1994.
118. Since the Essen European Council, the Council has reported twice a year to the European Council on the development of relations with the East European countries, including the structured relationship. The reports are usually annexed to the European Council Presidency Conclusions, published in the *EU Bulletin*.
119. As Nuttall warns in *European Political Co-operation*, p. 321.
120. On 27 February 1996, the EU and associates' foreign ministers decided to improve the structured relationship. A planning framework would be established for meetings spanning two presidencies; discussion topics for sectoral meetings would be specified. The Commission would prepare background documents for the meetings. Council of the European Union, General Secretariat, Press Release 4720/96 (Presse 33), 26 and 27 February 1996.
121. Emmanouilidis, 'The CEEC and CFSP', p. 17. One official in Brussels said in March 1996, however, that the EU is 'drowning in political dialogue'.
122. It also presented a report on the implementation of the pre-accession strategy, which noted that the structured relationship could be improved by concentrating on more concrete issues. Summaries of the reports are in *EC Bulletin* no. 11, 1995, pts. 1.4.46–8. See also *Agence Europe* no. 6616, 30 November 1995.
123. 'Just Do It', *The Economist*, 15 July 1995.
124. Henri de Bresson and Jan Krauze, 'M. Chirac prône à Varsovie l'entrée de la Pologne dans l'Union européenne "dès l'an 2000"', *Le Monde*, 13 September 1996. Both promises later had to be qualified, as the Commission (among others) made it clear that 2000 was an unrealistic deadline. The declarations on Poland reflect in particular the strength of the 'Weimar triangle' linking France, Germany and Poland since 1991.

125. Conclusions of the Presidency, Madrid European Council, 15 and 16 December 1995, *EU Bulletin* no. 12, 1995, pt. I.25.
126. In April 1996, the Commission sent questionnaires to the East European countries requesting information on their progress in adapting to the *acquis communautaire*. The replies were received at the end of July 1996. (Slovenia was included in this although it applied only in June 1996.)
127. Conclusions of the Presidency, Florence European Council, 21–2 June 1996, *EU Bulletin* no. 6, 1996, pt. I.9. Malta's new government, in office since November 1996, decided not to pursue its application for EU membership.
128. Poland was disappointed that the Madrid European Council did not signal that the Czech Republic, Hungary and Poland headed the accession queue. *Agence Europe* no. 6630, 18–19 December 1995.
129. See Senior Nello and Smith, *The Consequences*.
130. See Kirsty Hughes, *Eastward Enlargement of the EU: EU Strategy and Future Challenges*, European Programme Working Paper no. 2 (London: Royal Institute of International Affairs, 1996), p. 6.
131. Hugh Carnegy, 'Baltics May Have to Take "Second Best"', *The Financial Times*, 22 November 1996.
132. On these proposals, see: Danish Institute of International Affairs, *European Stability: EU's Enlargement with the Central and East European Countries*, report for the Danish Parliament (Copenhagen, 1997).
133. The idea had been repeatedly proposed by French Foreign Minister Hervé de Charette. The possible inclusion of Turkey in the Conference was not welcomed by all ministers. *Agence Europe* no. 6936, 17–18 March 1997.
134. Quoted in Tom Buerkle, 'EU Confirms Turkey's Right to Join, but Not Now', *International Herald Tribune*, 17 March 1997. Yet Germany (along with Greece) was the most reluctant to let Turkey participate in the Conference. 'How to Say No', *The Economist*, 1 November 1997.
135. See the Commission Opinion, 'Reinforcing Political Union and Preparing for Enlargement', COM (96) 90 final, 20 February 1996.
136. 'Mountains Still to Climb', *The Economist*, 21 June 1997 and Victor Smart, 'Enlargement Opens a Can of Worms', *The European*, 19–25 June 1997.
137. Presidency Conclusions, Amsterdam European Council, 16–17 June 1997.
138. European Commission, 'Agenda 2000', COM (97) 2000, 15 July 1997. It is composed of three parts: '1. For a Stronger and Wider Union'; '2. The Challenge of Enlargement'; and '3. The Opinions of the European Commission on the Applications for Accession: Summaries and Conclusions'.
139. 'Agenda 2000', part 1, p. 6. That six countries (five East European countries and Cyprus) were recommended for membership contrasts with the Amsterdam Treaty protocol on the institutions and enlargement. If all six were to join, an IGC would have to be convened sooner than if only five did so.
140. Lionel Barber and Michael Smith, 'EU Enlargement Plan Costs Attacked', *The Financial Times*, 16 September 1997.

141. This proposal was controversial. The Commission, which usually decides by consensus, took a vote on three options. Talks would be opened only with the Czech Republic, Hungary and Poland (the option supported by Santer); or with these three plus Estonia and Slovenia; or with all the applicant countries. Van den Broek pushed for adding Estonia and Slovenia to the three 'frontrunners' and only just won the argument. 'Eastward Ho, They Said Warily', *The Economist*, 19 July 1997, and Franco Papitto, 'Via Libera all'Europa dei Ventuno', *La Repubblica*, 16 July 1997.
142. All new member states must be able to apply the *acquis* upon accession, or following reasonable transition periods. The other applicant countries were farther behind in meeting the economic conditions. Only Slovakia was judged not to have satisfied the political conditions.
143. Lionel Barber, 'Row Threatens EU Enlargement Plans', *The Financial Times*, 15 September 1997 and David Evans, 'EU Farm Ministers Get First Bite at Reforms', *Reuter*, 5 September 1997.
144. Janet McEvoy, 'Differences Burst into Open on EU Enlargement', *Reuter*, 22 July 1997.
145. Sarah Helm, 'EC Holds Hand Out as States Make Grade', *The Independent*, 17 July 1997.
146. Presidency Conclusions, Luxembourg European Council, 12 and 13 December 1997, p. 2.
147. See Michael Smith, 'The European Union and a Changing Europe: Establishing the Boundaries of Order', *Journal of Common Market Studies*, vol. 34, no. 1, March 1996, pp. 18–23.

7 CONFLICT PREVENTION

1. Gabriel Munuera, *Preventing Armed Conflict in Europe: Lessons from Recent Experience*, Chaillot Paper 15/16 (Paris: Western European Union Institute for Security Studies, 1994), p. 3.
2. There have been internal conflicts (Northern Ireland, the Basque country) and disputes between member states (over Gibraltar), but no inter-state violent conflicts.
3. Zielonka, *Security*, p. 5.
4. A report by several research institutes asserted that 'it is economic success or failure that will determine the fate of the new democracies.' Falk Bomsdorf, et al., *Confronting Insecurity in Eastern Europe: Challenges for the European Community* (London: Royal Institute of International Affairs, 1992), p. 21.
5. 'EC-US Statement on Peaceful and Democratic Transformation in the East', EPC press release P.111/91, 9 November 1991.
6. Jenonne Walker, 'European Regional Organizations and Ethnic Conflict', in Regina Cowen Karp, ed., *Central and Eastern Europe: The Challenge of Transition* (Oxford: Oxford University Press, 1993), p. 45.
7. Jopp, *Strategic Implications*, p. 67.

8. Jacques Delors, 'European Unification and European Security', in *European Security after the Cold War Part I*, Adelphi Paper no. 284 (London: Brassey's, 1994), p. 11.
9. Delors, 'European Unification', p. 9.
10. The report is in Annex I, Lisbon European Council Presidency Conclusions, in *EC Bulletin* no. 6, 1992, pt. I.31.
11. In September 1995, for example, NATO made the resolution of intrastate disputes a condition for membership. This would clearly be an additional strong factor favouring conflict prevention.
12. Presidency Conclusions, Luxembourg European Council, 28–9 June 1991, Annex V, *EC Bulletin* no. 6, 1991, p. 18.
13. Reinhardt Rummel, 'The CFSP's Conflict Prevention Policy', in Martin Holland, ed., *Common Foreign and Security Policy: The Record and Reforms* (London: Pinter, 1997), p. 107.
14. See Renée de Nevers, 'Democratization and Ethnic Conflict', *Survival*, vol. 35, no. 2, Summer 1993. She suggests that to try to prevent ethnic conflict during democratization, the international community should emphasize the need to protect group rights (p. 46).
15. EPC press release P.111/91.
16. Munuera, *Preventing Armed Conflict*, p. 104.
17. The Community had not insisted so much on minority rights before. The June 1991 Luxembourg European Council stressed 'the need to protect human rights whether or not the persons concerned belong to minorities.' Presidency Conclusions, Annex V, *EC Bulletin* no. 6, 1991, p. 17.
18. Jopp, *Strategic Implications*, pp. 58–9.
19. Merritt, *Eastern Europe*, pp. 23–4.
20. Uvin, '"Do As I Say"', p. 68.
21. As Georg Sorensen argues in 'Introduction', in Sorensen, ed., *Political Conditionality*, p. 4.
22. See Lawrence Whitehead, 'Democracy by Convergence and Southern Europe: A Comparative Perspective' and Geoffrey Pridham, 'The Politics of the European Community, Transnational Networks and Democratic Transition in Southern Europe', in Geoffrey Pridham, ed., *Encouraging Democracy: The International Context of Regime Transition in Southern Europe* (Leicester: Leicester University Press, 1991).
23. Pridham, 'Politics', p. 243.
24. See Uvin, '"Do As I Say"', p. 70.
25. Munuera, *Preventing Armed Conflict*, pp. 79–83.
26. This mirrors the clash between the economic containment and interdependence approaches discussed in Section 2.3. Both approaches concentrate on generating reform 'from above'. But the revolutions of 1989 were driven 'from below'. Timothy Garton Ash makes this point in relation to West Germany's *Ostpolitik*, in Garton Ash, *In Europe's Name*, pp. 203–15.
27. Adrian Bridge, 'Bulgaria Torn by Row Over Kremlin Alliance', *The Independent*, 1 April 1996.
28. Bulgaria was also a problem case. Former communists had ruled Bulgaria since 1990; in December 1996, a reformist won the presidential

elections. Following public protests about corruption and the poor state of the economy, parliamentary elections were held early, in April 1997 and resulted in a defeat for the ruling Socialist party. But Bulgaria's relations with its neighbours have been relatively unproblematic. Official persecution of ethnic Turks ended with the toppling of the communist regime in November 1989; a good neighbour treaty was signed with Turkey in May 1992. Although Bulgaria does not acknowledge 'Macedonian' as a nationality, it was the first country to recognize FYROM (on 16 January 1992). The need for Western approval contributed to these developments.

29. Alfred Reisch, 'Meciar and Slovakia's Hungarian Minority', *RFE/RL Research Report*, vol. 1, no. 43, 30 October 1992. From February 1992, the CSCE High Commissioner for National Minorities sent observers to Slovakia (and Hungary, where there are an estimated 100,000 ethnic Slovaks). Munuera, *Preventing Armed Conflict*, p. 16.

30. Alfred Reisch, 'The Difficult Search for a Hungarian-Slovak Accord', *RFE/RL Research Report*, vol. 1, no. 42, 23 October 1992. Hungary's attitude on the minorities issue has not always been constructive, particularly under the Antall government (1990–4): it argued that it has a special obligation towards Hungarians living outside Hungary. 'Minorities: That Other Europe', *The Economist*, 25 December–7 January 1994, and Edith Oltay, 'Minorities as Stumbling Block in Relations with Neighbors', *RFE/RL Research Report*, vol. 1, no. 19, 8 May 1992.

31. Sharon Fisher, 'Turning Back?', *Transition*, vol. 1, no. 1, 30 January 1995, p. 62. Although no government had been formed after elections on 1 October 1994, Meciar's party and two small parties formed a voting bloc and took over the broadcast media and intelligence service and ousted the privatization minister.

32. Peter Javurek, 'US, EU Formally Express Disquiet on Slovak Turmoil', *Reuter*, 25 October 1995. The concern stemmed from the prime minister's suspected involvement in the kidnapping of the president's son.

33. *Agence Europe*, 18 November 1995, and 'Madness', *The Economist*, 2 December 1995. The EP was reacting to Meciar's attempts to expel an opposition party from parliament.

34. 'Nice New Friends', *The Economist*, 21 December 1996; *Agence Europe* no. 6922, 26 February 1997. The EU has urged Slovakia to approve a law on the use of minority languages.

35. 'Tongue-tied', *The Economist*, 13 September 1997.

36. European Commission, 'Agenda 2000: 3. The Opinions of the European Commission on the Applications for Accession. Summaries and Conclusions', COM (97) 2000, 16 July 1997.

37. Since 1993, Slovakia has signed dozens of agreements with Russia. 'The Visegrad Three ...', *The Economist*, 9 March 1996.

38. This was apparently because in Slovakia there was a marked deterioration. Because Romania is so much further behind (economically and politically) and further away (geographically), expectations for it are lower; it would not have joined the EU in the first enlargement eastwards, whereas Slovakia might have.

39. 'Getting Nastier', *The Economist*, 4 February 1995.
40. The Romanian government distributed a book blaming Hungarians for atrocities committed during the 1989 revolution and passed an education bill that limited minority language rights (which was condemned by the EP in July 1995). See Adrian Bridge, 'Romania Set for New Row with Hungary', *The Independent*, 26 August 1995 and 'Romania Slams EU Over Gypsy Resolution', *Reuter*, 18 July 1995.
41. 'Paris, Bonn Remind Romania of EU Entry Conditions', *Reuter*, 18 July 1995.
42. European Commission, 'PHARE Programme and Contract Information 1995: Multi-country and Cross-border Programmes no. 1', pp. 20–1.
43. 'PHARE Annual Report 1993', p. 52.
44. European Commission, 'PHARE Programme and Contract Information 1995: Multi-country and Cross-border Programmes no. 2', pp. 34–6.
45. *Final Report: Evaluation of the PHARE and TACIS Democracy Programme 1992–1997*, prepared by ISA Consult, Sussex University European Institute, and GSW Europe (Brighton and Hamburg, 1997).
46. Bomsdorf, et al., *Confronting Insecurity*, p. 9.
47. Elfriede Regelsberger, 'The Twelve's Dialogue with Third Countries – Progress Towards a *Communauté d'action?*', in Holland, ed., *Future*, p. 174.
48. Körmendy, 'The Hungarian View', p. 248, and Adamiec, *East-Central Europe*, pp. 24–5.
49. Milada Anna Vachudova, 'The Visegrad Four: No Alternative to Cooperation?', *RFE/RL Research Report*, vol. 2, no. 34, 27 August 1993.
50. 'PHARE Annual Report 1991', p. 5 and p. 9. In December 1991, a regional coordination group was established among the recipients' national aid coordinators, which was to evaluate proposals and agree on the sectors to which aid should be allocated. 'PHARE Annual Report 1992', pp. 10–11.
51. 'PHARE Annual Report 1994', pp. 11–12. The programme resulted from a December 1992 Commission proposal and a 1993 EP request; a pilot PHARE programme began in 1993.
52. 'PHARE Annual Report 1993', p. 52.
53. 'Concrete Heads', *The Economist*, 16 September 1995. On relations among the Visegrad countries, see George Kolankiewicz, 'Consensus and Competition in the Eastern Enlargement of the European Union', *International Affairs*, vol. 70, no. 3, 1994.
54. Frans Andriessen, Speech at the UK Presidency Conference, 'Europe and the World After 1992', London 7 September 1992.
55. 'Report of the Commission to the Council on the Promotion of Intra-regional Cooperation and "Bon Voisinage"', prepared for the General Affairs Council of 6–7 March 1995, p. 1.
56. Jopp, *Strategic Implications*, p. 56. See also Lippert, 'Relations', pp. 211–14.
57. *EC Bulletin* no. 4, 1994, pt. 1.3.21.
58. Interviews in Brussels, March 1996.

59. The report is in *EC Bulletin* no. 6, 1992, pt. I.31.
60. Presidency Conclusions, Essen European Council, SN 300/94, Annex IV, pp. 24–5.
61. 'Agenda 2000' part 1, p. 59, and part 3.
62. *Agence Europe* no. 5755, 22–3 June 1992.
63. *EC Bulletin* no. 6, 1992, pt. I.17.
64. Jenonne Walker contends that the EC made a Czech-Slovak customs union a precondition for continued association. In 'International Mediation of Ethnic Conflicts', *Survival*, vol. 35, no. 1, Spring 1993, p. 110.
65. Sharon Fisher, 'Czech-Slovak Relations Two Years After the Elections', *RFE/RL Research Report*, vol. 3, no. 27, 8 July 1994, p. 11.
66. In December 1991, the Community and the member states adopted criteria for recognizing new states in Eastern Europe, which included respect for the rule of law, democracy and human rights and guarantees for the rights of ethnic and national minorities. 'Declaration on the "Guidelines on the Recognition of New States in Eastern Europe and in the Soviet Union"', EPC Press Release P.128/91, 16 December 1991. These go well beyond international law standards for recognizing statehood.
67. The Gabcikovo dam dispute had been defused (see Section 7.3.3), but the issue of the Hungarian minority in Slovakia was still problematic.
68. Originally the Quadrangolare, then Pentagonale, then Hexagonale (as more states joined), this was an attempt by then Italian Foreign Minister Gianni De Michelis to increase Italy's presence in Eastern Europe. The initiative was to complement Community policy. Sergio Romano has argued that the undeclared aim was to prevent East European countries from falling completely under German influence. Sergio Romano, *Guida alla Politica Estera Italiana: Dal Crollo del Fascismo al Crollo del Comunismo* (Milan: Rizzoli, 1993), p. 205. See also Vojtech Mastny, ed., *Italy and East-Central Europe: Dimensions of the Regional Relationship* (Boulder: Westview, 1995).
69. Conclusions of the Presidency, Florence European Council, 21–2 June 1996, *EU Bulletin*, pt. I.14; European Commission, 'Report from the Commission to the Council on European Union Cooperation with the Central European Initiative (CEI)', COM (96) 601 final, 4 December 1996.
70. European Commission, 'Report on the Current State of and Perspectives for Cooperation in the Baltic Sea Region', COM (96) 609 final/3, 21 February 1996; *EU Bulletin* no. 10, 1994, pt. 1.3.21.
71. Andrzej Podraza, *The Western European Union and Central Europe: A New Relationship*, RIIA Discussion Paper no. 41 (London: Royal Institute of International Affairs, 1992), pp. 28–9.
72. See 'Rome Declaration on Peace and Cooperation, Issued by the Heads of State and Government Participating in the Meeting of the North Atlantic Council in Rome on 7–8 November 1991' in *NATO Review*, vol. 39, no. 6, December 1991.
73. In an attempt to rationalize the membership of the EU, WEU and NATO, three kinds of WEU membership were then created: full

membership (Greece became a member); associate membership, for those NATO members that are not EU members (Turkey, Iceland and Norway); and observers, for those EU members unwilling to become full WEU members (Ireland, Denmark, Austria, Finland and Sweden).
74. *Agence Europe* no. 5755, 22–3 June 1992.
75. At the time, the Community was negotiating only trade and cooperation agreements with the Baltic states. They were included in the Forum of Consultation to give them a greater sense of external security vis-à-vis Russia.
76. Podraza, *Western European Union*, p. 29.
77. Willem Van Eekelen, 'WEU Prepares the Way for New Missions', *NATO Review*, vol. 41, no. 5, October 1993, p. 21.
78. *Agence Europe* no. 5755, 22–3 June 1992.
79. Jopp, *Strategic Implications*, p. 31. In 1992, the WEU and NATO separately declared their willingness to support UN or CSCE peace-keeping missions; both were monitoring the UN embargo on the former Yugoslavia in the Adriatic. Their rivalry stemmed from the fact that some states (notably France) preferred to develop the WEU as Europe's primary defense organization, while others preferred NATO. Relations improved by the fall of 1992, when formal mechanisms of cooperation were agreed.
80. See 'Partnership for Peace: Invitation', *NATO Review*, vol. 42, no. 1, February 1994, p. 28.
81. Jopp, *Strategic Implications*, pp. 50–1.
82. 'Réunion des ministres des affaires étrangères d'Allemagne, de Pologne et de France – Déclaration commune' (Warsaw, 12 November 1993), in *La Politique Étrangère de la France: Textes et Documents*, November-December 1993 (Paris: French Foreign Ministry), pp. 64–5.
83. Jopp, *Strategic Implications*, pp. 51–2.
84. Turkey, an associate member, reportedly also objected to the idea. *Agence Europe* no. 6113, 24 November 1993. It certainly does complicate even further the variable geometry of membership in European organizations.
85. 'WEU Opens up to East Europe', *European Report* no. 1949, 12 May 1994. France at this stage would naturally have supported a WEU initiative over a NATO one.
86. Western European Union, 'Kirchberg Declaration', 9 May 1994. This was two months after the political dialogue with the associates had been strengthened (see Chapter 5). After Slovenia signed a Europe agreement, it became an associate partner, on 25 June 1996.
87. *Agence Europe* no. 5230, 14 May 1994.
88. There had been talk about requiring the Baltic states to declare their neutrality as a condition for concluding Europe agreements, but this was dropped. Andrew Marshall, 'Neutrality Price of Baltic Entry', *The Independent*, 31 October 1994.
89. The risk arises even with EU enlargement: the new member states could push for a tougher EU stance vis-à-vis Russia.
90. Munuera, *Preventing Armed Conflict*, p. 7.

91. For background on the dispute, see Vera Rich, 'Central Europe II: The Battle of the Danube', *The World Today*, vol. 48, no. 2, December 1992 and 'The Murky Politics of the Danube', *The World Today*, vol. 49, nos. 8–9, August–September 1993.

92. Sharon Fisher, 'The Gabcikovo-Nagymaros Dam Controversy Continues', *RFE/RL Research Report*, vol. 2, no. 37, 17 September 1993, p. 8.

93. Nicholas Denton and Ariane Genillard, 'Hungary Stokes Bitter Row Over Danube Dam', *The Financial Times*, 20 May 1992.

94. See Tony Barber, 'Danube Dam Splits Nations', *The Independent*, 9 January 1993, and Nicholas Denton and Anthony Robinson, 'Danube Dam Threatens to Open Floodgates of Hostility', *The Financial Times*, 29 October 1992. The Hungarian minority in Slovakia opposed the dam project, another source of tension between the Slovak government and the Hungarian minority. See Reisch, 'Meciar and Slovakia's Hungarian Minority', p. 19.

95. *Agence Europe* no. 5413, 19 January 1991.

96. Munuera, *Preventing Armed Conflict*, p. 10.

97. Karoly Okolicsanyi, 'Slovak-Hungarian Tension: Bratislava Diverts the Danube', *RFE/RL Research Report*, vol. 1, no. 49, 11 December 1992, p. 52.

98. Munuera, *Preventing Armed Conflict*, p. 11.

99. *Agence Europe* no. 5841, 21 October 1992, and 'Slovakia Delays Danube Dam Project', *The Financial Times*, 21 October 1992.

100. Lionel Barber, 'Danube Row Hits Plan to Widen EC', *The Financial Times*, 23 October 1992.

101. *Agence Europe* no. 5844, 24 October 1992 and Nicholas Denton and Ariane Genillard, 'Hungary Backed by Germany Over Dam', *The Financial Times*, 27 October 1992.

102. Anthony Robinson, 'End In Sight to Danube Dam Row', *The Financial Times*, 30 October 1992.

103. 'Tripartite Discussion on the Gabcikovo-Nagymaros System of Locks', EC Press Release IP/92/865, 29 October 1992. Czechoslovakia had not previously acknowledged the ICJ's jurisdiction.

104. Okolicsanyi, 'Slovak-Hungarian Tension', p. 53.

105. 'Czechoslovakia Told To Halt Dam', *The Financial Times*, 7 November 1992.

106. *Agence Europe* no. 5868, 30 November–1 December 1992. The agreement was signed on 21 December.

107. 'Gabcikovo Dam Talks Continue', *European Report* no. 1817, 2 December 1992.

108. Barber, 'Danube Dam Splits Nations'.

109. *Agence Europe* no. 5916, 10 February 1993.

110. 'Negotiations on Gabcikovo Dam Fail Again', *European Report* 20 February 1993.

111. *EC Bulletin* no. 1/2, 1993, pt. 1.3.13. The Visegrad-troika political dialogue meeting on 8 March would have provided another opportunity to pressure the disputants.

112. *Agence Europe* no. 5934, 6 March 1993. The Commission had suggested that two-thirds of the Danube's waters be kept in the river, allowing

one-third to be directed to the by-channel supplying the Gabcikovo power station. *Agence Europe* no. 5922, 18 February 1993.

113. *EC Bulletin* no. 3, 1993, pt. 1.3.14.
114. Ibid., pt. 1.3.15.
115. *Agence Europe* no. 5957, 8 April 1993.
116. *Agence Europe* no. 6020, 12–13 July 1993. In September 1997, the ICJ concluded that Hungary had acted improperly in suspending work on the dam. Both sides should compensate each other for whatever damage its conduct had caused, and seek a solution to the problem of water management. *European Report* no. 2255, 1 October 1997.
117. Munuera, *Preventing Armed Conflict*, p. 22. The Commission never actually threatened to delay the Europe agreement with Slovakia, although Hungary had asked it to do so. Instead, it emphasized that it would be in both countries' interests to reach an agreement. The Commission's mandates to negotiate Europe agreements with the Czech Republic and Slovakia, though, were approved on 5 April 1993, two days before the agreement to send the dispute to the ICJ.
118. Munuera, *Preventing Armed Conflict*, p. 23.
119. 'In France, Peace Plan for Europe is Outlined', *International Herald Tribune*, 16 April 1993.
120. David Buchan, 'Summit Backs Sovereign Bosnia', *The Financial Times*, 3 June 1993. Kohl's backing for the proposal may have been timed to ensure France's support for the Copenhagen European Council conclusions on enlargement.
121. David Buchan, 'New French Pact Aims to Avoid "Second Yugoslavia"', *The Financial Times*, 10 June 1993.
122. 'Helping Whom?', *The Economist*, 17 July 1993.
123. As Balladur and Mitterrand were from different parties, the Pact proposal was seen as an attempt by Balladur to try to increase the prime minister's involvement in foreign policy, thus limiting (socialist) President Mitterrand's role.
124. 'West Meets East', *The Economist*, 19 June 1993.
125. Jopp, *Strategic Implications*, p. 53 and Jonathan Eyal, 'France's False Sense of Security', *The Independent*, 27 January 1994.
126. Tom Dodd, 'Developing the Common Foreign and Security Policy', Research Paper no. 94/131, House of Commons Library, 19 December 1994, p. 12.
127. 'French Proposal for a Pact on Stability in Europe (Copenhagen, 22 June 1993)', statement translated by the Press Department of the French Embassy in London.
128. Conclusions of the Presidency, SN 180/93, pp. 16–17.
129. Council of the European Communities, General Secretariat, Press Release 7714/93 (Presse 128), 19 and 20 July 1993. Coreper (not the Political Committee) would submit the working group's proceedings to the Council. The working group would collaborate with EPC. Although Coreper 'won' this task, the CFSP machinery later took over.
130. Council of the European Communities, General Secretariat, Press Release 8907/93 (Presse 156), 4 October 1993. The Pact was then

discussed during the multilateral political dialogue with the associates, and with the US, Canadian and Russian foreign ministers. Andrew Marshall and Annika Savill, 'EC Pact to Calm Security Fears', *The Independent*, 6 October 1993.

131. Conclusions of the Presidency, Brussels European Council, 29 October 1993, *EC Bulletin* no. 10, 1993, pp. 7–8.
132. *Agence Europe* no. 6122, 6–7 December 1993, and no. 6125, 10 December 1993.
133. The long-established tradition of keeping member states' disputes off the collective agenda prevailed here.
134. Greek-Albanian relations were strained over the ethnic Greek minority in Albania. 'Border Blows', *The Economist*, 30 April 1994.
135. Annex I, Conclusions of the Presidency, Brussels European Council, 10–11 December 1993, *EC Bulletin* no. 12, 1993, p. 14.
136. Ibid.
137. Ibid., pt. I.9.
138. Council Decision 93/728/CFSP in OJ L339, 31 December 1993.
139. *Agence Europe* no. 6139, 31 December 1993. No 'operational expenditure' was entailed by the decision. The CFSP provides for two types of expenditure: administrative, met by the EC budget, and operational, met by either national contributions or the Council or Commission section of the EC budget. Who pays for joint actions was in 1994 a matter of some dispute, between member states and between the Council and EP. France, as host country, eventually agreed to pay the costs of the inaugural conference. Dodd, 'Developing', p. 7.
140. The Belgian, Greek and Germany presidencies (in 1993 and 1994) also appointed special representatives to discuss the Pact with third countries and organize the round tables. *Agence Europe* no. 6238, 27 May 1994.
141. 'Concluding Document from the Inaugural Conference for a Pact on Stability in Europe', *EU Bulletin* no. 5, 1994, p. 100.
142. The EU set up an ad hoc group of member state representatives, to form the round tables. *Agence Europe* no. 6239, 28 May 1994. The Commission chaired some round table meetings.
143. See the conference documents annexed to Council Decision 94/367/CFSP of 14 June 1994 on the continuation of the joint action, in OJ L165, 1 July 1994. The decision stipulates that expenditure relating to meetings convened by the EU would constitute administrative expenditure (charged to the EC budget), in so far as the costs exceeded those usually borne by host countries.
144. See 'Political Declaration adopted at the Conclusion of the Final Conference on the Pact on Stability in Europe and List of Good-Neighbourliness and Cooperation Agreements and Arrangements', *EU Bulletin* no. 3, 1995, p. 113.
145. *Agence Europe* no. 6236, 25 May 1994.
146. An interim assessment conference was held at the margins of the December 1994 CSCE summit in Budapest.
147. *Agence Europe* no. 6349, 3 November 1994.

148. See the Commission's report, requested by the Essen European Council, on the promotion of regional cooperation and good neighbourly relations in relation to the Pact's objectives. 'Report of the Commission to the Council on the Promotion of Intra-regional Cooperation and "Bon Voisinage"', prepared for General Affairs Council of 6–7 March 1995.
149. The CSCE has become progressively 'institutionalized', and was renamed the Organization for Security and Cooperation in Europe at its December 1994 summit in Budapest.
150. The final declaration of the Pact and a list of the agreements are in *EU Bulletin* no. 3, 1995, pt. 2.2.1.
151. Ibid., p. 112.
152. At the conference, however, Slovakian Prime Minister Meciar stated that he considered the concept of minority rights destabilizing. *Agence Europe* no. 6445, 22 March 1995.
153. Adrian Bridge, 'Slovaks Protest as their Freedoms are Whittled Away', *The Independent*, 1 April 1996.
154. 'Tongue-tied', *The Economist*, 13 September 1997.
155. 'Hungary Calls on Romania To Compromise in Talks', *Reuter*, 20 June 1995; Marie Jégo and Yves-Michel Riols, 'A Paris, le Chef de la Diplomatie Russe S'Oppose à Une Extension "Précipitée" de l'OTAN vers l'Est', *Le Monde*, 22 March 1995.
156. 'Whose Stability Pact?', *The Economist*, 18 March 1995.
157. 'Agenda 2000', part 1, p. 59.

8 EXPLAINING THE MAKING OF A FOREIGN POLICY TOWARDS EASTERN EUROPE

1. Buchan, *Europe*, p. 33.
2. Arguably, in much of the world this has always been the case, but the NATO-Warsaw Pact stand-off during the Cold War – based on the threat of nuclear annihilation – precluded much consideration of the non-military sources of insecurity.
3. See Peter Green, 'EU Membership Seen as Vital to East's Security', *International Herald Tribune*, 10 July 1997 and 'Welcome to Europe', *The Economist*, 19 July 1997.
4. See Heinz Kramer, 'The European Community's Response to the "New Eastern Europe"', *Journal of Common Market Studies*, vol. 31, no. 2, June 1993, p. 234.
5. Giles Merritt pointed out that until social security systems are reformed and state enterprises are privatized, Western aid would only subsidize inefficiency. Merritt, *Eastern Europe*, pp. 248–9.
6. See the contributions by the former Bulgarian President Zhelyu Zhelev and Polish Prime Minister Hanna Suchocka in Philip Morris Institute, *Is The West Doing Enough for Eastern Europe?*.

7. See 'Joining the Club', *The Economist*, 12 July 1997. One UK official has argued that the UK was the driving force behind EU policy towards Eastern Europe: it pushed for the Europe agreements, for trade concessions, for the Andreatta-Hurd initiative and for enlargement. Interview in London, December 1995.
8. An exception to this was Italy's right-wing government in 1994, which took a much harder stance on EU-Slovenian relations than earlier and later governments.
9. Simon Nuttall, 'The Commission and Foreign Policy-Making', in Geoffrey Edwards and David Spence, eds, *The European Commission* (Harlow: Longman, 1994), p. 294.
10. See Peter Ludlow, 'The European Commission', in Keohane and Hoffmann, eds, *The New European Community*, pp. 116–21 and Grant, *Delors*, pp. 278–84.
11. Although they are in line with CSCE norms, Germany's friendship treaties with its neighbours contain provisions for minorities, reflecting its support of German minorities. See Garton Ash, *In Europe's Name*, p. 401. Lothar Gutjahr notes that the emphasis on rights for German minorities came particularly from the CDU. In *German Foreign and Defence Policy after Unification* (London: Pinter, 1994), p. 53.
12. Sarah Helm, 'Eastern Expansion Sparks Row', *The Independent*, 16 December 1995.
13. As Ulrich Sedelmeier and Helen Wallace argue, in 'Policies towards Central and Eastern Europe', in Helen Wallace and William Wallace, *Policy-Making in the European Union* (Oxford: Oxford University Press, 1996).
14. As early as October 1989, Genscher stressed the need for the Community to reinforce cooperation with East European countries to facilitate their eventual accession to the EC. *Agence Europe* no. 5106, 7 October 1989.
15. In Michael Smith's words ('The European Union').
16. Had the Berlin Wall fallen ten years earlier, one wonders if they would have been as keen to join the Community.
17. Secretary Baker, 'A New Europe, A New Atlanticism: Architecture for a New Era', address to Berlin Press Club, 12 December 1989, US Department of State, Bureau of Public Affairs, Washington, D.C.
18. On Germany's preference for multilateral solutions, see Reinardt Rummel, 'The German Debate on International Security Institutions', in Marco Carnovale, ed., *European Security and International Institutions after the Cold War* (New York: St. Martin's, 1995).
19. See Buzan, et al., *European Security*, p. 129; Stark, 'L'Est de l'Europe'; and Romer and Schreiber, 'La France'.
20. 'Statement Concerning Central and Eastern Europe', Document no. 89/314, *EPC Documentation Bulletin*, vol. 5, no. 2, 1989.
21. In early 1990, UK Foreign Secretary Douglas Hurd said, 'It is fitting that it should be the Community – the most successful expression of our shared values and objectives as Europeans – which is throwing a lifeline to the rest of our family of nations.' Quoted in Timothy Garton Ash, 'Poor but Clubbable', *The Independent*, 19 January 1990.

22. In Hill's words ('Capability-Expectations Gap').
23. Which Stanley Hoffmann contrasted to the logic of diversity in 'Obstinate or Obsolete?'.

Bibliography

ARTICLES AND BOOKS

Acharya, Rohini. *Making Trade Policy in the EU*. Discussion Paper 61. London: Royal Institute of International Affairs, 1996.

Adamiec, Jolanta. *East-Central Europe and the European Community: A Polish Perspective*. RIIA Discussion Paper no. 47. London: Royal Institute of International Affairs, 1993.

Allen, David. 'West European Responses to Change in the Soviet Union and Eastern Europe', in Rummel, ed., *Toward Political Union* (1992).

——. 'Conclusions: The European Rescue of National Foreign Policy?', in Hill, ed., *The Actors* (1996).

Alting von Geusau, Frans A. M. *Beyond the European Community*. Leyden: A. W. Sijthoff, 1969.

Andreatta, Nino. 'Una Politica Estera per l'Italia', *Il Mulino*, no. 5, September/October, 1993.

Andriessen, Frans. 'Towards a Community of Twenty-Four'. Speech to the 69th Plenary Assembly of Eurochambers, Brussels, 19 April 1991, Rapid Database Speech/91/41.

——. Speech at the UK Presidency Conference, 'Europe and the World After 1992'. London, 7 September 1992.

Artisien, Patrick F. R., and Stephen Holt. 'Yugoslavia and the E.E.C. in the 1970s', *Journal of Common Market Studies*, vol. 28, no. 4, June 1980.

Baker, James. 'A New Europe, A New Atlanticism: Architecture for a New Era'. Address to Berlin Press Club, 12 December 1989. US Department of State, Bureau of Public Affairs, Washington, D.C.

Balázs, Péter. 'Trade Relations between Hungary and the European Community', in Marc Maresceau, ed., *The Political and Legal Framework of Trade Relations between the European Community and Eastern Europe*. Dordrecht: Martinus Nijhoff, 1989.

——. *The EU's Collective Regional Approach to its Eastern Enlargement: Consequences and Risks*. CORE Working Paper 1/1997. Copenhagen: Copenhagen Research Project on European Integration, 1997.

Baldwin, Richard. *Towards an Integrated Europe*. London: Centre for Economic Policy Research, 1994.

Bertsch, Gary K. *East-West Strategic Trade, COCOM and the Atlantic Alliance*. Paris: The Atlantic Institute for International Affairs, 1983.

Birnbaum, Karl E., and Ingo Peters. 'The CSCE: a Reassessment of its Role in the 1980s', *Review of International Studies*, vol. 16, no. 4, October 1990.

Bloed, Arie. *The External Relations of the Council for Mutual Economic Assistance*. Dordrecht: Martinus Nijhoff, 1988.

——, ed., *From Helsinki to Vienna: Basic Documents of the Helsinki Process*. Dordrecht: Martinus Nijhoff, 1990.

Bomsdorf, Falk, et al. *Confronting Insecurity in Eastern Europe: Challenges for the European Community*. London: Royal Institute of International Affairs, 1992.

Buchan, David. *Europe: The Strange Superpower*. Aldershot: Dartmouth, 1993.

Bulmer, Simon. 'Analysing European Political Cooperation: The Case for Two-Tier Analysis', in Holland, ed., *The Future of European Political Cooperation* (1991).

Burghardt, Günter and Fraser Cameron. 'The Next Enlargement of the European Union', *European Foreign Affairs Review*, vol. 2, no. 1, 1997.

Buzan, Barry, et al. *The European Security Order Recast: Scenarios for the Post-Cold War Era*. London: Pinter, 1990.

Cafruny, Alan, and Glenda Rosenthal, eds, *The State of the European Community Vol. 2: The Maastricht Debates and Beyond*. London: Lynne Rienner, 1993.

Clarke, Michael. 'Britain and European Political Cooperation in the CSCE', in Kenneth Dyson, ed., *European Detente: Case Studies of the Politics of East-West Relations*. London: Frances Pinter, 1986.

——. 'Foreign Policy Analysis: A Theoretical Guide', in Stelios Stavridis and Christopher Hill, eds, *Domestic Sources of Foreign Policy: West European Reactions to the Falklands Conflict*. Oxford: Berg, 1996.

Crawford, Beverly. 'The Roots of European Self-Assertion in East-West Trade', in Beverly Crawford and Peter Schulze, eds, *The New Europe Asserts Itself: A Changing Role in International Relations*. Berkeley: University of California, 1990.

Cutler, Robert M. 'Harmonizing EEC-CMEA Relations: Never the Twain Shall Meet?', *International Affairs*, vol. 63, no. 2, Spring 1987.

Danish Institute of International Affairs. 'European Stability: EU's Enlargement with the Central and East European Countries'. Report for the Danish Parliament. Copenhagen, 1997.

Dehousse, Renaud and Joseph H. H. Weiler. 'EPC and the Single Act: From Soft Law to Hard Law?', in Holland, ed., *The Future of European Political Cooperation* (1991).

de La Serre, Françoise. 'The EC and Central and Eastern Europe', in Leon Hurwitz and Christian Lequesne, eds, *The State of the European Community: Politics, Institutions, and Debates in the Transition Years 1989–1990*. Harlow: Longman, 1991.

—— and Christian Lequesne. 'France and The European Union', in Cafruny and Rosenthal, eds, *The State of the European Community* (1993).

Delors, Jacques. 'European Unification and European Security', in *European Security after the Cold War Part I*. Adelphi Paper no. 284. London: Brassey's, 1994.

de Nevers, Renée. 'Democratization and Ethnic Conflict', *Survival*, vol. 35, no. 2, Summer 1993.

de Schoutheete, Philippe. *La Coopération Politique Européenne*. Brussels: Editions Labor, 1980.

Deutsch, Karl, et al. *Political Community and the North Atlantic Area: International Organization in the Light of Historical Experience*. Princeton: Princeton University Press, 1957.

Dienstbier, Jiri. 'Central Europe's Security', *Foreign Policy*, no. 83, Summer 1991.

Dodd, Tom. 'Developing the Common Foreign and Security Paper'. Research Paper no. 94/131. London: House of Commons Library, 1994.

Duchêne, François. *Jean Monnet: The First Statesman of Interdependence*. New York: W. W. Norton and Co, 1994.

Ehlermann, Claus-Dieter. 'Aid for Poland and Hungary, First Assessment', *European Affairs*, no. 4, 1989.

———. *Increased Differentiation or Stronger Uniformity*. RSC Working Paper no. 95/21. Florence: European University Institute, 1995.

Ehrhardt, Carl. 'EEC and CMEA Tediously Nearing Each Other', *Aussenpolitik*, vol. 28, no. 2, 1977.

———. 'The EC in the Network of its Bilateral Agreements', *Aussenpolitik*, vol. 31, no. 4, 1980.

Emmanouilidis, Janis. 'The CEEC and CFSP – More Than a First Acquaintance with the Second Pillar?', *CFSP Forum*, nos. 3 and 4, 1996.

Franck, Christian. 'Belgium: Committed Multilateralism', in Hill, ed., *National Foreign Policies* (1983).

———. 'Belgium: The Importance of Foreign Policy to European Political Union', in Hill, ed., *The Actors* (1996).

Garton Ash, Timothy. *The Magic Lantern: The Revolution of '89 Witnessed in Warsaw, Budapest, Berlin, and Prague*. New York: Random House, 1990.

———. *In Europe's Name: Germany and the Divided Continent*. London: Vintage, 1993.

Genscher, Hans-Dietrich. 'Toward an Overall Western Strategy for Peace, Freedom and Progress', *Foreign Affairs*, vol. 61, no. 1, Fall 1982.

George, Stephen. 'European Political Cooperation: A World Systems Perspective', in Holland, ed., *The Future of European Political Cooperation* (1991).

Ginsberg, Roy. *Foreign Policy Actions of the European Community: The Politics of Scale*. Boulder: Lynne Rienner, 1989.

———. 'Concepts of European Foreign Policy Revisited: Narrowing the Theoretical Capability-Expectations Gap', paper presented at the European Community Studies Association conference, Seattle, May 1997.

Grant, Charles. *Delors: Inside the House That Jacques Built*. London: Nicholas Brealey, 1994.

Grieco, Joseph. *Cooperation Among Nations: Europe, America, and Non-Tariff Barriers to Trade*. Ithaca: Cornell University Press, 1990.

Gutjahr, Lothar. *German Foreign and Defence Policy after Unification*. London: Pinter, 1994.

Haas, Ernst. *The Uniting of Europe: Political, Economic and Social Forces 1950–1957*. London: Stevens and Sons, 1958.

———. 'Turbulent Fields and the Theory of Regional Integration', *International Organization*, vol. 30, no. 2, Spring 1976.

——— and Edward Thomas Rowe. 'Regional Organizations in the United Nations: Is There Externalization?', *International Studies Quarterly*, vol. 17, no. 1, 1973.

Ham, Peter van. *The EC, Eastern Europe and European Unity: Discord, Collaboration and Integration Since 1947*. London: Pinter, 1993.

Hayes-Renshaw, Fiona and Helen Wallace. *The Council of Ministers*. London: Macmillan, 1997.

Hill, Christopher, ed., *National Foreign Policies and European Political Cooperation*. London: George Allen and Unwin, 1983.

——. 'European Foreign Policy: Power Bloc, Civilian Model – or Flop?', in Rummel, ed., *The Evolution of an International Actor* (1990).

——. 'The Capability-Expectations Gap, or Conceptualizing Europe's International Role', *Journal of Common Market Studies*, vol. 31, no. 3, September 1993.

——, ed., *The Actors in Europe's Foreign Policy*. London: Routledge, 1996.

—— and William Wallace. 'Introduction: Actors and Actions', in Hill, ed., *The Actors* (1996).

Hoffmann, Stanley. 'Obstinate or Obsolete? The Fate of the Nation-State and the Case of Western Europe', *Daedalus*, Summer 1966.

——. 'French Dilemmas and Strategies in the New Europe', in Robert Keohane, Joseph Nye, and Stanley Hoffmann, eds, *After the Cold War: International Institutions and State Strategies, 1989–1991*. Cambridge, MA: Harvard University Press, 1993.

Holland, Martin, ed., *The Future of European Political Cooperation: Essays on Theory and Practice*. London: Macmillan, 1991.

——. 'Introduction: EPC Theory and Empiricism', in Holland, ed., *The Future of European Political Cooperation* (1991).

——. *European Community Integration*. London: Pinter, 1993.

Hughes, Kirsty. *Eastward Enlargement of the EU: EU Strategy and Future Challenges*. European Programme Working Paper no. 2. London: Royal Institute of International Affairs, 1996.

Hurrell, Andrew. 'International Society and the Study of Regimes: A Reflective Approach', in Volker Rittberger, ed., *Regime Theory and International Relations*. Oxford: Clarendon Press, 1995.

ISA Consult, Sussex University European Institute, and GJW Europe, *Final Report: Evaluation of the PHARE and TACIS Democracy Programme 1992–1997*. Brighton and Hamburg, 1997.

Ifestos, Panayiotis. *European Political Cooperation: Towards a Framework of Supranational Diplomacy?*. Aldershot: Avebury, 1987.

James, Harold and Marla Stone, eds, *When the Wall Came Down: Reactions to German Unification*. London: Routledge, 1992.

Jepperson, Ronald L., Alexander Wendt and Peter J. Katzenstein. 'Norms, Identity, and Culture in National Security', in Katzenstein, ed., *The Culture of National Security* (1996).

Jopp, Mathias. *The Strategic Implications of European Integration*. Adelphi Paper no. 290. London: Brassey's, 1994.

Kahler, Miles. 'The United States and Western Europe: The Diplomatic Consequences of Mr. Reagan', in Kenneth Oye, Robert Lieber and Donald Rothchild, eds, *Eagle Defiant: United States Foreign Policy in the 1980s*. Boston: Little, Brown and Co, 1983.

Katzenstein, Peter J., ed., *The Culture of National Security: Norms and Identity in World Politics*. New York: Columbia University Press, 1996.

244 Bibliography

Katzman, Julie. 'The Euro-Siberian Gas Pipeline Row: A Study in Community Development', *Millennium*, vol. 17, no. 1, 1988.

Keohane, Robert. *After Hegemony: Cooperation and Discord in the World Political Economy*. Princeton: Princeton University Press, 1984.

——. 'Neoliberal Institutionalism: A Perspective on World Politics', in Robert Keohane, *International Institutions and State Power*. Boulder: Westview Press, 1989.

—— and Stanley Hoffmann, eds, *The New European Community: Decisionmaking and Institutional Change*. Boulder: Westview Press, 1991.

—— and Stanley Hoffmann. 'Institutional Change in Europe in the 1980s', in Keohane and Hoffmann, eds, *The New European Community* (1991).

Kirk Laux, Jeanne. *Reform, Reintegration and Regional Security: The Role of Western Assistance in Overcoming Insecurity in Central and Eastern Europe*. Working Paper no. 37. Ottawa: Canadian Institute for International Peace and Security, 1991.

Klotz, Audie. *Norms in International Relations: The Struggle Against Apartheid*. Ithaca: Cornell University Press, 1995.

Kolankiewicz, George. 'Consensus and Competition in the Eastern Enlargement of the European Union', *International Affairs*, vol. 70, no. 3, 1994.

Körmendy, Istvàn. 'The Hungarian View: An EC Associate's Perspective from Central Europe', in Rummel, ed., *Toward Political Union* (1992).

Kowert, Paul and Jeffrey Legro. 'Norms, Identity, and Their Limits: A Theoretical Reprise', in Katzenstein, ed., *The Culture of National Security* (1996).

Kramer, Heinz. 'The European Community's Response to the "New Eastern Europe"', *Journal of Common Market Studies*, vol. 31, no. 2, June 1993.

Krenzler, Horst-Günter and Henning C. Schneider. 'The Question of Consistency', in Regelsberger, de Schoutheete de Tervarent, Wessels, eds, *Foreign Policy of the European Union* (1997).

Lasok, D. and J. W. Bridge. *Law and Institutions of the European Communities*. London: Butterworths, 1991.

Lindberg, Leon. *The Political Dynamics of European Economic Integration*. Stanford: Stanford University Press, 1963.

Lippert, Barbara. 'EC-CMEA Relations: Normalisation and Beyond', in Geoffrey Edwards and Elfriede Regelsberger, eds, *The European Community and Inter-regional Cooperation*. London: Pinter, 1990.

——, Rosalind Stevens-Ströhmann, et al. *German Unification and EC Integration: German and British Perspectives*. London: Pinter, 1993.

——. 'Relations with Central and Eastern European Countries: The Anchor Role of the European Union', in Regelsberger, de Schoutheete de Tervarent and Wessels, eds, *Foreign Policy of the European Union* (1997).

Lucron, Claude-Pierre. 'Contenu et Portée des Accords entre la Communauté et la Hongrie, la Pologne et la Tchécoslovaquie', *Revue du Marché Commun*, no. 357, April 1992.

Ludlow, Peter. 'The Politics and Policies of the European Community in 1989', in Centre for European Policy Studies. *The Annual Review of European Community Affairs 1990*. London: Brassey's, 1990.

——. 'The European Commission', in Keohane and Hoffmann, eds, *The New European Community* (1991).

MacLeod, Ian, Ian Hendry and Stephen Hyett. *The External Relations of the European Communities: A Manual of Law and Practice*. Oxford: Clarendon Press, 1996.

Maresceau, Marc. 'Les Accords Européens: Analyse Générale', *Revue du Marché Commun et de l'Union Européenne*, no. 369, June 1993.

Marsh, Peter. 'The Development of Relations Between the EEC and the CMEA', in Avi Shlaim and G. N. Yannopoulos, eds, *The EEC and Eastern Europe*. Cambridge: Cambridge University Press, 1978.

——. 'E.E.C. Foreign Economic Policy and the Political Management of East-West Economic Relations', *Millennium*, vol. 9, no. 1, Spring 1980.

——. 'The European Community and East-West Economic Relations', *Journal of Common Market Studies*, vol. 23, no. 1, September 1984.

Maslen, John. 'The European Community's Relations with the State-Trading Countries, 1981–1983', *Yearbook of European Law*, no. 3, 1983.

——. 'The European Community's Relations with the State-Trading Countries, 1984–1986', *Yearbook of European Law*, no. 6, 1986.

——. 'A Turning Point: Past and Future of the European Community's Relations with Eastern Europe', *Rivista di Studi Politici Internazionali*, no. 4, 1988.

Mastanduno, Michael. 'The Management of Alliance Export Control Policy: American Leadership and the Politics of COCOM', in Gary K. Bertsch, ed., *Controlling East-West Trade and Technology Transfer: Power, Politics, and Policies*. Durham: Duke University Press, 1988.

Mastny, Vojtech, ed., *Italy and East Central Europe: Dimensions of the Regional Relationship*. Boulder: Westview, 1995.

Mearsheimer, John J. 'Back to the Future: Instability in Europe after the Cold War', *International Security*, vol. 15, no. 1, Summer 1990.

Menkveld, Paul. *Origin and Role of the European Bank for Reconstruction and Development*. London: Graham and Trotman, 1991.

Menon, Anand, Anthony Forster and William Wallace. 'A Common European Defence?', *Survival*, vol. 34, no. 3, Autumn 1992.

Merritt, Giles. *Eastern Europe and the USSR: The Challenge of Freedom*. London: Kogan Page, 1991.

Michalski, Anna and Helen Wallace. *The European Community: The Challenge of Enlargement*. London: Royal Institute of International Affairs, 1992.

Milner, Helen. 'International Theories of Cooperation Among Nations: Strengths and Weaknesses', *World Politics*, vol. 44, no. 3, April 1992.

Moïsi, Dominique. 'French Policy Toward Central and Eastern Europe', in William Griffith, ed., *Central and Eastern Europe: The Opening Curtain?*. Boulder: Westview, 1989.

Monar, Jörg. 'Political Dialogue with Third Countries and Regional Political Groupings: The Fifteen as an Attractive Interlocutor', in Regelsberger, de Schoutheete de Tervarent, and Wessels, eds, *Foreign Policy of the European Union* (1997).

Moravscik, Andrew. 'Negotiating the Single European Act', in Keohane and Hoffmann, eds, *The New European Community* (1991).

——. 'Preferences and Power in the European Community: A Liberal Intergovernmentalist Approach', *Journal of Common Market Studies*, vol. 31, no. 4, December 1993.

Morawiecki, Wojciech. 'Actors and Interests in the Process of Negotiations Between the CMEA and the EEC', *Legal Issues of European Integration*, vol. 15, no. 2, 1989.

Munuera, Gabriel. *Preventing Armed Conflict in Europe: Lessons from Recent Experience*. Chaillot Paper 15/16. Paris: Western European Union Institute for Security Studies, 1994.

Neuwahl, Nanette. 'Foreign and Security Policy and the Implementation of the Requirement of "Consistency" under the Treaty on European Union', in David O'Keeffe and Patrick Twomey, eds, *Legal Issues of the Maastricht Treaty*. London: Chancery Law Publishing, 1994.

North Atlantic Assembly. *East-West Economic Relations*. Brussels: North Atlantic Assembly, 1984.

Notzold, Jurgen. 'Political Preconditions of East-West Economic Relations', *Aussenpolitik*, vol. 36, no. 1, 1985.

Nuttall, Simon. 'Interaction between European Political Co-operation and the European Community', *Yearbook of European Law*, no. 7, 1987.

——. *European Political Co-operation*. Oxford: Clarendon Press, 1992.

——. 'The Commission and Foreign Policy-Making', in Geoffrey Edwards and David Spence, eds, *The European Commission*. Harlow: Longman, 1994.

——. 'The Commission: The Struggle for Legitimacy', in Hill, ed., *The Actors* (1996).

Nye, Joseph. 'Neorealism and Neoliberalism', *World Politics*, vol. 40, no. 2, January 1988.

——. 'Soft Power', *Foreign Policy*, no. 80, Fall 1990.

Olson, Mancur. *The Logic of Collective Action: Public Goods and the Theory of Groups*. Cambridge, MA: Harvard University Press, 1971.

Palankai, Tibor. *The European Community and Central European Integration: The Hungarian Case*. Occasional Paper Series no. 21. New York: Institute for East-West Security Studies, 1991.

Pelkmans, Jacques and Anna Murphy. 'Catapulted into Leadership: The Community's Aid and Trade Policies Vis-à-Vis Eastern Europe', *Journal of European Integration*, vol. 14, nos. 2–3, 1991.

Philip Morris Institute for Public Policy Research. *Is the West Doing Enough for Eastern Europe?*, 1994.

Pijpers, Alfred. 'European Political Cooperation and the CSCE Process', *Legal Issues of European Integration*, vol. 10, no. 1, 1984.

——. 'European Political Cooperation and the Realist Paradigm', in Holland, ed., *The Future of European Political Cooperation* (1991).

Pinder, John. 'Economic Integration and East-West Trade: Conflict of Interests or Comedy of Errors?', *Journal of Common Market Studies*, vol. 16, no. 1, September 1977.

——. *The European Community and Eastern Europe*. London: Pinter, 1991.

Podraza, Andrzej. *The Western European Union and Central Europe: A New Relationship*. RIIA Discussion Paper no. 41. London: Royal Institute of International Affairs, 1992.

Press and Information Office of the Federal Government of Germany. *European Political Co-operation (EPC)*. Bonn, 1982.

Pridham, Geoffrey, ed., *Encouraging Democracy: The International Context of Regime Transition in Southern Europe*. Leicester: Leicester University Press, 1991.

——. 'The Politics of the European Community, Transnational Networks and Democratic Transition in Southern Europe', in Pridham, ed., *Encouraging Democracy* (1991).

Putnam, Robert. 'Diplomacy and Domestic Politics: The Logic of Two-Level Games', *International Organization*, vol. 42, no. 3, Summer 1988.

Ransom, Charles. *The European Community and Eastern Europe*. London: Butterworths, 1973.

Redmond, John. 'The Wider Europe: Extending the Membership of the EC', in Cafruny and Rosenthal, eds, *The State of the European Community* (1993).

Regelsberger, Elfriede. 'The Twelve's Dialogue with Third Countries – Progress Towards a *Communauté d'action*?', in Holland, ed., *The Future of European Political Cooperation* (1991).

——, Philippe de Schoutheete de Tervarent and Wolfgang Wessels, eds, *Foreign Policy of the European Union: From EPC to CFSP and Beyond*. Boulder: Lynne Rienner, 1997.

Rhein, Eberhard. 'The Community's External Reach', in Rummel, ed., *Toward Political Union* (1992).

Rich, Vera. 'Central Europe II: The Battle of the Danube', *The World Today*, vol. 48, no. 12, December 1992.

——. 'The Murky Politics of the Danube', *The World Today*, vol. 49, nos. 8/9, August/September 1993.

Richardson, Jeremy. 'Interests, Ideas and Garbage Cans of Primeval Soup', in Jeremy Richardson, ed., *European Union: Power and Policy-Making*. London: Routledge, 1996.

Risse-Kappen, Thomas. 'Exploring the Nature of the Beast: International Relations Theory and Comparative Policy Analysis Meet the European Union', *Journal of Common Market Studies*, vol. 34, no. 1, March 1996.

Rollo, J. M. C. and Helen Wallace. 'New Patterns of Partnership', in Gianni Bonvicini, et al., *The Community and the Emerging European Democracies: A Joint Policy Report*. London: Royal Institute of International Affairs, 1991.

Romano, Sergio. *Guida alla Politica Estera Italiana: Dal Crollo del Fascismo al Crollo del Comunismo*. Milan: Rizzoli, 1993.

Romer, Jean-Christophe, and Thomas Schreiber. 'La France et l'Europe Centrale', *Politique Étrangère*, no. 4/95, Winter 1995.

Ross, George. *Jacques Delors and European Integration*. Cambridge: Polity Press, 1995.

Rummel, Reinhardt, ed., *The Evolution of an International Actor: Western Europe's New Assertiveness*. Boulder: Westview, 1990.

—— ed., *Toward Political Union: Planning a Common Foreign and Security Policy in the European Community*. Boulder: Westview, 1992.

——. 'The German Debate on International Security Institutions', in Marco Carnovale, ed., *European Security and International Institutions after the Cold War*. New York: St. Martin's, 1995.

———. 'The CFSP's Conflict Prevention Policy', in Martin Holland, ed., *Common Foreign and Security Policy: The Record and Reforms*. London: Pinter, 1997.

Sandholtz, Wayne. 'Choosing Union: Monetary Politics and Maastricht', *International Organization*, vol. 47, no. 1, Winter 1993.

Scharpf, Fritz. 'The Joint-Decision Trap: Lessons from German Federalism and European Integration', *Public Administration*, vol. 66, no. 3, Autumn 1988.

Schmitter, Phillipe. 'Three Neofunctional Hypotheses about International Integration', *International Organization*, vol. 23, no. 1, Winter 1969.

Sedelmeier, Ulrich and Helen Wallace. 'Policies towards Central and Eastern Europe', in Helen Wallace and William Wallace, eds, *Policy-making in the European Union*. Oxford: Oxford University Press, 1996.

Senior Nello, Susan. *EC-East European Economic Relations: Cooperation Agreements at the Government and Firm Levels*. EUI Working Paper no. 85/183. Florence: European University Institute, 1985.

———. *Recent Developments in Relations Between the EC and Eastern Europe*. EUI Working Paper no. 89/381. Florence: European University Institute, 1989.

———. *The New Europe: Changing Economic Relations Between East and West*. New York: Harvester Wheatsheaf, 1991.

——— and Karen E. Smith. *The Consequences of Eastern Enlargement of the European Union in Stages*. RSC Working Paper no. 51/97. Florence: European University Institute, 1997.

Sjöstedt, Gunnar. *The External Role of the European Community*. Westmead: Saxon House, 1977.

Smith, Hazel. *European Union Foreign Policy and Central America*. London: Macmillan, 1995.

Smith, Michael. 'The European Union, Foreign Economic Policy and the Changing World Arena', *Journal of European Public Policy*, vol. 1, no. 2, Autumn 1994.

———. 'The European Union and a Changing Europe: Establishing the Boundaries of Order', *Journal of Common Market Studies*, vol. 34, no. 1, 1996.

Smith, Michael E. *The 'Europeanization' of European Political Cooperation: Trust, Transgovernmental Relations, and the Power of Informal Norms*. Center for German and European Studies Working Paper 2.44. Berkeley: University of California, 1996.

Sorensen, Georg, ed., *Political Conditionality*. London: Frank Cass, 1993.

———. 'Introduction', in Sorensen, ed., *Political Conditionality* (1993).

Spence, David. *Enlargement without Accession: The EC's Response to German Unification*. RIIA Discussion Paper no. 36. London: Royal Institute for International Affairs, 1991.

Stark, Hans. 'L'Est de l'Europe et l'Allemagne: des rapports complexes', *Politique Étrangère*, no. 4/91, Winter 1991.

Taylor, Paul. *The Limits of European Integration*. New York: Columbia University Press, 1983.

———. 'A Conceptual Typology of International Organization', in A. J. R. Groom and Paul Taylor, eds, *Frameworks for International Co-operation*, London: Pinter, 1990.

——. 'The European Community and the State: Assumptions, Theories and Propositions', *Review of International Studies*, vol. 17, no. 2, April 1991.

——. *The European Union in the 1990s*. Oxford: Oxford University Press, 1996.

Teschke, Benno. 'The Incorporation of the Five New Länder into the European Community: Political, Legal and Economic Aspects', *European Access*, no. 2, April 1992.

Thatcher, Margaret. *The Downing Street Years*. London: HarperCollins, 1993.

Uvin, Peter. '"Do As I Say, Not As I Do": The Limits of Political Conditionality', in Sorensen, ed., *Political Conditionality* (1993).

van den Broek, Hans. 'Why Europe Needs a Common Foreign and Security Policy', *European Foreign Affairs Review*, vol. 1, no. 1, July 1996.

Van Eekelen, Willem. 'WEU Prepares the Way for New Missions', *NATO Review*, vol. 41, no. 5, October 1993.

Wæver, Ole. 'Three Competing Europes: German, French, Russian', *International Affairs*, vol. 66, no. 3, July 1990.

——. 'Identity, Integration and Security: Solving the Sovereignty Puzzle in E.U. Studies', *Journal of International Affairs*, vol. 48, no. 2, Winter 1995.

Walker, Jenonne. 'European Regional Organizations and Ethnic Conflict', in Regina Cowen Karp, ed., *Central and Eastern Europe: The Challenge of Transition*. Oxford: Oxford University Press, 1993.

——. 'International Mediation of Ethnic Conflicts', *Survival*, vol. 35, no. 1, Spring 1993.

Wallace, Helen with Adam Ridley. *Europe: The Challenge of Diversity*. London: Routledge and Kegan Paul, 1985.

—— and William Wallace. *Flying Together in a Larger and More Diverse European Union*. Working Document 87. The Hague: Netherlands Scientific Council for Government Policy, 1995.

Wallace, William. 'Political Cooperation: Integration through Intergovernmentalism', in Helen Wallace, William Wallace and Carol Webb, eds, *Policy-Making in the European Community*. Chichester: John Wiley and Sons, 1983.

——. 'From Twelve to Twenty-Four? The Challenges to the EC Posed by the Revolutions in Eastern Europe', in Colin Crouch and David Marquand, eds, *Towards Greater Europe? A Continent Without an Iron Curtain*. Oxford: Blackwell, 1992.

Waltz, Kenneth. *Theory of International Politics*. Reading, MA: Addison-Wesley, 1979.

Weiler, Joseph and Wolfgang Wessels. 'EPC and the Challenge of Theory', in Alfred Pijpers, Elfriede Regelsberger and Wolfgang Wessels, eds, *European Political Cooperation in the 1980s: A Common Foreign Policy for Western Europe?*. Dordrecht: Martinus Nijhoff, 1988.

Wellenstein, Edmund. 'The Relations of the European Communities with Eastern Europe', in David O'Keeffe and Henry G. Schermers, eds, *Essays in European Law and Integration*. Deventer, the Netherlands: Kluwer, 1982.

Wendt, Alexander. 'Anarchy is What States Make of It: The Social Construction of Power Politics', *International Organization*, vol. 46, no. 2, Spring 1992.

——. 'Collective Identity Formation and the International State', *American Political Science Review*, vol. 88, no. 2, June 1994.

White, Brian. 'Analysing Foreign Policy: Problems and Approaches', in Michael Clarke and Brian White, eds, *Understanding Foreign Policy: The Foreign Policy Systems Approach*. Aldershot: Edward Elgar, 1989.

Whitehead, Lawrence. 'Democracy by Convergence and Southern Europe: A Comparative Perspective', in Pridham, ed., *Encouraging Democracy* (1991).

Woolcock, Stephen. *Western Policies on East-West Trade*. London: Routledge and Kegan Paul, 1982.

Zielonka, Jan. 'Introduction: Eastern Europe in Transition', in Gary K. Bertsch, Heinrich Vogel, and Jan Zielonka, eds, *After the Revolutions: East-West Trade and Technology Transfer in the 1990s*. Boulder: Westview, 1991.

——. *Security in Central Europe*. Adelphi Paper no. 272. London: Brassey's, 1992.

OFFICIAL DOCUMENTS

General EU Documents

Bulletin of the European Communities (*EC Bulletin*, later *EU Bulletin*)
Commission Press Releases
Council Secretariat Press Releases
The Community Budget: The Facts in Figures. Luxembourg: OOPEC.
EIB Information
EIB Financing
European Political Cooperation Documentation Bulletin (*EPC Documentation Bulletin*)
EPC Press Releases
Eurostat
General Report on the Activities of the European Communities info PHARE (Commission)
Official Journal of the European Communities (OJ)
PHARE: Infocontract (Commission)
Review of the Council's Work

European Commission Documents (in chronological order)

External Relations Information no. 1/89, 'The European Community's Relations with Comecon and its East European Members', January 1989.

'Action Plan for Coordinated Aid to Poland and Hungary', COM (89) 470 final, 27 September 1989.

'Implications of Recent Changes in Central and Eastern Europe for the Community's relations with the countries concerned', SEC (90) 111 final, 23 January 1990.

'The Development of the Community's Relations with the Countries of Central and Eastern Europe', SEC (90) 196, final, 1 February 1990.

'Action Plan: Coordinated Assistance from the Group of 24 to Bulgaria, Czechoslovakia, the German Democratic Republic, Romania and Yugoslavia', SEC (90) 843 final, 2 May 1990.

'Association Agreements with the Countries of Central and Eastern Europe: A General Outline', COM (90) 398 final, 27 August 1990.

'The European Community and German Unification', *EC Bulletin Supplement 4/90*.

London Office, 'Background Report: The European Community and German Unification', 2 October 1990.

The European Community and its Eastern Neighbours. Luxembourg: OOPEC, 1990.

'First Annual Report from the Commission to the Council and the European Parliament on the Implementation of Economic Aid to the Countries of East and Central Europe as of 31 December 1990' ('PHARE Annual Report 1990'), SEC (91) 1354 final, 24 July 1991.

'Europe and the Challenge of Enlargement', *EC Bulletin Supplement 3/92*.

'Towards a Closer Association with the Countries of Central and Eastern Europe', SEC (92) 2301 final, 2 December 1992.

PHARE, Assistance for Economic Restructuring in the Countries of Central and Eastern Europe: An Operational Guide. Luxembourg: OOPEC, 1992.

'Second Annual Report from the Commission to the Council and the European Parliament on the Implementation of Community Assistance to the Countries of East and Central Europe (PHARE) in 1991' ('PHARE Annual Report 1991'), COM (93) 172 final, 10 May 1993.

'Towards a Closer Association with the Countries of Central and Eastern Europe', SEC (93) 648 final, 18 May 1993.

'European Community Relations with the Countries of Central and Eastern Europe', Background Brief BB 17, June 1993.

'PHARE General Guidelines 1993–1997', 5 July 1993.

Europe in a Changing World: The External Relations of the European Community. Luxembourg: OOPEC, 1993.

'European Union Relations with the Countries of Central and Eastern Europe', Background Brief BB 19, January 1994.

'PHARE: A Performance Review 1990–1993', April 1994.

'What is PHARE?', May 1994.

'PHARE General Guidelines 1994–1997', 1 June 1994.

'Trade and Aid in Relations between the European Union, the Countries of Central and Eastern Europe and the Countries of the Commonwealth of Independent States', MG/PRH/FW/vf, 9 June 1994.

'The Europe Agreements and Beyond: A Strategy to Prepare the Countries of Central and Eastern Europe for Accession', COM (94) 320 final, 13 July 1994.

'Follow up to Commission Communication on "The Europe Agreements and Beyond: A Strategy to Prepare the Countries of Central and Eastern Europe for Accession"', COM (94) 361 final, 27 July 1994.

'The Economic Interpenetration between the European Union and Eastern Europe', *European Economy*, no. 6, 1994.

252   *Bibliography*

'PHARE Programme and Contract Information 1995: Multi-country and Cross-border Programmes no. 1'.

'PHARE Programme and Contract Information 1995: Multi-country and Cross-border Programmes no. 2'.

'Report on the Implementation of Macro-Financial Assistance to Third Countries in 1994', *European Economy*, no. 2, 1995.

'Third and Fourth Annual Reports from the Commission to the Council and the European Parliament on the Implementation of Community Assistance to the Countries of East and Central Europe (PHARE) in 1992 and 1993' ('PHARE Annual Report 1992' and 'PHARE Annual Report 1993'), COM (95) 13 final, 20 February 1995.

'Report of the Commission to the Council on the Promotion of Intra-Regional Cooperation and "Bon Voisinage"', prepared for the General Affairs Council of 6/7 March 1995.

'Preparation of the Associated Countries of Central and Eastern Europe for Integration into the Internal Market of the Union', COM (95) 163 final, 3 May 1995.

'On the Inclusion of Respect for Democratic Principles and Human Rights in Agreements between the Community and Third Countries', COM (95) 216 final, 23 May 1995.

'PHARE 1994 Annual Report' ('PHARE Annual Report 1994'), COM (95) 366 final, 20 July 1995.

'Reinforcing Political Union and Preparing for Enlargement', COM (96) 90 final, 20 February 1996.

'The PHARE Programme Annual Report 1995' ('PHARE Annual Report 1995'), COM (96) 360 final, 23 July 1996.

'Report from the Commission to the Council and the European Parliament on the Implementation of Macro-Financial Assistance to Third Countries in 1995', COM (96) 695 final, 8 January 1997.

'Agenda 2000', COM (97) 2000, 15 July 1997.

European Parliament Documents

'Report on the European Community's Relations with the East European State-Trading Countries and COMECON', Rapporteur: Mr. E. A. Klepsch (the Klepsch Report), Working Document 425/7, 9 January 1975.

'Report drawn up on behalf of the Committee of External Economic Relations on relations between the European community and the East European state-trading countries and the CMEA (COMECON)', Rapporteur: Mr. U. Irmer (the Irmer Report), Document 1-531/82, 28 July 1982.

'Report drawn up on behalf of the Committee on External Economic Relations on relations between the European Community and the Council for Mutual Economic Assistance (CMEA) and the Eastern European Member states of the CMEA', Rapporteur: Mr. Hans-Joachim Seeler (the Seeler Report), PE Doc A2-187/86, 19 December 1986.

'Report of the Committee on Institutional Affairs on the Structure and Strategy for the European Union with regard to its Enlargement and the Creation of a Europe-Wide Order', Rapporteur: Klaus Hänsch, Document A3-0189/92, 21 May 1992.

European Council Conclusions

(additional to those in the *EC Bulletin* and *EPC Documentation Bulletin*)
European Council in Edinburgh, 11–12 December 1992, Conclusions of the Presidency, SN 456/92.
European Council in Copenhagen, 21–2 June 1993, Conclusions of the Presidency, SN 180/93.
European Council Meeting on 9 and 10 December 1994 in Essen, Presidency Conclusions, SN 300/94.
Cannes European Council 26 and 27 June 1995, Presidency Conclusions, SN 211/95.

Other International Organizations

European Bank for Reconstruction and Development, 'Political Aspects of the Mandate of the European Bank for Reconstruction and Development' (no date).
'Rome Declaration on Peace and Cooperation, Issued by the Heads of State and Government Participating in the Meeting of the North Atlantic Council in Rome on 7–8 November 1991', in *NATO Review*, vol. 39, no. 6, December 1991.
'Partnership for Peace: Invitation', in *NATO Review*, vol. 42, no. 1, February 1994.
UN Economic Commission for Europe, 'Economic Survey of Europe in 1991–1992'.
UN Economic Commission for Europe, *Economic Bulletin for Europe*.
Western European Union, 'Kirchberg Declaration', 9 May 1994.
World Bank, *World Debt Tables 1991–1992: External Debt of Developing Countries Volumes 1 and 2*. Washington, DC: The World Bank, 1991.

Member State Documents

French Foreign Ministry, *La Politique Étrangère de la France: Textes et Documents*.
'French Proposal for a Pact on Stability in Europe, Copenhagen (22 June 1993)'. Statement translated by the Press Department of the French Embassy in London.
Italian and UK Foreign Ministers, Text of Letter on Andreatta-Hurd Initiative, Coreu, December 1993.

NEWS SOURCES

Agence Europe
Associated Press
The Daily Telegraph
The Economist

The European
European Report
The Financial Times
The Guardian
The Independent
International Herald Tribune
Le Monde
The New York Times
La Repubblica
Reuter
RFE/RL Research Institute, *Report on Eastern Europe*, *Research Reports*, and
 Transition
Il Sole 24 Ore
The Times
The Washington Post

Index

Entries in bold indicate tables; n denotes endnote.